AF608151

Confucianism, A Habit of the Heart

Confucianism, A Habit of the Heart

Bellah, Civil Religion, and East Asia

Edited by

Philip J. Ivanhoe and Sungmoon Kim

Cover photo of Robert N. Bellah taken by Andreas Guther
Cover image of Confucius courtesy of Bigstockphoto.com

Published by State University of New York Press, Albany

Printed in the United States of America

For information, contact State University of New York Press, Albany, NY
www.sunypress.edu

Production, Diane Ganeles
Marketing, Anne M. Valentine

Library of Congress Cataloging-in-Publication Data

Confucianism, a habit of the heart: Bellah, civil religion, and East Asia / edited by Philip J. Ivanhoe and Sungmoon Kim.
pages cm
Includes bibliographical references and index.
ISBN 978-1-4384-6013-0 (hardcover : alk. paper)
ISBN 978-1-4384-6014-7 (e-book)
1. Confucianism. 2. Civil religion. I. Ivanhoe, P. J., editor.

BL1855.C685 2015
299.5'12—dc23 2015015577

10 9 8 7 6 5 4 3 2 1

We dedicate this volume to Robert N. Bellah,
whose work and personal example
has been and remains an inspiration.

Because good social science is always morally serious, we can transpose Weber's saying that only a mature man can have the calling for politics into the statement that only a mature person can have the calling for sociology. Moral vacuity creates cognitively trivial work.

—Robert N. Bellah, "The Ethical Aims of Social Inquiry"

Contents

Acknowledgments ix

Introduction 1
Sungmoon Kim and Philip J. Ivanhoe

1. Confucianism as Civil Religion 25
Fenggang Yang

2. The Revival of Confucianism in the Sphere of Mores and the Reactivation of the Civil Religion Debate in China 47
Sébastien Billioud

3. Inside the Revival of Confucianism in Mainland China: The Vicissitudes of Confucian Classics in Contemporary China as an Example 71
Guoxiang Peng

4. The Politics of Confucianism in Contemporary China 85
Anna Sun

5. Obstacles to the Globalization of Confucianism 99
Richard Madsen

6. Beyond a Disciplinary Society: Reimagining Confucian Democracy in South Korea 113
Sungmoon Kim

7. The Experience of Village Leaders during the *Saemaul* Movement in the 1970s: Focusing on the Lives of the Male Leaders 139
Do-Hyun Han

8. Contemporary Japanese Confucianism from a Genealogical Perspective 169
Takahiro Nakajima

9. The Bildungsroman of the Heart: Thick Naturalism in Robert Bellah's *Religion in Human Evolution* 183
Yang Xiao

10. Can We Imagine a Global Civil Religion? 205
Robert N. Bellah

Contributors 223

Index 229

Acknowledgments

We gratefully acknowledge the support of the Department of Public Policy of City University of Hong Kong and the support provided by a grant from the Academy of Korean Studies funded by the Korean government (MEST) (AKS-2011-AAA-2102). An earlier version of Chapter 7 was previously published in Korean as "1970 년대 새마을운동에서 마을 지도자들의 경험세계: 남성지도자들을 중심으로" in <사회와 역사> 88 (Dec. 2010), pp. 267-305; we are grateful to the journal's editor for permission to reprint. We thank all the contributors for their work and patience and offer special thanks to Nancy Ellegate for shepherding this volume through the process of revision, refinement, and publication.

Introduction

Sungmoon Kim and Philip J. Ivanhoe

Like many before and since, 1967 was an eventful year and especially so in America. There were half a million American troops fighting in Vietnam, the civil rights movement was calling on and inspiring all Americans to live up to their high ideals, feminist thinkers and activists were overturning the persistence of patriarchy, the counterculture movement was in full swing, and Robert Bellah first published "Civil Religion in America." However one views the excesses and shortcomings of this year and the decade in which it occurred, there is no denying that 1967 marked a period when a new and revealing sense of national self-consciousness began to dawn across the land. Americans were forced to step back from the ongoing activities of individual and national life and the larger events occurring around the world and reflect upon who they were and the direction in which they and their country were heading. This reflection was often painful, at times traumatic, and resulted in a very different trajectory for the nation and its people. Bellah's essay was not only a part of this process, a cause of these developments, but it also captured what was going on in the hearts and minds of the American people at this critical juncture in their history. He argued that apart from the various institutionalized religions of America, there was a "religious dimension"[1] to American culture, what he called "American civil religion."[2] This civil religion lacks the formal institutional structure of more familiar religions; it has no headquarters, mailing address, hierarchy, or designated leader, and yet it can be found throughout the culture and commands a special kind of reverence. It is most definitely not a national religion or even a celebration of the nation; rather it is "the subordination of the nation to ethical principles that transcend it in terms of which it should be judged."[3]

In other words, it is a civil religious expression of what Alexis de Tocqueville described as one of our "habits of the heart"—the underlying, unofficial, often unselfconscious assumptions, orientations, beliefs, practices, symbols, and styles of reasoning that inform, shape, and guide life in society.[4]

American civil religion is evident in the clear and ubiquitous references to God and his plan that are woven into the fabric of our national character. Almost no political event fails to acknowledge and celebrate that we are a nation "under God." The eye of providence appears on the Great Seal of the United States and upon the one-dollar bill, along with the dual mottos "He favors our endeavors" (*Annuit cœptis*) and a "new order of the ages" (*Novus ordo seclorum*). Our currency makes clear that it is *in God* (not the government or even the people) that we place our highest trust, but it leaves unspecified how one conceives of God. Most Americans are sure that there is a higher power guiding and judging their actions and whose plan they seek to bring to fruition; this makes clear that no secular authority or individual is the ultimate moral standard for deciding what is right and wrong, for them as individuals or for *we the people*. The government can be wrong, individual citizens can be mistaken, the entire nation can be catastrophically off course, but we can and will find our way back and make progress toward a better life for ourselves and all the world when we discover, heed, and subordinate ourselves to "this higher criterion."[5]

This ability to judge and reassess every facet of our individual and collective lives is what allows us to talk about how we or the nation can from time to time "lose our way" or "fail to live up to our highest ideals," while at the same time never abandoning a deep sense of our special moral mission on earth. Our shared civil religion provides us with bedrock, a place to stand, when we sense that our all-too-human efforts have failed; we turn to it in times of turmoil and find there the humility of our finitude, the solace of forgiveness, the promise of rebirth, the encouragement of hope, the strength of our convictions, and the inspiration to strive to further improve and realize a great yet still only dimly perceived goal: the ultimate, collective expression of America: "The land that never has been yet—And yet must be [illegible]"[6] In light of this sketch of Bellah's idea of civil religion, it should be clear how fitting it was for him to give voice to this notion as the decade of the sixties was grinding to a close. This was a time of great soul-searching, fierce recrimination, immense liberation, widespread confusion, and deep frustration. It was an age in which people were forced to reexamine and reevaluate their personal ideals and their vision of America. In light of the perspective and wisdom that is granted only with the passing of time, most Americans feel it was a time in which the nation made great strides toward becoming a more moral, just, and caring society and in developing new ideals not only about how our society should be but also concerning its proper role and place in the world.

Not even Bellah could have predicted how influential and in some ways notorious his idea of a civil religion would become. Much like Kuhn's concept of a scientific revolution, the idea of civil religion nearly eclipsed the many other profound contributions its author has made and continues to make in the course of his career, several of which are trenchantly described and analyzed in chapter 9 and advanced in chapter 10 of this work. The idea generated a vast secondary literature, and again like Kuhn's concept of scientific revolution, it often was misunderstood and at times employed in ways wholly contrary to its import and intention. Bellah's notion proved far larger than its original context and too powerful to be constrained by its original time and place. It has commanded the attention and inspired people throughout the world to look for or agitate on behalf of their own civil religion. This extension, appropriation, and development has occurred throughout East Asia, which is most fitting, both theoretically and poetically, for traditions such as Confucianism seem especially suited to be understood as a civil religion and East Asia was the focus of Bellah's early research and publication.[7] *Confucianism, A Habit of the Heart* thus marks both an extension and a return for Bellah and his theory.

In what sense, though, is Confucianism the civil religion of East Asian societies? The very fact that one points to an explicit tradition, with a long and variegated history, immediately raises questions, because one of the characteristic marks of a civil religion, in Bellah's sense of the term, is that it is not associated with *any* particular faith tradition. Some authors argue, and quite plausibly, that Confucianism is no longer, if it ever was, a religious tradition because it lacks the institutional structure required to have such a tradition. Nevertheless, Confucianism has been and remains one among several *habits of the heart* for most East Asian people: a set of general moral principles, life orientations and aims, and styles of reasoning describing what a good person and a good society are like and how one fosters personal moral development and social harmony. Such a habit of the heart reveals itself in many of the fundamental attitudes and unselfconscious behaviors of a people and, as in the earlier examples, it manifests itself in the symbols that permeate and subtly guide a culture.

If we look across East Asian societies for correlates to the aforementioned examples drawn from American culture, we get a very different message, depending on the culture we explore. For example, South Korea appears to offer good and even unequivocal evidence that Confucianism is indeed its civil religion or at the very least a core part of such. The National Emblem of the Republic of Korea has at its center the Supreme Ultimate (*taeguk* 太極) symbol, found also on its national flag, surrounded by the five petals of the Rose of Sharon, Korea's national flower. On Korea's national flag, the *taeguk* symbol is surrounded by four of the eight trigrams from the Chinese classic the *Book of Changes* (*Yijing* 易經), a core Confucian text. The *taeguk* symbolizes the harmonious balance of *yin* 陰 and *yang* 陽, the two fundamental forces in the universe, which are the origin of all things. The four trigrams on the flag represent Heaven, Earth, the sun, and the moon. These symbols date back to the earliest periods of Korean history and find even more remote precedents in China. If we look to Korean currency, we find clearer and more explicit manifestations of the culture's underlying Confucian character. The most common notes, the 1,000 and 5,000 *won* (元) denominations, both bear clear symbols of Korea's traditional Confucian culture. The obverse side of the 1,000 *won* note bears a traditional portrait of Yi Hwang 李滉 (1501–1570), one of the two most prominent Korean Confucian scholars of the Joseon dynasty; the 5,000 *won* note bears the likeness of the other, Yi I 李珥 (1536–1584), who joined in a widely celebrated debate with Yi Hwang about some of the most fundamental claims of Confucian philosophy.[8]

When we turn to the People's Republic of China, we find a very different set of national symbols. The National Emblem consists of a representation of the "Gate of Heavenly Peace" (*Tiananmen* 天安門), the main entrance to the "Forbidden City" (*zijincheng* 紫禁城, more commonly known as the "Former Palace," *gugong* 故宮), which served as the imperial palace throughout the Ming and Qing dynasties. However, most significantly and some would say ironically, it was from atop the Gate of Heavenly Peace that Mao Zedong announced the founding of the People's Republic of China in 1949. The golden image of the Forbidden City rests in a red circle; above it stand the five gold stars that appear on the national flag. The largest star, at the top and centered, represents the Communist Party of China; the four smaller stars arrayed beneath it represent the four social classes as defined by Maoist thought: proletarian workers, peasants, the petty bourgeoisie, and nationally based capitalists. Clearly, all of these symbols represent and display the power of the Communist Party. Chinese currency reinforces this impression in an even more direct and totalizing fashion. The obverse of every common denomination of Chinese paper money: the one, five, ten, twenty, fifty, and one hundred *yuan* (元) notes, or *renminbi* (人民幣), all contain the same image of Chairman Mao. In terms of these important aspects of civil society, symbols that permeate and subtly guide the culture, the most likely candidate for the "civil religion" of China is Maoism. But this would violate another key feature of Bellah's conception of what a civil religion is, for Maoism in China is unambiguously a self-conscious, state-sponsored, institutionalized set of beliefs and practices. The notion of civil religion can tolerate none of these.

When we turn and look for the general moral principles; life orientations and aims; widely shared, meaning-laden symbols; and styles of reasoning about what a good person and a good society are like and how one fosters personal moral development and social harmony, we find some basis for making the case that Confucianism might be the civil religion of China or at least an important part of it. Characteristically Confucian conceptions and practices concerning, for example, the relationship between parents and children and those that stretch across generations still define a great deal of belief and activity in China. General views about the role of the family and the relationship between self and society remain in the background and often come to the fore in contemporary Chinese culture. Confucian influence can also be seen in widely held beliefs and practices concerning the nature, practice, and aims of education. All of these important social phenomena are supported by shared stories, images, and examples from traditional literary sources that resonate and inform the lives of most Chinese people today. Nevertheless, the picture in China is more ambiguous and decidedly mixed, the state ideology and its various symbols dominate much of civil society, they crowd out and do not tolerate direct competition much less challenge; while Confucianism remains an enduring influence and source of moral inspiration in contemporary China, it is by no means the only such source, and there is no clear need for it to or reason to think it will assume such a role.

The current precarious and uncertain state of the Confucian tradition in China has prompted a number of concerned scholars to work at promoting the tradition as the much-needed moral foundation and guide for a rapidly transforming China, and such concern has led to increased interest in Bellah's conception of civil religion and his related interpretation and use of Tocqueville's notion of habits of the heart. A number of the contributions to this volume explore the many faces and complex workings of such attempts at a Confucian revival in China, Korea, and Japan. Several of these mention a parallel movement among a number of Chinese scholars to promote Confucianism as a national rather than civil religion.[9] A number of those who hope to make Confucianism the official national religion of China seek to enlist Bellah's ideas about civil religion in their cause, but, as noted earlier, such efforts often misconstrue and corrupt

Bellah's conception of civil religion. A civil religion can be promoted but never officially founded, sanctioned, or supported; it can and must draw upon particular historical religious traditions but must never speak from or represent any such tradition or school. To do so would undermine one of the most essential functions and appeals of a civil religion; it would align it with the government, official culture, and law, which are some of the most important forces against which civil religion stands as a moral judge and practical challenge. Civil religion must forever stand apart from and look beyond and above any secular, institutionalized authority; it must remain somewhat enigmatic in form and open to ongoing revision and development. It expresses no particular creed or doctrine but finds its strong and enduring voice in the collective history and aspirations of a people. For these reasons it might turn out that the true civil religion of East Asian societies cannot be associated, even loosely, with any single tradition. Perhaps the less exclusive traditions of East Asia give rise to a civil religion that is more of an amalgam of traditions: Daoist, Confucian, Buddhist, among others, and that collectively these and other sources supply the habits of the heart underlying life in these rich and complex societies.

Our first contribution, "Confucianism as Civil Religion," by Fenggang Yang, explores the vibrant contemporary movement among Mainland New Confucians to revive Confucianism as a resource for the moral reconstruction of China, an aim the author shares. Yang focuses on a group of thinkers whose goal is to make Confucianism the "state religion" of China, an aim the author does not share. As an alternative, Yang advocates the development of a new civil religion "based on both Confucianism and Christianity, which would serve not only China but also East Asia, the Pacific region, even possibly 'all under Heaven' " (p. 25). Yang's essay provides a helpful historical context within which to better understand the current interest in Confucianism as a civil religion in China; he explores the earlier harsh criticisms and campaigns against Confucianism, the subsequent collapse of Marxism-Leninism-Maoism as a normative standard and guide, and the recent avid advocacy of a return to and elevation of Confucian tradition. He also surveys some of the challenges involved in understanding Confucianism as a religion and explores the potential dangers of establishing Confucianism, or any tradition, as the state religion of China.

Yang also discusses one of the commonly encountered objections Mainland New Confucians make against liberal democracy: that "its legitimacy comes solely from popular votes of equal citizens" (p. 37). The thought is that such a political system inevitably leads to fragmented and selfish forms of individualism, problems for which Confucianism purportedly offers a ready-made and decisive solution. Careful readers will question whether these Mainland New Confucians have an accurate and adequate grasp of the nature of contemporary liberal democracy, for they fail to account for or appreciate the rule of law or the roles of rights, which are specifically designed to alleviate many of the problems they attribute to such societies. Yang takes their comments in a different direction by exploring the role that religion has always played in societies such as America, and this leads him to connect his analysis with Bellah's conception of civil religion and the possibility of Confucianism serving this role in China. As noted earlier, Yang rejects the latter possibility and instead contends that a combination of Confucianism and Christianity offers the best possibility for the development of a civil religion in China. He supports this proposal by claiming, "Christianity has become one of the major religions among the Chinese" (p. 40), and hence in some sense it is an important element among the Chinese habits of the heart. He further argues that Christianity offers "important resources for civil religion in China," foremost among these is that it provides a way, perhaps the *best* way, "to critically evaluate and purge its feudalist remnants, including gender inequality" (p. 40). Yang concludes his essay by suggesting that this new amalgam of Confucianism and Christianity "may serve well not only China or the greater China but also much of East Asia, the Transpacific region, even 'all under Heaven' " (p. 26), pointing toward themes that will take center stage in the concluding contributions to this volume.

Our second contributor, Sébastien Billioud, shifts the focus on the contemporary Confucian revival from the level of theoretical possibility to that of everyday norms and practices in "The Revival of Confucianism in the Sphere of Mores and the Reactivation of the Civil Religion Debate in China." This more practical perspective allows us to see a far greater range of Confucian civil religious norms, feelings, beliefs, and activities and gives us insights not only into where "the sphere of Chinese mores" currently is but also where it might be heading. Among Billioud's case studies are Mrs. D., formerly a member of the People's Liberation Army but now the owner of a vegetarian restaurant in Shenzhen who found "inner peace and life direction" through her contemporary reappropriation of Confucian tradition. Mrs. D. sponsors "classics reading sessions for children or conferences for adults' (p. 50) that count among their regular members many of her customers as well as several of her employees. Another case study focuses on Mr. Y., a university professor in Beijing and disciple of the Mainland New Confucian Jiang Qing. Mr. Y. organized and now leads a Confucian academy where he gathers "a group of well-educated young people (students and young professionals) for whom Confucianism now becomes a real spiritual resource" (p. 51).

Billioud does a splendid job describing the personal dimensions and deep subjective significance of these newly developed forms of Confucian spiritual practice, but he also carefully explores the role that the systematic views of thinkers such as Mou Zongsan, Wang Caigui, and Jiang Qing play in this growing social phenomenon. He also shows how the revival of Confucian practice often spills over into unexpected aspects of life, well outside any strict conception of Confucian circles. For example, Billioud describes the moral training regimen organized by the Taiwanese Buddhist monk the Venerable Master Jingkong, in which "selected candidates follow a six-month training course during which they live in the community and are mainly exposed to traditional Confucian values" (p. 54). Preliminary indications are that such "promotion of the Confucian classics or core elements of Confucian ethics by Buddhist organizations is quite a widespread phenomenon" (p. 55).

Another important dimension of Billioud's contribution is his survey and discussion of various contemporary debates concerning the notion of civil religion. He focuses on the views of mainland scholar Chen Ming, Paris-based Ji Zhe, and our first contributor, Yang Fenggang, professor of sociology and director of the Center on Religion and Chinese Society at Purdue University, as representing a distinctive perspective in this debate, one that explicitly rejects, for principled reasons, establishing Confucianism as any sort of national teaching or state religion. This puts them in direct opposition to contemporary mainland figures such as Jiang Qing and Kang Xiaoguang or the earlier view of Kang Youwei. Billioud goes on to explore some of the challenges associated with the possibility of Confucianism as a civil religion, for example the dangers of it becoming a vehicle for cultural nationalism as it has been in other contexts (i.e., Japan and Taiwan) and the profound difficulty posed by the condemnation and persecution of Confucianism by the CCP, still fresh in recent memory. Among the most fascinating possibilities he proposes is the idea that Confucianism might develop into what Jean-Paul Willaime calls a "common religion" that is "a civil religion with a primarily social—rather than political—orientation" (p. 58).

In our next contribution, "Inside the Revival of Confucianism in Mainland China: The Vicissitudes of Confucian Classics in Contemporary China as an Example," Peng Guoxiang offers a revealing survey and personal evaluation of the recent history, current state, and future potential of the Confucian classics in China and beyond. In the past, the classical texts of

Confucianism commanded a central role in the life of the tradition not only as scriptures to be venerated and studied but also texts that inspired a rich and extensive tradition of commentary. Not surprisingly, study groups on the classics and schools for teaching the classics to young people are widespread and popular manifestations of the contemporary Confucian revival. Peng's contribution thus gives us a clear and revealing lens through which we can consider not only the roles the classics have played as repositories of Confucian habits of the heart and scriptural authority but also a reflection on what part they might and should play in contemporary Chinese and world culture.

As Peng's title suggests, the recent history of the Confucian classics within China is a tale of vicissitudes and challenges, and the current state of play is no less tumultuous or rife with danger. As noted in chapters 1 and 2, the Chinese classics and the tradition as a whole suffered fierce condemnation and criticism by the CCP since the founding of the People's Republic of China and down through the 1970s. Focusing on the classics brings this general attack into clear focus, for throughout this period the Confucian classics were banned from all formal education; "during this period the term 'classics' (i.e., canonized) could only refer to works of the Marxist-Leninist tradition" (p. 72). When this rocky relation came to be replaced with increased attention to the classics by the party and the government, during the 1980s, there was a surge of interest, among academics, in the Confucian classics. After 2000, this interest spread to society in general and served as an important facet of the widespread Confucian revival. Nevertheless, in the wake of this most welcome attention were unwelcome and unappealing consequences. Roughly, these can be described as the politicization and commercialization of the Confucian classics.

Other contributions to this volume explore some of the many ways the revival of Confucianism is being politicized. Those advocating that Confucianism be established as China's official national religion often are closely aligned with or at the center of movements advocating cultural nationalism; they typically contrast their beliefs and policies with those advocating various forms of "Western" democracy and human rights. Most who advocate Confucianism as China's civil religion work to distance themselves from this kind of national or state-sponsored model. In addition to these attempts to have the tradition directly represent the state, Peng explores how Confucianism has been implicated in recent government calls for building "a harmonious society," where harmony is largely understood not as the blending of different voices, which is what traditional Confucian sources advocate, but obedience to a single authoritative voice.

Alongside and sometimes in step with such politicization is the parallel threat of commercialization and commodification of the tradition. There is a fairly widespread inclination among people and governmental agencies with no deep understanding or real interest in the tradition to hop on board and ride the current wave of interest in Confucianism to profit themselves. This can be seen at the level of individuals teaching or selling products connected with the classics, from new translations and commentaries to CDs and television programs, or governmental agencies seeking to cash in on such programing and the tourist revenues associated with revived interest in visiting Confucian sites.

Peng laments that the best aspect of the Confucian classics, their ability to guide and inspire moral values, is being crushed beneath the twin pressures of politicization and commercialization. He notes the remarkable fact that "the Confucian classics have not been officially adopted into the officially sanctioned education system at any level and are not part of the general education requirements in universities" (p. 76). This lack of serious attention to and engagement with the classics is a powerful impediment to them regaining a proper and prominent place within Chinese culture and society and works against them taking what Peng sees as their destined place upon the even larger stage of world culture.

In her lucid and revealing contribution, "The Politics of Confucianism in Contemporary China," Anna Sun begins by introducing three "snapshots" taken from contemporary Chinese society to highlight a range of political possibilities for Confucianism in China. First, she notes that in recent publications the government seems inclined to regard Confucianism not only as a religion but one of the five "major religions" within China. This would mark a profound change in the official stance and attitude toward Confucianism, though it would leave as an open question what the state would do from this new stance and with this new attitude. Second, she recounts the remarkable but difficult to decipher incident concerning the thirty-one-foot-tall bronze statue of Confucius that suddenly appeared in front of the National History Museum, which is located on the border of Tiananmen Square, and just as quickly disappeared, whisked inside the museum for display. This event gave rise to a frenzy of speculation about the symbolism, possible internal political struggles, and final meaning of these actions. Third and finally, she introduces the "Qufu Church Controversy," which concerned the planned construction of a Protestant church in Qufu, Confucius's native home. This plan generated heated protests from various "Confucian" individuals and groups who objected in various ways to the building of such a prominent Christian structure on the "sacred" ground of

Confucianism. Sun takes these snapshots as representative of three different political dimensions of contemporary Confucianism. The first represents the "politics of epistemology," the second stands for the "politics of the religion question," the third manifests the "politics of Confucian nationalism."

The "politics of epistemology" concerns the formidable difficulties associated with our understanding of the phenomenon of religion: what precisely is religion, and how do we know one when we see one? Related to this question are the very real consequences that come with any view or typology of religion: once institutionalized classifications of religion play significant roles "in knowledge production as well as policymaking" (p. 88). The "politics of the religion question" is connected to what is at stake for the Chinese state (and one might add to those outside of the state both within and beyond China) in declaring and treating Confucianism as a religion. The CCP is an adamantly atheistic political party. As noted in several of the other contributions to this volume, it has had a profoundly antagonistic relationship with Confucianism as well as other religious traditions, throughout most of its history. And yet now, for a variety of reasons, arising from both domestic and foreign concerns, the government has grown increasingly more engaged with religion. Today, we find the government explicitly approving of Confucianism and at least tacitly endorsing certain interpretations of Confucian ethics as a kind of state morality. At the extreme, some within the government want to make Confucianism China's national religion, and surely hints of such a view have manifested themselves in recent statements and actions, among them the appearance and subsequent disappearance of the statue of Confucius on Tiananmen Square. The "politics of Confucian nationalism" was manifested in the "Qufu Church Controversy," but like the other forms of politics associated with the revival of Confucianism, this one too has an ambiguous and evolving nature. The intolerance displayed by some who protested the building of the church was in several cases conjoined with a growing national pride and related hypersensitivity to insults, real or imagined, to the dignity of Chinese culture (represented in this case by the sacred ground of Confucianism). Such growing nationalism is evident in a range of contemporary phenomena in China and has risen along with the fortunes of the Chinese economy and its corresponding greater influence on global political, military, and economic affairs. National pride, however, is a two-edged sword and not always in the hands of the government. Some who want to make Confucianism a national religion make clear that their ultimate goal is not just to influence or even convert the CCP but to replace it with a "Confucian" form of government. One man's patriot can be another man's traitor, a nation's revolutionary, or a people's savior.

All these forms of politics are inextricably intertwined with the question of Confucianism as a civil religion, for whatever form such advocacy takes, it must be based on a belief that Confucianism is a religion (the politics of epistemology), that viewing it as such will have profound consequences (the politics of the religion question), and that the imperative to take up this cause is an overriding concern with the current state and future prospects of China (the politics of Confucian nationalism). Sun dedicates the remaining sections of her essay to this set of issues, which she identifies as the "Politics of Confucianism as a Civil Religion."

In "Obstacles to the Globalization of Confucianism," Richard Madsen draws attention to and seeks to explain why, unlike the other major East Asian religions of Daoism and Buddhism, Confucianism has not traveled as well or settled in as comfortably in North America, Europe, and other parts of the world. This anomaly is not only intellectually curious but practically important, especially for those, like several of our contributors, who see Confucianism as an important resource not only for East Asian people but also for all the people of the world.

Madsen argues that part of the reason lies in the particular historical formation of our current notion of "Confucianism." While the Confucian tradition has a long and varied history in East Asia, Confucianism as a world religion is a recent phenomenon, arguably coming into being at the Parliament of World Religions in 1893. Madsen notes that the Chinese ambassador to this meeting "gave a famous speech proclaiming that China too had a national religion and that religion was Confucianism" (p. 101). The more scientific spirit of the age, along with a strong desire on the part of Chinese intellectuals to present their national religion in the best possible light, conspired to shear Confucianism of its more mysterious, other-worldly, and metaphysically arresting features and shape it into a purely humanistic philosophy of life. This transformation tended to render Confucianism more amendable to some but less intriguing and inspiring for the average person. It became a form of life most attractive to intellectuals, particularly academics, and less distinctively a world religion in any robust sense of the term.

Another challenge for Confucianism has been its association with the ruling class. Historically, Confucianism has been understood as offering "a guide to cultivating elites who will be fit to govern" (p. 109). This has led to it becoming a target for the CCP throughout much of its history. Wholly apart from this aspect of its legacy, the explicitly political nature and focus of much Confucian thought at times has tended to limit its appeal to those who take a strong interest in the political dimensions of human life. Moreover, the particular political character of Confucianism, which calls for the subordination of the self to the group and the greater good, has made it quite attractive to authoritarian regimes and makes it appear incompatible with Western individualism, a current that runs well beyond the societies of Europe and North America. The liberal tradition, with its profound commitment to the dignity and rights of each person, conflicts with the generally more communal character of Confucianism and with specific beliefs, attitudes, and practices that traditionally have reinforced things like gender inequality. Given all these obstacles, is there any reason to hope that Confucianism will be welcomed and embraced outside of East Asia?

Madsen contends that there is certainly room for improvement and suggests there may yet be room for hope if Confucianism "dissociates itself from political power, comes to terms with the rights and freedoms that Western Enlightenment liberalism has made possible, and re-embeds itself to some degree in the myths and rituals that give meaning to ordinary life" (p. 109). While all of these are daunting challenges, they remain more than notional possibilities. For one thing, living traditions are not closed off from reform and self-transformation; for another, there are clear and impressive examples, in Taiwan and South Korea, of how strongly Confucian societies can accommodate all of the changes that Madsen claims are needed to revive the tradition. One lesson that recent history seems to teach is that such reforms cannot be ordered from the top down, "Confucianism that is developed from the ground up . . . will be more credible globally than that promoted from the top down" (p. 109). Here we return to a theme found in many of the contributions to this volume: a true civil religion, whether particular or global in nature, must take shape and command the hearts and minds of the people. Habits of the heart flow forth freely and spontaneously; they cannot be engineered by a central authority and stamped upon the soul.

In the next two chapters, Sungmoon Kim and Do-Hyun Han examine how Confucian habits of the heart have been revitalized in two different stages of contemporary Korean society—before and after democratization. Taken together, the sociological and political implications of these two chapters are of critical significance because they powerfully show that Confucianism as social capital and practice can not only be compatible with but even bolster both authoritarian and democratic regimes, implying that the relatively stable social semiotics underlying Confucian habits of the heart does not necessarily prevent it from developing into multifaceted (democratic, nondemocratic, or antidemocratic) social actions and strategies.[10]

In "Beyond a Disciplinary Society: Reimagining Confucian Democracy in South Korea," Sungmoon Kim examines why South Korea, arguably the most Confucianized society in the contemporary world, has remained (and still remains) one critical exception to the recent fascination with Confucian constitutionalism and Confucian democracy among East Asian scholars, even if "Koreans are still deeply saturated with Confucian habits and mores in their daily social life" (p. 114). The virtual lack of interest in Confucian democracy in today's Korea, argues Kim, has a great deal to do with the failure of what can be called the "New Confucianism Movement" initiated by a group of Confucian-minded philosophers and social scientists in the late 1990s and early 2000s, especially its critical failure to present Confucianism in a way that resonates with the increasing democratic sensitivity of the general Korean public (particularly young Koreans).

Kim pays special attention to Chaibong Hahm's political theory of postmodern Confucianism, which undergirded the theoretical foundation of the whole intellectual movement during this period and which Hahm presented as a discourse that would best capture the Koreans' Confucian habits of the heart. Kim argues that Hahm's Confucian political theory, at the heart of which lies a poignant critique of Western modern epistemology and the reaffirmation of Neo-Confucian cosmology and metaphysics (along with associated social and political assumptions), failed to accommodate much less resonate with the active participatory citizenship and strong democratic civil society that were increasingly characterizing Korean politics in the postdemocratic context, because it could hardly come to terms with the new "Confucian-democratic" social habits and mores that had taken hold throughout Korean society. In Kim's view, Hahm's postmodern Confucianism, though helpful for understanding why the modern onto-epistemology underlying Western liberal democracy is both at odds with Confucian ontology and the normative ideas affiliated with it and unpalatable to the Koreans' (Confucian) moral sensibilities, only reaffirms premodern Confucianism in the name of postmodern Confucianism ("postmodern" in the sense of overcoming the limitations of modern Western epistemology and political theory), thus failing to reinvent Confucianism as democracy-enhancing political theory and social practice. In particular, Kim contends, Hahm's strong emphasis on "discipline" as the core element of the Confucian habit of the heart only tended to alienate the Korean public from a serious exploration of a new mode of democracy in their given societal and cultural context by making Confucian democracy look like another version of East Asian developmentalism or soft authoritarianism.

Kim's core claim vindicates Fenggang Yang's worry about recent attempts to revive Confucianism by some Mainland Chinese scholars—that is, unless such a revival genuinely reflects the general public's deep Confucian moral sensibilities and political aspirations, not only can it turn out to be a sort of phantom social phenomenon, having no meaningful social moorings, but, more problematically, it can be socially dangerous and politically oppressive. Kim's essay can and should serve as a cautionary reminder to some Chinese scholars of why they should be extremely cautious about what they are asking for (i.e., the revival of Confucian monism) while at the same time further encouraging them to develop modes of Confucian political theory attractive not only to Confucian intellectuals but, more crucially, to ordinary Chinese citizens.

In his contribution, entitled "The Experience of Village Leaders during the *Saemaul* Movement in the 1970s: Focusing on the Lives of the Male Leaders," Do-Hyun Han shows how a plethora of Confucian social capital organized through the *Saemaul* (New Village or New Community) movement launched in 1970 nurtured and supported Park Chung Hee's authoritarian government, thereby (although implicitly) belying one of the dominant theses among contemporary Confucian theorists, namely, the thesis about the happy congruency between Confucian communitarianism and (national) democratic empowerment. As a sociologist, though, Han's primary focus in this chapter is not so much on refuting the congruency thesis as such or on examining the complex nature of what can be called Park's "Confucian authoritarianism," which enabled the regime's remarkable political and economic "success," but, by drawing on some powerful empirical evidence (consisting mainly of interviews), on showing how the *Saemaul* movement, otherwise known as a government-originated and government-coerced political project, often functioned as a community project in which local leaders and ordinary peasants participated with great enthusiasm, devotion, and self-sacrifice.

Han's central finding is that the *Saemaul* movement, which he notes was inspired and partially based upon the model of the traditional Korean Confucian *hyang'yak* (Community Compact), as a voluntary community project carried out in local villages was possible due to the "Confucian values, orientations, and practices" (p. 139) or habits of the heart of the local leaders who actually carried out the movement. "The Confucian orientation and values of those who participated in the *Saemaul* movement provided both the initial motivation and sustaining perseverance required to implement this large-scale and dramatic social initiative," says Han (p. 140). What is worth noting is that in contrast to most Korean social scientists, who understand the *Saemaul* movement as essentially a purely secular economic developmental plan, Han captures its driving force in terms of Confucian civil religion by drawing attention to strong religious—Christian in appearance but Confucian in actual content—elements widely found in the ordinary discourse of its actual carriers in Korean localities. It is the Confucian habit of the heart, asserts Han, that transformed the ground-level leaders, unpaid volunteers, into "incarnations of the spirit of community development or priests of the Korean civil religion" (p. 162) who devoted themselves to the rebirth of the village. Such participants were motivated by traditional Confucian views about self-cultivation and its proper aims to train and discipline themselves to develop the abilities and skills needed to transform their local communities and the larger state into a flourishing and harmonious social order. They were guided, in ways that still inform the lives of many East Asian people, by an ideal that sees learning and self-improvement as inextricably tied to more comprehensive social welfare and inspired by their beliefs about and at times meetings with a charismatic leader: Park Chung Hee, whom many perceived in terms of the Confucian ideal of a virtuous ruler. In the absence of such Confucian underpinnings, it is implausible to think that the *Saemaul* movement would have commanded such loyalty and been as successful as it proved to be.

According to Han, by participating in the movement, the *Saemaul* leaders underwent a kind of spiritual self-transformation and then each became active "proselytizers" of this transformative experience by helping local farmers to personally embody the spirit of community. For instance, successful (or "self-reliant") village leaders participated in a "training program," in which they invited six to ten leaders of less successful ("basic" or "self-help") villages for a few days' visit to their homes, during which they offered the chance for "field training": an opportunity to gain the know-how to "live better," the famous catchphrase of the movement. In each of these cases, the visitors were fully accommodated by their hosts; this would not have been possible without tremendous yet voluntary sacrifices on the part of the hosts (and their wives). In other words, says Han, "after 'conversion,' they [the village leaders] became preachers and were ready to be 'martyrs.'" (p. 162).

Our next contribution, by Takahiro Nakajima, "Contemporary Japanese Confucianism from a Genealogical Perspective," explores a range of different features and qualities of what he refers to as the "Confucian boom" in contemporary Japan. His essay thus concerns the general theme of our anthology by exploring the revival of Confucianism in East Asia and its role as a habit of the heart among the Japanese people; as readers will see, this revival takes a very specific form in Japan, manifesting both similarities and differences from what we find in China and Korea. For example, like the increased contemporary interest in Confucianism in China and Korea, the Japanese revival of Confucianism always has a spiritual dimension, with a number of people arguing explicitly that Confucianism is and must be understood as a religion, in the fullest sense of that term. Also like what we find in China and Korea, the Confucian boom in Japan often is associated with if not explicitly tied to movements of national revitalization and claims about how Confucianism is part of an essential and authentic "national spirit." On the other hand, in a number of important respects, the Confucian revival in Japan is quite distinctive.

One of the distinguishing characteristics of contemporary Japanese interest in Confucianism is that it is almost exclusively focused on the figure of Confucius and study of the *Analects*. Other major figures and classical texts from the tradition are largely ignored. Behind this intense interest in the *Analects* and its traditional author is a widely held belief in the existence of a pure "Confucian spirit" that can and must be extracted from the text and internalized within each person. This spiritual essence is then to serve as an unwavering moral guide, offering the opportunity to recover a profound religious sensibility. Nakajima explores a variety of contemporary Japanese discourses focused on reviving Confucianism that develop contrasting interpretations of the role of Confucius and the nature of the *Analects* from this common starting point, which supplies a shared reference across the genealogies he traces.

An interest in "cultural cultivation" (*kyōyō* 教養) is shared by many proponents of the Confucian revival in Japan. This process consists of a range of practices, from recitation and study of the *Analects* to more formal regimens of meditation. Yasuoka Sadako advocates *kyōyō* for children, insisting that it can produce "adults with firm principle" (p. 171). As Nakajima is careful to point out, like many who emphasize such training, Yasuoka's aim is to recover an ideal past essence or character that is held up as authentically Japanese. Such policies are encouraged for students at all levels of education and by educators, both within and outside the profession. For example, Saitō Takashi, a professor at Meiji University, is a prominent proponent of *kyōyō* as the only sure way to recover Japan's "national character." Nakajima points out that in Saitō's writings, we "easily find an echo from prewar Japan, when it was commonly said that we Japanese understand the essence of the *Analects* better than the Chinese" (p. 172).

Katō Tōru, another Meiji University professor, offers one of the rare criticisms of this kind of essentialist and nationalistic view, arguing that such nostalgic readings obscure "the dangerous or critical aspect of the *Analects*" (p. 173), a criticism that also has been leveled at contemporary popular Confucian advocates such as Yu Dan. The idea is that the *Analects* is a fundamentally political text and one deeply concerned with political legitimacy; it often has been the source of revolutionary inspiration and remains so today. Katō's emphasis on the revolutionary character of the *Analects* rests on an explicitly religious reading of Confucius and his teachings, and in doing so he was building on and acknowledges the work of people like Shirakawa Shizuka. Shirakawa presented a bold religious interpretation of the *Analects* that offered a stark contrast with widely accepted secular humanistic understandings of the text and its traditional author and used this reading to launch fierce criticisms of the Japanese establishment. Kaji Nobuyuki follows this line of argument as well, offering an elaborate theory of how Confucius himself attained a powerful religious consciousness. Kaji relies upon this religious reading of the *Analects* as a foundation for criticizing modern Western values such as "democracy, individualism, and feminism" (p. 176–77) and advocating the restoration of a traditional, conservative form of life. Here we see another important point of contact between these Japanese revivalists and the Mainland New Confucians. This critique of Western values and call to return to an authentic Confucian tradition is also seen in the influential work of authors such as Yasuoka Masahiro, who combined this political and cultural orientation more explicitly and intimately with the issue of *kyōyō*, discussed previously, but who turned away from a religious reading of the *Analects*, insisting that Confucius was a philosopher and moralist.

Nakajima concludes his chapter with the observation that contemporary Japanese discourses about reviving Confucianism have more or less turned in a great circle but never broken out of the general perspectives and approaches found in prewar Japan. The Confucian revival remains mired in essentialist notions of a pure Japanese spirit and national essence and is closely tied to criticisms of modern "Western" values. In these respects, we see strong similarities with certain currents running through the resurgence of Confucianism in other East Asian cultures and especially in China. Nakajima bemoans this recurrent, conservative nostalgia and holds out the hope and promise not of Confucianism as a civil or national religion but "a new approach to Confucianism," what he calls "Critical Confucianism," as the path toward a more accurate and revealing understanding of the tradition, its contemporary possibilities, and future potential.

As noted in the opening sections of this introduction, this volume is both an extension and a return for Bellah and several of his key theories about religion. It is a return to the East Asian cultures that served as the focus of Bellah's early research and publications and has always remained among his deepest and most abiding interests. It is an extension to take as its central theme his theory of civil religion and his general, ethically charged approach to social scientific research and apply and develop them in new and revealing ways. The last two contributions step back from the application of Bellah's theories and turn toward a more synoptic analysis and further development of them.

In his chapter, "The Bildungsroman of the Heart: Thick Naturalism in Robert Bellah's *Religion in Human Evolution*," Xiao Yang relates the central issues of this volume to larger themes in our understanding of religion. In this way, his work serves as a bridge between much of what the volume contains up to this point and Bellah's latest work, including his concluding essay to this volume. Xiao begins by noting the important relationship between Bellah's earlier arguments in *Habits of the Heart* and his recent, monumental volume *Religion in Human Evolution*—how the latter work should be read as offering "a general theory of culture as habits of the heart, of which religion is an essential dimension" (p. 184). Most importantly, in this volume, Bellah enlists the resources of disciplines from the natural sciences, such as biology, evolutionary psychology, cognitive science, and child psychology, in order to develop a nonreductive humanistic naturalism concerning religious phenomena. This establishes a new point of view, distinct from those who seek to deploy the natural sciences either to debunk or to defend the status of religion. Bellah seeks neither; his aim is to understand and explain; the effect is often to amaze and inspire.

Religion in Human Evolution offers a general theory of religion as a cultural system, and as Xiao points out, one of its most fascinating claims, defended in the first part of the book, is how the human proclivity to play "gives rise to culture, especially ritual and myth, which are the key components of religion" (p. 187). This shows how Bellah's project not only sheds light upon the origin, nature, and role of religion, but also how it contributes to a more general understanding of the character of human nature. Bellah provides a grand narrative of the evolution of religion, which both defends and qualifies his earlier claim of religion as a cultural system. It defends this claim by showing how all religions share core structural features and a similar course of development but qualifies it by illustrating how religion is always "embodied, social, personal, emotional, experiential, developmental, and historical" (p. 187).

One of the most revealing and powerful claims Xiao defends is the parallel he draws between Bellah's *Religion in Human Evolution* and Hegel's *Lectures on the Philosophy of Religion*. Xiao notes that both works and few others share the virtue of providing a general theory of religion and tying this theory to in-depth analyses of a broad range of religions from around the world. This insight reminds us that the notions of civil religion and habits of the heart, which have served as the guiding themes of our volume, are equally at home and powerfully revealing in China and the modern West. The combination of grand theoretical construction and extensive and meticulous application is breathtaking in both Bellah's and Hegel's works. So too is the profound shared theme that "nothing is ever lost." Xiao brilliantly summarizes this point, saying, "Hegel and Bellah try to tell the universal history of religion as *Bildungsroman* of humankind" (p. 192). As Bellah himself describes it, in order to fully realize our humanity we must "live again those moments that belong to us in the depths of our present, to draw living water from the well of the past" (p. 192).

Nothing is ever lost for each individual, for each tradition or culture, and for the general phenomenon of religion as well. Every stage of our experience draws upon and reconfigures elements of our history, and these elements echo and are reflected and refracted throughout the world's religions and cultures. In these ways, the habits of the heart we find in individual lives and particular societies, while in certain respects clearly distinctive of specific historical trajectories, are also, at the same time, traveling along shared trajectories. They do not, though, always travel in straight lines, and as Xiao insightfully explains, this is a major strength of Bellah's account, for this "crucial insight allows Bellah to hold the view that there is 'progress' in the sense that new capacities are acquired as humankind moves from tribal and archaic religions to Axial Age religions. Yet he can at the same time reject the view that there is progress in all aspects in general" (p. 197).

The implications of *Religion in Human Evolution* are dramatic and diverse; it is pointedly opposed to antifoundationalism and postmodernism but offers a revolutionary form of grand narrative that goes far beyond traditional versions of universal history in both its open-ended interpretative capacity and its incorporation of insights from the natural sciences. In regard to our concern with habits of the heart and the possibility of Confucianism as a civil religion, *Religion in Human Evolution* seems to say not only that traditions like Confucianism will always have a civil religious dimension but also that they will always point beyond their specific place, time, and culture, drawing "living water from the well of the past" and pointing the way forward to a more grand and global future.

Our final contribution—"Can We Imagine a Global Civil Religion?"—carries forward many of the claims discussed in Xiao's essay and refocuses and extends the central themes of this volume. In it, Robert Bellah takes up again an idea he first raised in his provocative, inspiring, and influential essay "Civil Religion in America": the possibility of a "world civil religion" (p. 205). In its original context, this idea was suggested as a possible response to what Bellah termed the "third time of trial" for America, the contemporary period when the nation and its people would seek to work out a viable and satisfying answer to the question of America's place in the world, which of course includes the question of what kind of world Americans want to help build. While the idea of a global civil religion initially sounds naïve or idealistic in the sense of being impractical, understanding it in terms of a conception of what role America should serve in the world and what kind of world that might be situates the idea in the historical and still ongoing context of America's quest for its true destiny and in the very real and practical challenges of where and how to use the resources, position, power, and influence of the nation. Seen in this way, the question of a global civil religion, a religion for what Confucians would describes as "all under Heaven," is revealed to be a concern of every nation and every person on earth who aims at contributing to the construction of "a viable and coherent world order" (p. 205). Any such order, if it is to be something we choose rather than something imposed upon us, will require a global civil society, and, as Bellah and others before him have argued, "any actual civil society will have a religious dimension" (p. 207).

What makes the question of a global civil religion more pressing now than it has been in the past is the emergence of alternatives or as we see it pretenders to the crown. For example, in his essay "Mammon and the Culture of the Market," Harvey Cox brilliantly argues that "the emerging global market culture . . . is generating an identifiable value-laden, 'religious' world-view" (p. 207). While none can deny its power, influence, or importance, there are severe problems with the global market as a contender for a world civil religion. For one thing, there is the profound incivility of its structure: the market is indifferent to human inequality or any strong moral value. The market tracks and rewards efficiencies, but it serves no greater or humane end. Moreover, it is not concerned about pressing problems such as environmental degradation; "externalities" such as the value a virgin forest has for humans beings have no firm place in its calculations. Rather than offering a foundation for a stable and satisfying global civil society, the market, untamed, presents one of the greatest threats to it.

A global civil religion requires a shared moral and spiritual perspective, but some, for example Michael Walzer, argue that humanity in general has no common life, history, or culture that might provide the basis of such common cause. Just as change is said to be the only constant, the only thing humanity purportedly has in common is its particularity: its different cultures. Bellah argues against this view, insisting that many of us in the modern world actually live in numerous overlapping communities linked by shared rules and norms and that underneath the precious and remarkable variety of world cultures are common needs, themes, and aspirations that are parts of our long and complex evolutionary inheritance. Drawing upon his recent magnum opus *Religion in Human Evolution,* discussed in chapter 9, Bellah presents a variety of examples and arguments to support his contention that we in fact share much more than many realize. He goes on to note that the emergence of transnational movements like socialism, feminism, and environmentalism add strength, complexity, and capacity to this underlying common set of challenges, experiences, and concerns. In addition, technologies facilitating high-speed, long-distance travel and instant global, mass communication are working to knit the people of the world more closely together into what some call the global village. The question, though, remains: how do we mobilize such resources into the common cause of a global civil society?

One answer, offered by people such as Jürgen Habermas, is basically political; what is needed is a radical new political vision, "an obligatory cosmopolitan solidarity" that is capable of breaking down the divisions inherent in nations and the universal pressures of the global economy. If such solidarity requires a global form of government, the prospects do not look promising nor, we would argue, are they appealing. If cosmopolitan solidarity remains more of an abstract personal ideal, it seems hardly strong enough to exert the kind of influence that the task requires. And so while the goal is something all people of goodwill can endorse, they still are in need of a firm foundation and ample motivation to launch what Bellah, citing William James, describes as "the moral equivalent of war" against the growing force of global economic forces. Here we return to the core themes of this volume, now understood not only as the habits of the heart or civil religion of this or that particular culture but of humanity as a whole. Bellah concludes his essay with the following declaration and idea: "I am convinced that religious motivation is a necessary factor if we are to transform the growing global moral consensus and the significant beginnings of world law into an effective form of global solidarity and global governance, an actually existing global civil society with a spiritual dimension drawing from all the great religions of the world" (p. 219).

The contributions to this volume explore some of the many ways Bellah's notion of civil religion and the related idea of habits of the heart resonate within, inspire, and challenge contemporary East Asian Confucian societies and the potential these ideas have to support a greater, global civil order. These essays mark the opening stage of a powerful, potentially fruitful, and even revolutionary debate in the cultures of East Asia, which are undergoing a period of transformation and critical self-reflection not wholly unlike what characterized America in the 1960s. East Asian societies not only have to ask what form their own lives and nations should take but also what role they will play in the evolving global order. Our hope is that this debate persuades the people of contemporary East Asian societies to reflect upon, reclaim, rebuild, reform, and refine their heritages, Confucian as well as others, and that it further leads societies—East, West, and all between—to reflect deeply upon and draw strength from the civil religions and habits of the heart that lie beneath and stand ready to provide guidance and inspiration to us all.

Notes

1. "Civil Religion in America," reprinted in *The Robert Bellah Reader*, ed. Robert N. Bellah and Steven M. Tipton (Durham and London: Duke University Press, 2006), 225. (First published in *Daedalus* 96.1 [Winter 1967]: 1–21.)

2. Ibid.

3. Ibid.

4. Alexis de Tocqueville, *Democracy in America*, trans. George Lawrence, ed. J. P. Mayer (New York: Anchor Books, 1969), 287. This idea served as the central and organizing theme in a highly insightful and influential book by Bellah and others written many years later. See Robert N. Bellah, Richard Madsen, William M. Sullivan, Ann Swidler, and Steven M. Tipton, *Habits of the Heart: Individualism and Commitment in American Life* (Berkeley: University of California Press, 1985).

5. Bellah et al., *Habits of the Heart*, 229.

6. Langston Hughes, "Let America Be America Again," reprinted in *The Collected Poems of Langston Hughes* (New York: Alfred A. Knopf, 1994), 189–191. (First published in *Esquire* (July 1939): 92.

7. Bellah obtained a joint PhD degree in sociology and Far Eastern languages from Harvard University. His first book, which was based upon his dissertation, was *Tokugawa Religion: The Cultural Roots of Modern Japan*, second ed. (New York: Free Press, 1985).

8. The obverse side of the 50,000 *won* note bears a traditional portrait of Shin Saimdang 申師任堂 (1504–1551), a famous woman artist, writer, calligrapher, and poet, who also was the mother of Yi I. She is commonly referred to as "Wise Mother" (*Eojin Eomeoni* 어진 어머니) and is revered as a model of Confucian ideals.

9. The term *guojiao* is variously translated as "national religion" or "state religion" and appears both ways in this volume. Regardless of which translation one chooses, the sense is that Confucianism would be the official religion of China, much as the Church of England is the official Christian church of England.

Advocates of the *guojiao* ideal, such as Kang Youwei 康有爲 (1858–1927) and Jiang Qing 蔣慶, recognize and defend freedom of religion and reject coercion on the part of the state when it comes to matters of religious faith or practice.

10. For a theoretical discussion on this plasticity of Confucianism as social practice, see Sungmoon Kim, "Confucianism in Contestation: The May Struggle of 1991 in South Korea and Its Lesson," *New Political Science* 31.1 (2009): 49–68.

1

Confucianism as Civil Religion

Fenggang Yang

Since the beginning of the twenty-first century, Mainland New Confucians (*dalu xinrujia* 大陆新儒家; hereafter, MNC) have made important statements and stirred up effervescences of discussion. Some of the most captivating statements include the necessity to revive Confucianism for the moral reconstruction of China, the necessity to avert the development of liberal democracy in China, and the necessity to make Confucianism the "state religion" (*guojiao* 国教) of China.[1] There are certainly varied positions among them regarding these important issues, but there have been plenty of expressions or sentiments that affirm the desirability, if not outright necessity, of these developments. Either taking the soft position of desirability or the hard position of necessity, MNC have shown a combative spirit against opposition and criticism, especially attacking what they perceived as political liberals, culturally Westernized, and Christians in China and the West. The combative approach is an indication of their frustration, albeit misguided, because in the current social, cultural, and political contexts, almost all of their goals are beyond reach. Yet, taking Confucius as their model, they are exhibiting a spirit of striving for a noble goal regardless of the improbability (*Analects* 14.41).[2]

At the onset, let me state as clearly as possible my position on these issues. First, I share MNCs' desire to revive Confucianism for the moral reconstruction of China. Second, I share much of their criticism of liberal democracy, more precisely the particular version of liberal democracy that seems dominant among Chinese liberals. Finally, I disagree with those MNC about making Confucianism the state religion. As an alternative, I suggest the development of civil religion based on both Confucianism and Christianity, which would serve not only China but also East Asia, the Pacific region, even possibly "all under Heaven" (*tianxia* 天下). In this chapter, I focus the discussion on Confucianism as religion or civil religion and only touch upon the other two issues briefly.

Changing Attitudes toward Religion

To begin with, China observers must realize that an important change of attitudes toward religion has happened in China, even though the religious policy based on atheism by and large has remained suppressive. Throughout the twentieth century, Chinese intellectuals commonly perceived religion negatively. Now it has become a value-added term among many intellectuals, especially for some MNC. The negative perception of religion might come from the introduction and appropriation of European Enlightenment thoughts. It was then reinforced and radicalized by Marxism-Leninism-Maoism (hereafter, MLM). The appropriated Enlightenment heritage served as the basis for the antisuperstition campaigns by political regimes and the antireligion movements by intellectuals since the New Culture movement in the 1910s and 1920s.[3] MLM ideology compelled the communist authorities to suppress religion as a reactionary social and political force. The ultraleftist regime went even further to eradicate religion and completely banned religion from 1966 to 1979. This stunning experiment spectacularly failed, as did a series of social engineering experiments. The failures came to be acknowledged by some Communist Party leaders. In the late 1970s, as Deng Xiaoping emerged as the paramount leader, the Chinese Communist Party took a detour path, initiating economic reforms and opening-up toward the capitalist world. Some religions have been granted limited social and physical space for practice. However, until now leftist intellectuals have never stopped despising religion.[4] When they dislike some social phenomenon, they say that it is so bad that it must be religion or of religion.

The leftist intellectual who took the lead in criticizing Confucianism was Ren Jiyu (1916–2009). It might appear paradoxical that this scholarly man remained an MLM loyalist until his death. In fact, however, he was the man who was single-handedly picked by Chairman Mao Zedong and entrusted to establish the Institute of World Religions (IWR) in 1964, two years before the launching of the Cultural Revolution when all religions were banned. The IWR mission was, as has been recalled and reemphasized repeatedly, to apply MLM to criticize theism and defeat religion.[5] Carrying on the mission assigned by Mao, after the official ending of the Cultural Revolution, Ren Jiyu mounted assaults on Confucianism as a religion, blaming it as the culprit responsible for China's social and political problems, including the calamities of the Cultural Revolution and, preposterously, the personality cult of Mao. Ren's assertions about Confucianism as a religion met with lukewarm reaction or indifference by most scholars of religion, philosophy, and history. Many researchers of Confucianism merely took advantage of increased resources to fill positions in established institutions. However, when Ren's disciple Li Shen turned Ren's assertions into a systematic articulation in the two-volume *The History of China's Confucianism* (*Zhongguo rujiao shi* 中国儒教史) around the turn of the twenty-first century,[6] unexpectedly, many researchers of Confucianism revolted. In hindsight, these researchers must have been looking for an opportunity to vent their dissatisfaction over the assaults on Confucianism; it was only that their dissatisfaction had been subdued by their deference to the founder of the IWR and paradoxical benefactor of religious studies. Li's book became the perfect target for various reasons. The strict press censorship could have prevented their dissatisfaction from becoming public, had they not found a new media—the internet. Suddenly, the website Confucius2000.com became the most important platform for discussing Confucianism from all positions.[7]

Apparently, after two decades of slow brewing, the reevaluation of Confucianism accelerated in the twenty-first century. Instead of following the MLM call for deepening criticism, many scholars of the younger generations have gone in the opposite direction and taken it upon themselves to revive Confucianism. More importantly, unlike the senior MLM loyalists or the secularist liberals, the younger MNC have broken the black spell hanging over religion and begun to assert that Confucianism is so good that it *must* be a religion, one that is on par with other great world religions. Many of them have gone even further, asserting that Confucianism must be the best of all religions because it is rational and humanistic, thus avoiding the religious wars, extremism, and fanaticism caused by those religions that emphasize an irrational faith in the transcendent. Such belligerent assertions may not be a simple demonstration of arrogance but more of ignorance, the blame for which should be placed squarely on the atheist education that has been the norm in China for more than half a century.

Overall, times have changed. Despite the restrictions of religious policy, all kinds of religions have revived and are thriving in China. In spite of the official ideology of atheism, many intellectuals have gone beyond official discourses about religion. The cultural approach in the study of religion is the key that unlocked this dramatic change of attitudes toward religion.[8] In this context of religious appreciation, many new Confucians desire to call Confucianism a religion or make it into a religion.

Engaging Mainland New Confucians

The new attitude toward religion in regard to Confucianism took me off guard when I first encountered it in person in the summer 2006. I began my career as a religious studies scholar at Renmin University in China in the mid-1980s. I left for the United States to study the sociology of religion in 1989. Until 2006, I had paid no more than casual attention to the ongoing discussion of Confucianism in China. I knew about Ren Jiyu's criticism of Confucianism as religion and Fang Keli's criticism of overseas new Confucianism, both of which are advanced from the MLM standpoint.

However, Confucianism is so integral to Chinese culture that it is inevitably a topic of interest in empirical studies of Chinese societies or diasporic communities. In my dissertation-turned-book on Chinese Christians in America, I produced a sociological analysis of Chinese Christians' appropriation of Confucianism in their Christian lives and identity reconstruction.[9] In a series of articles I contributed, responding to an invitation from the editors of *China's Religion* (*Zhongguo zongjiao* 中国宗教), the official journal of the State Administration of Religious Affairs, I included a short piece describing the status of Confucianism and Daoism in the United States. The editors of the journal initially flinched, telling me that Confucianism was not recognized as a religion in China so it would not be appropriate to publish such an article in their journal. I persuaded them by emphasizing the merit of sociological description without taking a normative position. Eventually, the article was published in 2001.[10]

During many research and lecture tours in China since the year 2000, I became aware of the discontent in regard to Li Shen's books. Still, it was a surprise that in May 2006, after a long journey of multiple flights crossing the Pacific, upon my arrival at Shandong University, my host asked me about my views on Confucianism. I had little to offer on the spot as I was thinking only about the short course on the sociology of religion I was about to teach there. A more dramatic shock came a few weeks later at Shandong Academy of Social Sciences. Following a presentation of my sociological studies of religions, during which I mentioned nothing about Confucianism, a young scholar raised a question and demanded to know my position regarding the question of Confucianism as religion. The exchanges on that occasion were quite bewildering for me. First, one old scholar simply reiterated the MLM ideological position toward religion in general, insisting that religion would die out and it was justified for the authorities to suppress religion. Yet, several young scholars admonished me for applying Western or Christian standards to define religion, which would exclude Confucianism. They wanted to call Confucianism a religion, as if that would boost its value in China and the world. That was a wakeup call for me to engage the MNC.

Intrigued by the new attitude toward religion MNC, in summer 2006 I began to seek out scholars of Confucianism for the purposes of both learning and understanding. Almost all Chinese universities have individual scholars studying and teaching about Confucianism. These scholars are commonly in humanities disciplines, including philosophy, history, and literature. Moreover, many research centers, institutes, and associations of Confucian studies have been established. I also conducted fieldwork observations and interviews about various revivals of Confucianism, including scripture reading groups of Confucian classics on university campuses and at elementary schools, teaching sessions at the recently restored Confucius temples, the Han Chinese Clothing (Hanfu 汉服) shops, Confucian conferences, and, of course, the televised Confucius Birthday Commemoration ceremonies.[11] After much research, I came to realize that both scholars and those working in grassroots revival movements have made important statements that deserve serious examination and honest discussion by all people who are concerned about the present situation and future of China.[12] Here are only a few representative examples that have been captivating for me. I have heard them so many times from different people on various occasions, so much so that it may not be necessary to attribute the statements to particular individuals, although I could provide references to those who may be interested.

First, it is necessary to revive Confucianism after the multiple injuries it has suffered throughout the twentieth century. The MNC have made attempts through numerous conferences, websites, and print publications to reevaluate each of these injuries, often distorting their true nature and turning them upside down completely. The injuries, which were indeed severe, include the abolishment of the "imperial examination system" (*keju* 科举) in 1905 (MNC call for reviving the *keju*), the abolishment of the dynastic monarchy in the Republican Revolutions, including the so-called Second Revolution against Yuan Shikai's restoration of the monarchy (MNC argue that a constitutional monarchy is the best form of polity for China), the wholesale criticism of Confucianism during the May Fourth and New Culture movements (MNC want to overturn the evaluation of these movements), the adoption of Marxism as the official ideology for the nation-state since 1949 (MNC emphasize that Marxism is part of a more general destructive Westernization that should be reversed, although this suggestion has been expressed no more than timidly and in a muted fashion), and the rampaging corruption and social anomie that has occurred during the social transition to a market economy (MNC are ostensibly critical of the capitalist market economy).

Second, Confucianism is reclaimed to be the original and continuous mainstream of Chinese culture that had made China strong for thousands of years. MNC like to repeat that Chinese civilization is not only one of the oldest civilizations in the world, it is also the only one that has remained uninterrupted. They contend that Confucianism should not be held responsible for all the negative social and political problems in Chinese history. Instead, these problems should be viewed as due to non-Confucian forces; Confucianism has done nothing but temper the problems and ameliorate the situation. Had there not been Confucianism, they claim, these problems would be much worse and China would have been cast into a new dark age.

Third, Confucianism is believed to be the best spiritual foundation for practical solutions of the major social and political problems of China today. It can provide the foundation for morality and social order. It can restore the people's national confidence to face and withstand the imperialistic or expansionist Christian civilization of the West.

Fourth, they argue that the political system of liberal democracy does not and will not work in China, even if it has worked in the West. Indeed, even if it has worked in the West up to now, it has manifested internal crises that will lead to its self-destruction in the future. The key deficiency of liberal democracy, as the MNC view it, is its single-dimensional legitimacy of political authority—democratic votes of equal citizens. Such a political structure based on individualistic philosophy cannot be stable, harmonious, and advantageous for communities and societies. Besides, the politicians selected through the democratic process are in practice controlled by the capitalists or the large corporations, individuals driven by material greed instead of moral values. In comparison, Confucianism provides a political philosophy that is collectively based upon the welfare of the family, the community, and the nation.

Finally, regarding Confucianism as religion, I find that there are still secularist Confucians who have little interest in the religious dimension of Confucianism and insist on its irreligious nature, but many MNC demand respect for Confucianism as a religion, appealing to the authorities to recognize Confucianism as one of the legally permitted religions or outright calling for establishing Confucianism as the state religion of China. In the eyes of state religion advocates, Marxism-Leninism-Maoism is the de facto state religion since 1949, and it as an easy step to replace MLM with Confucianism. One way in which this aim has been advanced is by a call to Confucianize (*ruhua* 儒化) the Chinese Communist Party. MNC seem to like everything about the current power structure except the substance of its MLM—for example, that it is elitist, efficient, and maintains order.

I wrote an article in preparation for the conference of Chinese Confucian-Christian dialogue held in Hong Kong in early summer 2007,[13] in which I made some arguments about the problems of making Confucianism a religion. Briefly, my main points were that Confucianism functioned like a state religion in dynastic times, which resulted in many negative social consequences as is common with state religions everywhere. Efforts to make Confucianism a religion in the early twentieth century failed and would fail again because Confucianism lacks some crucial components of religion. However, it may be possible to construct Confucianism into a civil religion or a "public teaching" (*gongjiao* 公教), and Christianity has become an integral part of Chinese culture that provides ideational and institutional resources for the construction of a Chinese civil religion.

Before I made the suggestion of treating Confucianism as civil religion at that conference, I was not aware of the civil religion discussion by Chen Ming, one of the outspoken MNC. Since then, I have read his writings and had several conversations with him in person. It seems to me that Chen Ming's position has been evolving in his discussion of civil religion, but after all he seems to continue to hold on to a strategic approach. That is, he treats Confucianism as a kind of civil religion as a strategic step toward eventually establishing it as the state religion. In contrast, my discussion of civil religion in my 2007 article is from a sociological perspective, describing a possibility in social development. As any good sociologist would do, I tried to be as detached as possible about the subject matter. In the following section I reiterate and further develop some of the points first made in that article.

Problems of Making Confucianism a Religion

Confucianism has a religious dimension or religious elements. This has become recognized after many able expositions by new Confucians in modern times. On the other hand, many scholars recognize that the religious dimension of Confucianism is thin and weak. Some oft-quoted statements by Confucius or his disciples make this clear. For example, "How can you understand death without understanding life first?"; "Respect the spirits and gods, but keep some distance from them"; and "The subjects on which the Master did not talk were: extraordinary things, feats of strength, disorder, and gods." Overall, Confucianism offers little articulation about supernatural beings and life beyond death, lacks a clearly defined doctrine of beliefs, and lacks an organization of clergy and believers.

Regarding the supernatural, Confucius and his followers talk about "Heaven" (*tian* 天), "Heaven's Mandate" (*tianming* 天命), or "Heavenly Reason" (*tianli* 天理), but these are vague expressions. In real life, to meet their personal spiritual needs, many Confucians have to resort to Buddhism, Daoism, or folk religion. Such examples are plentiful and easy to find, and I will offer one instance that I found during the period of fieldwork focusing on Confucianism. In the renowned old city of Pingyao in Shanxi Province, which I visited in fall 2006, the Confucius temple stood on a patch of land twice the size of the county court, which makes it hard to say the county governor was not a Confucian scholar. The innermost structure in the county court was called "the Great Immortal's Building," where the three rooms on the first floor served as the private space—a dining and resting place for the county governor. Interestingly, upstairs is a hall for the Fox Spirit, "the immortal that protects the seal" (*baoyin daxian* 保印大仙). Apparently, the county governors offered worship to the Fox Spirit for the protection of their position. Many Confucian scholars made similar appeals to folk deities, let alone the commoners.

Confucianism did not develop its own clergy other than the "scholar-officials" (*rushi* 儒仕) who were embedded in the imperial political system. The transmission of Confucianism from generation to generation was primarily maintained by the compulsory inculcation mandated by the imperial examination system at the upper level of society and the perpetuation of traditional family structure at the lower level of society. There were Confucius temples, but they were reserved only for the scholar-officials who passed certain levels of imperial examination. There were "Confucian academies" (*shuyuan* 书院), but they seemed not very different from the Communist "Party schools" (*dangxiao* 党校) nowadays.

Some MNC believe that they could develop a Confucian clergy, design rituals, and rebuild Confucian temples for the religious activities of Confucianism. However, even if Confucianism could obtain official recognition as a religion, a major problem is to establish its sacredness among the people. Would the state promulgate Confucian religion by applying the state apparatus? The history of the PRC has shown us that forced promulgation of a system of beliefs by the government cannot help a philosophy or ideology establish and maintain its sacredness. In reality, in Hong Kong, Taiwan, Singapore, the United States, and Canada where one is free to choose one's religion, very few people identify themselves as believers in Confucianism.

In a survey of Chinese spiritual life conducted by the Horizon Group in 2007, when Confucianism was deliberately presented to the respondents, extremely few chose it as their religion.

It is not rare to hear MNC say that only the common folk need the transcendental dimension of religion and it is for promoting Confucian ethics that they advocate setting up Confucianism as a religion. In other words, they themselves do not believe it religiously but would make efforts to promulgate Confucianism as a religion among the common people. What an astonishing pseudo-religion! However, pseudo-religion brings more problems than solutions. In the 1980s, the Singaporean government incorporated Confucian ethics into the religious studies curriculum in middle schools, but this endeavor ended after less than ten years because the curriculum was stirring up religious controversies.[14]

Another problem is about religious belonging. If Confucianism is recognized as a religion parallel to other religions, who could belong to it? Can Buddhists, Daoists, or Christians claim to be believers in Confucianism as well? As de Bary and Tu Weiming have effectively argued, Confucianism is synonymous with Chinese culture.[15] Confucianism is the common cultural heritage of most of the Chinese people in China and in the diaspora. If Confucianism belongs exclusively to Confucian believers, that would deprive adherents of other religions of their right to share this common cultural heritage. If people could identify with more than one religion, and many people assert that the Chinese have never been exclusive in their religion, then what is the point of making Confucianism independent of and parallel to other religions to begin with? In reality, the 2007 Chinese Spiritual Life Survey shows that when respondents were allowed to choose to identify with more than one religion, only 1 percent of people did so, and extremely few of them included Confucianism as one of them. It is evident that most Chinese do not consider Confucianism a religion at all.

Of course, under the principle of religious freedom, Confucians are free to construct a religion and ask for state recognition. In fact, there have been religious sects in Taiwan that are very much Confucian, including treating Confucian classics as part of their holy scriptures and venerating Confucius in religious rituals. However, the reality is that such sects, including Yiguandao, Xuanyuanjiao, Tiandijiao, among others, are independent from one another and not united under the single banner of Confucianism. In other words, making Confucianism a religion will result not in one single religion of Confucianism but multiple religions of Confucianism. Is this what MNC call for? In Indonesia, there is a single religion of Confucianism as one of the six state-recognized religions.[16] However, the number of its followers is relatively small, whereas more Chinese in Indonesia adhere to Christianity and Buddhism. None of these examples or scenarios seem to appeal to the desire of MNC.

Furthermore, the suggestion to establish Confucianism as the state religion of China is not only dubious but also dangerous. Looking back at human history, from the ancient Roman empire to the Chinese imperial dynasties, from the early modern nation-states of Europe and Japan to the contemporary Islamic nations, state religions have always resulted in dire consequences: dictatorship and despotism, repressing scientific and technological development, violating human rights, and causing religious violence and ethnic wars. Some MNC suggest that such problems are due to the religious monopoly. Instead of monopoly, they suggest a mild version of a state religion, modeling it on the Anglican Church of Britain, in which Confucianism holds the most privileged status for state functions while other religions are accepted so long as they are submissive to the orthodoxy of Confucianism. However, this is anachronistic. The separation of state and religion started in the United States of America, but it has become a modern principle adopted by more and more states. When Kang Youwei and his contemporaries looked around about a hundred years ago, there were still quite a few European countries that maintained a state religion. One such state was the rapidly modernizing Japan of that time, long before it brought the calamities of World War II. By now, the national-religion model is clearly on its way to extinction among industrialized societies. Religious pluralism has become inevitable in the process of modernization and globalization. The American experiment has demonstrated that only through the separation of state and religion and the equal treatment of all religions by the government can religious wars and violent conflicts be avoided and social harmony achieved.

One of the strategies MNC have adopted is to redefine religion so that Confucianism can be included. Some MNC have argued that Confucianism is a different kind of religion, either a philosophical religion, a cultural religion, a humanistic religion, or a spiritual religion. They insist that the current definition of religion is based on the ethnocentric standard of the West and that makes it unfair and unacceptable. It is true that the most common understandings of religion nowadays are very much defined on the model of Christianity, especially Protestantism. However, that in itself does not necessarily mean they are unfair. Just like many concepts we use nowadays, such as philosophy, science, society, nation, politics, democracy, republic, among others, the concept of religion is not only a *Western* one but also a *modern* one. Modern scholarship has its intrinsic logic and should not be changed in whatever way one wishes. The imperial logic of "pointing at a deer to call it a horse" (*zhi lu wei ma* 指鹿为马) is outdated now. Without following logic and working on certain parameters in coming up with a definition, it will take us nowhere and lead only to political squabbling.

Sociologically speaking, there are three major social forces contending to define religion in the modern or modernizing world: scholars, believers, and the government.[17] Moreover, there are scholars of multiple disciplines and multiple theoretical schools, believers of multiple religions and religion-like systems, and contending forces within and outside the government. Consequently, it is difficult, if not impossible, to reach a complete consensus about the definition of religion. However, avoiding definition, which is a strategy followed by many Western scholars, is not a real solution either. Definition matters. It matters even more in China. It can be an issue of life and death for believers of certain sects, and an issue of maintaining social and political order on the part of the authorities. Therefore, in spite of the difficulties, social scientists must rely on scientific principles to advance the understanding of complex social phenomena. As I noted recently, "Social scientists do not have to give in to the postmodernist abandonment of science. For the purpose of the social-scientific study of religion in contemporary society, the definition of religion must be a simple abstraction that is broad enough to include all religions but sufficiently specific to distinguish religion from other similar concepts."[18]

In my recent book, I propose a definition of religion with a classification that is based on Durkheim's definition but integrates Taylor's substantive definition:

> *A religion is a unified system of beliefs and practices about life and the world relative to the supernatural that unite the believers or followers into a social organization of moral community.* This definition includes four essential elements of a religion: (1) a belief in the supernatural, (2) a set of beliefs regarding life and the world, (3) a set of ritual practices manifesting the beliefs, and (4) a distinct social organization of a moral community of believers and practitioners.[19]

From this definition, we may classify religious phenomena and closely related social phenomena that compete with religion (see table 1.1).

In contrast to fully developed religions, whose four components are fully developed, semi-religions are those with underdeveloped beliefs and organization, and quasi-religions are those belief systems that are intrinsically embed-

Table 1.1. A Definition of Religion with Classification

	Supernatural	*Beliefs*	*Practices*	*Organization*	*Examples*
Full religion	Yes	Yes	Yes	Yes	Christianity, Buddhism, Islam
Semi-religion	Yes	Underdeveloped	Yes	Underdeveloped	Folk or popular religion, magic, spiritualities
Quasi-religion	Yes	Yes	Yes	Diffused	Civil religion, ancestor worship, guild cults
Pseudo-religion	No	Yes	Yes	Yes	Atheism, communism, fetishism

ded in other institutions without a stand-alone organization. This includes civil religion, which is inseparable from the state; ancestor worship, which is inseparable from the family; and vocation cults, which are difficult to be separated from the trade guilds. This is essentially what C. K. Yang called "diffused religion," and its primary function is to reinforce the secular institution to which it is attached.[20] Because it is so embedded or even parasitic, when the old state, the family, or the guild collapses, the corresponding quasi-religion will also collapse, leaving residual fragments in folklore. Quasi-religious Confucianism collapsed along with the demise of dynastic monarchy. In the early twentieth century, Kang Youwei led the Confucian Religion (*Kongjiao* 孔教) movement, which was tightly linked to the threshold of monarchy. After the short-lived emperor Yuan Shikai died, Confucian Religion vanished as well, although the residual movement has lingered on outside mainstream Chinese societies, such as in Hong Kong or Indonesia.[21]

However, what appear to be weaknesses of Confucianism as a religion can be the exact strengths in the development of civil religion. As civil religion, it is not, and need not become, a fully developed religion, and it may be carried out through schools and celebrated by all religions in a society.

Civil Religion for China?

One of the reasons many MNC advocate making Confucianism the state religion of China is to address what they see as a grave deficiency of liberal democracy—that its legitimacy purportedly comes solely from popular votes of equal citizens. This criticism may be merited for the particular version of liberal democracy—that is, the secularist liberal democracy—that has dominated the thinking of Chinese liberals. The democratic mechanisms of elections and checks and balances of different branches are concerned with negative aspects of morality—limiting corruption. However, a healthy society also needs the positive contribution of moral people. From a Durkheimian perspective, social norms need some kind of sacred foundation. The French Enlightenment thinker Rousseau made it even clearer: "No state has ever been founded without religion serving as its base."[22] He went on to suggest the need for a civil religion. The founding fathers of the United States of America were greatly learned in the Enlightenment tradition in addition to the Protestant heritage. They commonly valued religion as providing the moral foundation of society. The collective memory of Americans is that the founding fathers believed the United States to be the new "promised land" or new Israel, a city on the hill to become an example for all nations. "Religion, particularly the idea of God, played a constitutive role in the thought of the early American statesmen."[23] American presidents have always called God to bless America. Nowadays, Americans make the pledge of allegiance to the American flag for the "one nation under God" and express "In God we trust" on many occasions, including printing this on the dollar bill and many automobile license plates. The French scholar Alexis de Tocqueville observed that churches served as moral associations for American democracy.[24] Overall, in addition to popular votes, the United States of America has always maintained some kind of sacred legitimacy of the polity, the political authority of democratically elected government, and the American way of life. The sociologist Robert Bellah called this sacred dimension "civil religion in America."

Like China, the United States of America is a multiethnic, multireligious country. Just like other modern nation-states, the United States needs to cultivate in its citizens a national identity. In fact, American diversity exceeds China in terms of the numbers of ethnic groups and religions. Americans have come from many countries around the world. Almost every religion that has ever existed anywhere in the world in the whole human history may find followers in the United States today. Besides, there are conflicting political parties and interest groups. How can such a diverse country maintain its unity and social harmony? Do Americans share some core values? How do these values get transmitted through generations as the United States becomes ever more diverse in religion and ethnicity? Some scholars have suggested that there is an American creed or an American way of life,[25] which include the core values of liberty, democracy, equality, justice, and, above all, God. These universal values are sanctified by sacred symbols and rituals, maintained and carried over through civil religion.

According to Bellah and many other scholars, civil religion is a set of beliefs and rituals—related to the past, present, and future of a people or nation—that are understood in some transcendental fashion. It provides a national identity, serves as a basis for social cohesion, but also transcends the state and nation by expecting the nation-state to be better than it is. Civil religion embraces patriotism, but not nationalism. The universalistic principles it observes that transcend nationality are represented in the pledge of allegiance to the American flag: "I pledge allegiance to the Flag of the United States of America, and to the Republic for which it stands: one Nation, under God, indivisible, with Liberty and Justice for all."

In America, civil religion is manifested in the people's daily life, including the most important holidays of Memorial Day, Thanksgiving, Independence Day, the presidential inauguration, and so on. During such holidays, through ceremonies and rituals, citizens learn and appreciate common values. The Washington Monument, Jefferson Memorial, Lincoln Memorial, and Arlington National Cemetery, among others, are sacred places in civil religious space for commemorating their heroes. Through the sacred symbols, rituals, and freely shared universal values, civil religion provides sacred legitimacy to the political authority. Without the sacred legitimacy, citizens may lose respect for the authorities and that may lead to anarchism, or they may respect out of fear only, which is common under totalitarian tyranny.

It is worth emphasizing, as Robert Bellah emphasizes, that American civil religion is not the worship of the nation-state, it is not used to subdue the masses, or to exclude particular religions. On the contrary, American civil religion places the state under the power of God. The state that is subjected to the authority of God is best for everyone's liberty and justice. In a democratic political system, decisions made through democratic processes can sometimes be wrong and harmful, and leaders elected democratically make mistakes and become corrupt. Americans often invoke the words of Lord Acton, that power leads to corruption and absolute power leads to absolute corruption. The democratically elected president of the United States is vested with the highest executive power and is the top military commander. Besides being responsible to the American people by submitting reports to Congress, the president is expected to be accountable to God. When in office, the president is under the restraint of Congress, the judiciary system, and the watch of the media. But all of these may fail to check and balance the power of the president, especially in the second term, when he or she no longer needs to worry about a reelection. When they are sworn in, government officials and judges, including the president, place their hands on the Bible, and their oaths of the office often include the words "So help me God." Outside observers might see this as merely a religious custom devoid of substance, but, understood in terms of civil religion, this is at least an expression of the wish of the citizens that the government officials elected to power are subject to God's authority. When people's opinion, the media's scrutiny, and the checks and balances of the other branches of power all fail to work, a president or official who genuinely believes in God will take into account the issue of eternal judgment by the omniscient and omnipotent God who rewards the good and punishes the evil. In this way, civil religion functions as the last safeguard to inhibit political leaders from making grave mistakes.

Bellah maintains that American civil religion believes in a transcendental God. American presidents always conclude their speeches with "God bless America." Congress starts its yearly session with a prayer to God. Americans believe the United States is "one nation under God." However, as pointed out by Bellah, the God in civil religion is not particular, so that Christians, Jews, and other religious adherents may take the God as their own supreme or only God.

The idea of civil religion in America gives me inspiration to think about the possibility of developing some kind of civil religion for China. Instead of establishing Confucianism as the state religion, which would result in grave consequences, as discussed earlier, it is perhaps feasible and more helpful to develop some kind of civil religion based on Confucianism, as most Chinese people share the common cultural heritage and most Confucian values. The Chinese notion of "heaven" (*tian* 天) is so readily available for civil religion, which can be interpreted by different religions in reference to their own divinity, thus affirming the inclusive spirit that has existed since the ancient times of Chinese civilization. Making Confucianism the civil religion need not and should not entail rejecting any other specific religion. It is important to emphasize that there would be no civil religion without some shared values, and it is up to people of all religions to articulate the set of shared values that they follow.

A crucial remaining question is whether there can there be civil religion in China without Christianity? First of all, we must face the reality that Christianity has become one of the major religions among the Chinese. Multiple social surveys have indicated that about one-third of the Chinese in North America identify with Christianity (including Catholicism and Protestantism), next only to the category of "no religion" in proportion. About 20 percent of Chinese identify with Buddhism. Few choose other religions. In Mainland China, Protestantism and Catholicism have at least fifty million believers, which is more than two times the current population of Taiwan. The numbers of Christians in various Chinese societies and communities has been growing, particularly in Mainland China.

More importantly, Christianity provides important resources for civil religion in China. One of the greatest challenges to the revival of Confucianism is how to critically evaluate and purge its feudalist remnants, including gender inequality. Core Confucian concepts such as loyalty (*zhong* 忠) and filial piety (*xiao* 孝) all require modern reinterpretation. Simplistic return to the past amounts to fundamentalism, which is detrimental to individuals and the larger society. After the May Fourth and New Culture movements, upon learning about Western ideas of liberty and equality and democratic practices, how many people would still stick to the imperial conception of loyalty, which entails that "if the emperor wants you dead, you must die"? How many would be willing to practice the kind of filial piety portrayed in Ba Jin's *The Family*? How many women would want to put on the fetters of wifely submission? The Chinese American scholar Lin Yusheng[26] argues that the continuance of Chinese tradition must be subject to creative transformation. In this regard, I see that Christianity makes possible the creative transformation of traditional Chinese culture. In my 1999 sociological study of Chinese Christians in America, I find that Christianity provides a kind of lever with which Confucian ethics is creatively transformed and selectively inherited. For instance, filial compliance (*xiaoshun* 孝顺) is changed into filial respect (*xiaojing* 孝敬): tradition stresses *xiaoshun*—compliance is better than respect; the Chinese Christians, by contrast, value *xiaojing*—honor your parents—which they like to point out is the only commandment among the ten commandments that comes with promises of earthly blessings. This is the case not only among Chinese Christians overseas but also in China.[27] This example of creative transformation is not simply replacing the Confucian notion of *xiao* with something totally new. Instead, it underlines or highlights what is already in Confucianism, as *xiaojing* is well expressed by Confucius himself, notwithstanding the later developments of Confucianism that buried it with simple obedience *xiaoshun*.

Some MNC worry that the exclusive nature of Christianity may cause conflicts with other religious believers and those with no religion. They have such worries because Christianity is monotheistic. However, they seem to have not appreciated enough the Christian emphasis on individual freedom and the Enlightenment exposition of God-given freedom. People are created free, which logically includes the freedom to search for one's own religion. Following the Enlightenment expositions, this God-given freedom has become socially sanctioned and legally protected. Historically, religious tolerance was first advocated in Europe and religious freedom first implemented in the United States of America, where Christians constitute the majority of the population. This historical fact did not come inadvertently, but with some intrinsic logic in monotheism and its view of human nature. In other words, the monotheism of Christianity that matured through the Enlightenment treats each individual as a free agent who is at liberty to choose what religion to adhere to, although Christian evangelicals would never forfeit an opportunity for trying to persuade, instead of coerce, people to convert and return to God the creator. Given this understanding of freedom by Christians, it is not surprising to see that some Chinese Christian lawyers have risen up in recent years to defend the freedom of belief for followers of so-called religious cults. It is not that these Christian lawyers agree with the beliefs of those they defend, but they would fight for their freedom and human rights. If they can do so for such cases under the current difficult political situation, we can hope for even better performance under less suppressive authorities. In any case, looking at Christian-dominated European and American societies, religious and cultural pluralism has become the social norm. It is not only legally sanctioned but also practiced in daily life and deeply rooted in the minds of the people.

A New Proposition for Civil Religion of Tianxia

My initial suggestion for developing Confucianism as a civil religion for China, which was made in the 2007 conference, unfortunately was drowned amid emotional reactions by certain Confucians to other points I had made. That kind of emotional reaction is probably due to the unfortunate limits of the kind of "dialogue" in which participants are pigeonholed into one or the other opposing camp. In such a setup, some of the participants from both camps manifested a combative spirit, which, to me, betrays their harmonious rhetoric. What was most disturbing to me was that some of the Confucians had a false sense of exclusive ownership of Confucianism, which, to me, belies the great breadth of Confucianism for "all under Heaven" (*tianxia* 天下). In my view, Confucianism does not exclusively belong to the self-proclaimed Confucians. Rather, anyone, Chinese or non-Chinese alike, may appropriate from this rich spiritual heritage. Similarly, anyone may appropriate from the rich spiritual heritage of Christianity.

In retrospect, would I say that my beliefs and experiences have tinted my scholarly arguments in my earlier article? Probably so. On the meta-methodological level, no one can escape from that kind of tinting. Our scholarship is inevitably informed by our experiences and beliefs. Now, coming again to the table of an interdisciplinary dialogue, I feel compelled to make my peculiar or idiosyncratic vantage point known. That is, I write this chapter as a sociologist of religion, even though this is not a typical sociological research study describing and explaining some facts. Moreover, this sociologist of religion has been a Christian for about twenty years and has lived both in China and the United States for about an equal length of time beyond preschool childhood—more than twenty years on each side of the Pacific.

With that autobiographical information laid out in front of you, let me restate my position on Confucianism, which may be informed by my Christian beliefs and living experiences in China and America. In my view, Confucianism might develop into some sort of civil religion, but at the present this is only a possibility, not a reality. Whether or not the development succeeds in the future will depend upon multiple factors, especially political factors in Chinese society. Furthermore, it will also depend upon interactions between Christians and Confucians[28]—not only Chinese Confucians on one side vis-à-vis Western Christians on the other side but also the other possible pairings—Chinese Christians and Chinese Confucians, Chinese Christians and Western Confucians, and Western Christians and Western Confucians. The encounter between Matteo Ricci and Chinese Confucians in late Ming and early Qing eras was one kind. Then there have been the Boston Confucians, most of whom are non-Chinese. My question is, how much are their efforts known to other Western Christians? My guess is that it is still limited, not yet reaching many Christian theologians and philosophers. There have been dialogue conferences between Western Christians and Chinese Confucians, but it is still rare to have such conferences bringing together Chinese Christians and Chinese Confucians. However, the relationship of Chinese Christians and Chinese Confucians is probably the most crucial for the construction of Chinese civil religion. Moreover, the simple classification of Westerners and Chinese is no longer clear in itself in the era of globalization, as there are ethnic Chinese scholars in Western universities and Caucasians regularly teaching in Chinese universities.

Furthermore, today I would like to take one step further to make an even bolder suggestion: The kind of civil religion I envisage, based on

Confucianism and Christianity, if successfully constructed or developed, may not only serve China or the greater China well but also much of East Asia, the Transpacific region, even "all under Heaven." As many people know, Christians comprise a significant minority in the Chinese societies of Taiwan (about 5%), Hong Kong (about 10%), Singapore (15%), and the United States (30%). In South Korea, at least a third of the population has become Christian. Meanwhile, globalization leads to even greater mixing of peoples who migrate across the Pacific Ocean. East Asians are the fastest growing immigrant ethnic/racial minority in the United States, Canada, and Australia. The Pacific region has become increasingly integrated economically and socially. Along with economic and social integration, some level of cultural fusion is inevitable. I believe that the most promising fusion would be the development of a new kind of civil religion that is based on Confucianism and Christianity.

Admittedly, this is a vision, perhaps merely my wishful thinking. Nonetheless, it is a vision that emerges out of a free spirit, which is also coming from the loving and holy spirit. I must add that it is a vision also inspired by the Confucian spirit of "striving for the noble goal without relenting to the said improbability" (*zhi qi bu ke er wei zhi* 知其不可而为之). Even if it may not be realized within the next few decades, perhaps not until the twenty-second century, nonetheless we may endeavor with faith, love, and hope.

Fortunately, we have had some predecessors and role models for this seemingly improbable endeavor of constructing civil religion based on Confucianism and Christianity. We may trace this to the encounter of Jesuits and Confucians in Ming and early Qing periods. Both Matteo Ricci and Xu Guangqi were well versed in Christianity and Confucianism. Then, the founding father of the first republic in all of Asia—Dr. Sun Zhongshan (Sun Yatsen 孙中山), was a Christian and Confucian revolutionary. The first Chinese student in America, Rong Hong (Ying Wing 容闳), was a Christian who expressed his love of China by bringing cohorts of Chinese students to study in the United States. There also have been the educator Yan Yangchu 晏阳初; the scholar Lin Yutang 林语堂; the founder of Nankai University, Zhang Boling 张伯苓; and many more Chinese Christians who inherited much of Confucianism and strove for a better society. There may have been numerous Confucians who have appreciated or inherited much of Christianity. Meanwhile, significant efforts have been made on the part of Americans to reach out and integrate Confucianism into the American system. Just to name a few, the statue of Confucius stands side by side with the Judeo-Christian prophet Moses on the building of the US

Supreme Court; there have been Confucian scholars teaching at American universities: Tu Weiming, Yu Yingshih, and others.

This chapter does not end with a conclusion. I would like to think it merely marks a beginning. Despite myriad dangers and problems ahead, let us take faith and hope for the new era of peace and harmony in *tianxia*, all under Heaven.

Notes

1. There are at least two possible translations of the term *guojiao* in English, one is "national religion," as in some of the chapters in this volume, and the other is "state religion." I believe "state religion" is a more accurate translation, which has been widely used in the literature in discussion of the Confucianist movement in the early Republic (e.g., C. K. Yang, *Religion in Chinese Society* [Berkeley: University of California Press, 1961], 364; William Theodore de Bary, Wing-tsit Chan, Richard John Lufrano, and Joseph Adler, *Sources of Chinese Tradition*, vol. 2 [New York: Columbia University Press, 2011], 265) and the proposals by Mainland New Confucians (e.g., Guanghu He, "Thirty Years of Religious Studies in China," in *Social Scientific Studies of Religion in China*, ed. Fenggang Yang and Graeme Lang [Leiden: Brill, 2012], 39; David Ownby, "Kang Xiaoguang: Social Science, Civil Society, and Confucian Religion," *China Perspective* 4 (2009): 101; Ping-Cheung Lo, "Jiang Qing's Arguments on the Inevitable and Permanent Conflict between the Christian Faith and Chinese Culture and on Establishing Confucianism as the State Religion," in *The Renaissance of Confucianism in Contemporary China*, ed. Ruiping Fan [Dordrecht: Springer, 2011], 163; Daniel A. Bell, *China's New Confucianism: Politics and Everyday Life in a Changing Society* [Princeton: Princeton University Press, 2010], 187).

2. *Analects* 14.41. "Zilu was passing the night at Stone Gate and the gatekeeper there asked him, 'From whom do you come?' Zilu replied, 'From Master Kong.' The gatekeeper replied, 'Isn't he the one who keeps at it even though he knows it won't work out?' "

3. Rebecca Nedostup, *Superstitious Regimes: Religion and the Politics of Chinese Modernity* (Cambridge: Harvard East Asian Center, 2010).

4. Fenggang Yang, *Religion in China: Survival and Revival under Communist Rule* (New York: Oxford University Press, 2012).

5. It is ironic that the IWR in the Chinese Academy of Social Science has become a bastion for religious studies with a growing tendency of scholarly objectivity. Moreover, quite a few scholars of the IWR have spoken favorably about certain aspects of certain religions. Right before his death, however, Ren made a final stride to whip up a few militant atheists to fight for the original mission of MLM studies of religion. So far the militant atheist endeavor has to be carried out mainly outside the IWR in a muffled voice.

6. Li Shen, *The History of Confucianism*, 2 vols. (Shanghai: Shanghai Renmin Press, 1999 and 2000).

7. Anna Sun, "Confusions over Confucianism: Controversies over the Religious Nature of Confucianism, 1870–2007" (PhD dissertation, Princeton University, 2009).

8. Fenggang Yang, "Between Secularist Ideology and Desecularizing Reality: The Birth and Growth of Religious Research in Communist China," *The Sociology of Religion: A Quarterly Review* 65.2 (2004): 101–119.

9. Fenggang Yang, Chinese Christians in America: Conversion, Assimilation, and Adhesive Identities (University Park: Penn State University Press, 1999).

10. Fenggang Yang, "Confucianism and Daoism in the United States," *China's Religion* (Beijing) 2 (2001): 52–53.

11. The Confucian revivals have been well documented in a series of articles by Sébastien Billioud and Joël Thoraval, including "*Jiaohua*: The Confucian Revival in China as an Educative Project," *China Perspectives* 4 (2007): 4–20; "The Contemporary Revival of Confucianism: *Anshen liming* or the Religious Dimension of Confucianism," *China Perspectives* 3 (2008): 88–106; "*Lijiao*: The Return of the Ceremonies to Honour Confucius in Mainland China Today," *China Perspectives* 4 (2009): 82–100. See also Daniel A. Bell, *China's New Confucianism: Politics and Everyday Life in a Changing Society* (Princeton: Princeton University Press, 2008).

12. Fenggang Yang, "Cultural Dynamics in China: Today and in 2020," *Asia Policy* 4 (July 2007): 41–52.

13. It has been published first as "A Sociological Perspective on Confucianism as Religion" (in Chinese), *Journal of Lanzhou University (Social Sciences)* 36.2 (2008): 2–8, then reprinted in *New Views and Perspectives on Confucianism as Religion* (in Chinese), ed. Chen Ming (Guiyang: Guizhou Renmin Press, 2009), 222–235, and reprinted in *A Confucian-Christian Dialogue in Contemporary Context* (in Chinese), ed. Luo Bingxiang and Xie Wenyu (Guilin: Guangxi Normal University Press, 2010), 549–567.

14. Eddie C. Y. Kuo, "Confucianism as Political Discourse in Singapore: The Case of an Incomplete Revitalization Movement," in *Confucian Traditions in East Asian Modernity: Moral Education and Economic Culture in Japan and the Four Mini-Dragons*, ed. Tu Weiming (Cambridge, MA, and London: Harvard University Press, 1996); Lin Weiyi, "Xinjiapo ruxue zai tizhi nei de liuchuan" (Singaporean Confucianism's spread within the established institutions), in *Rujia sixiang zai shijie de chuanbo yu fazhan (The Spread and Development of Confucianism in the World)*, ed. Zhang Liwen (Shijiazhuang: Hebei University Press, 2005), 108–127.

15. William Theodore de Bary, *Neo-Confucian Orthodoxy and the Learning of the Mind-and-Heart* (New York: Columbia University Press, 1981); Tu Weiming, "Cultural China: The Periphery as the Center," in *The Living Tree: The Changing Meaning of Being Chinese Today*, ed. Tu Weiming (Stanford: Stanford University Press, 1994).

16. Wang Aiping, *Yindunixiya Kongjiao yanjiu* (A Study of Confucian Religion in Indonesia) (Beijing: Zhongguo Wenshi Chubanshe, 2010).

17. For a more elaborated discussion about the definition problem, see Fenggang Yang, *Religion in China: Survival and Revival under Communist Rule* (New York: Oxford University Press, 2012), chap. 2.

18. Ibid., 36.

19. Ibid.

20. Yang, *Religion in Chinese Society.*

21. See Sun, "Confusions over Confucianism." Also see Liu Yi's chapter in *Confucianism and Spiritual Traditions in Modern China and Beyond*, ed. Fenggang Yang and Joseph Tamney (Leiden: Brill, 2011), and Gan Chunsong's book, *Zhidu Ruxue* (Institutional Confucianism).

22. See Jean-Jacques Rousseau, *On the Social Contract*, ed. and trans. Donald A. Cress (Indianapolis: Hackett, 1983 [1762]), 96, 99.

23. Robert Bellah, "Civil Religion in America," *Journal of the American Academy of Arts and Sciences* 96.1 (Winter 1967): 1–21.

24. Alexis de Tocqueville, *Democracy in America*, trans. and ed. Harvey C. Mansfield and Delba Winthrop (Chicago: University of Chicago Press, 2000).

25. Will Herberg, Protestant-Catholic-Jew: An Essay in American Religious Sociology, second ed. (Garden City: Doubleday, 1960); Gunnar Myrdal, An American Dilemma: The Negro Problem and Modern Democracy (New York: Harper and Row, 1944); Horace Meyer Kallen, Cultural Pluralism and the American Idea (Philadelphia: University of Pennsylvania, 1956); Hans Kohn, American Nationalism: An Interpretative Essay (New York: Macmillan, 1957); Philip Gleason, "American Identity and Americanization," in Harvard Encyclopedia of American Ethnic Groups, ed. Stephan Thernstrom, Ann Orlov, and Oscar Handlin (Cambridge: Harvard University Press, 1980), 31–58; Nathan Glazer, "Is Assimilation Dead?" Annals of the American Academy of Political and Social Sciences 530 (November 1993): 122–136; Kathleen Neils Conzen, David A. Gerber, Ewa Morawska, George E. Pozzetta, and Rudolph J. Vecoli, "The Invention of Ethnicity: A Perspective from the U.S.A.," *Journal of American Ethnic History* 12 (Fall 1992): 3–41.

26. Lin Yusheng. *Creative Transformation of Chinese Traditions* (Beijing: Sanlian Bookstore, 1996).

27. Huang Jianbo and Yang Fenggang, "Survey Report: Family Ethic and Work Ethic of Christians in a Northern Coastal City," *Journal of Christian Culture* 11 (2004): 326–354.

28. Besides, believers of other religions in China will also play important roles in the process, including Buddhists, Daoists, Muslims, among others.

2

The Revival of Confucianism in the Sphere of Mores and the Reactivation of the Civil Religion Debate in China

SÉBASTIEN BILLIOUD

In *Habits of the Heart*, their study on "individualism and commitment in American life," sociologists Robert N. Bellah and Richard Madsen and their colleagues emphasize that it makes particular sense to study the mores of a society, which "include consciousness, culture, and the daily practices of life," because it is in their sphere, "and the climates of opinion they express, that we are apt to discern incipient changes of vision—those new flights of the social imagination that may indicate where society is heading."[1]

This remark is certainly as relevant in the circumstances of contemporary China as it was for the study of the transformation of American culture when the book was written in the 1980s. The focus of this chapter is precisely incipient changes of vision and new flights of social imagination developing today in a prevailing context that social scientists have sometimes described as the "individualization of Chinese society," and by which is meant the deep and increasing social trend of affirmation, for now around three decades, of the individual in all dimensions of his or her life (family, work, leisure, sexual orientations, etc.).[2] While such an individualization paves the way for an increasing individualism within Chinese society (and, by the same token, for a value crisis that, sometimes, is not without echoes of Bellah's dark statements on American society[3]), it also paradoxically enables the affirmation of forms of subjectivity that, in the end, recreate or reactivate collective links and values. The quick developments of religion or the NGO sector with adepts involved in their communities or volunteers dedicating time and energy to a cause exemplify such a trend.

At the same time, this general movement of individualization of Chinese society, with its two opposite directions (individualism, renewed collective links), interfaces with another important phenomenon at work today in the PRC: an evolving relation of the Chinese people to time and its various dimensions. This evolution—itself directly linked to the expansion, over the past thirty years, of people's "field of experience" and "horizon of expectations,"[4] or, in other words, to a process of "ideological decolonization" and reconciliation with a longer memory span[5]—translates into a striking comeback of the reference to the "past" in people's life. Such a reference is, to a large extent, a process of the production of collective memory (rather than history) with all its shares of retrospective dreams and reinventions. Although it interacts in a complex way with an official manipulation of memory (and history) that crystallizes, for example, in all kinds of state-fostered commemorations (from tutelary figures of Chinese civilization to Maoist epics), it cannot be reduced to such a political dimension either. Official and ideological "production of the past" does not impact the future, it sanctifies the present. By contrast, collective production of memory "in the space of the people" (*minjian* 民間) may turn into resources able to inform and shape the future. Somehow, its development in today's China might even herald—even though one should remain cautious since this is just here a hypothesis that requires further research—an entry into what historian François Hartog terms a new "regimen of historicity," by which is meant a reorganization of the articulations between past, present, and future.[6]

This popular production of memory translates into all kinds of "fevers," from Ming studies[7] to national learning (*guoxue* 國學)[8] or even a revived Maoist nostalgia.[9] But, most importantly for us here, it also translates, since approximately the beginning of the new century, in a popular movement of so-called "Confucian revival" that takes a variety of different forms in the realms of education, self-cultivation, ritualism, and so forth.[10] The phenomenon is complex and, in the more general context previously described, it is fueled by different elements. In another study,[11] I introduce an analytical framework structured around three ideal types of motivations frequently encountered in the rank of the "promoters of Confucianism": adhesion to some elements of the Confucian worldview, whatever they may be and even if such an adhesion is not exclusive; the power of the *renminbi* 人民幣 (material motivation, that is, taking advantage of the bonanza provided by the "Confucian fever" by marketing relevant products, be they books, DVDs, ritual activities or performances, etc.), and, finally, political motivation. In the present chapter, I will no longer confine myself to "promoters of Confucianism." In its first part I primarily discuss, based on fieldwork and ethnographic literature, motivations that can be encountered among ordinary people and the way rediscovered Confucian values again become a "habit of the heart." Therefore, little attention will be paid to material motivations here. They are in any case much less important for ordinary people than, in some cases, for activists. Political considerations only reappear in the second part of the chapter, when I link these revitalized "habits of the heart" with recent discussions on a possible Confucian civil religion.

New Flights of Social Imagination: Confucianism as a "Habit of the Heart"

To what extent does Confucianism become again a "habit of the heart" in Chinese society today and its core values meaningful to the people? Raising these questions, we immediately face two intertwined difficulties. First, a problem of definition and delimitation of our subject matter: due to the complex history of Confucianism, a wide range of practices and values may be associated with this tradition. What are we talking about when we speak about Confucian core values? The second difficulty is somehow the reverse side of the first one: people may embrace Confucian values without necessarily relating them to this tradition and without claiming any Confucian identity.[12] In this chapter I consider Confucianism in a broad and inclusive sense without restricting it to any set of clearly defined practices (e.g., participation in ritual activities in a temple or at a grave, ancestor worship, etc.).[13] Since I am interested in the way ordinary people are again referring to Confucianism as a source of meaning, I mainly concentrate on reactivated elements of Confucian religiosity in people's lives. In order to provide evidence of the expanding dissemination of these values today, I introduce different contexts in which they are nowadays rediscovered and often endorsed: the first example is the one of groups openly claiming a Confucian identity. The second example brings us beyond these Confucian circles to the cases of Buddhist societies and syncretistic religious organizations. Since very little concrete empirical evidence is so far available to researchers about the return of Confucianism as a habit of the heart, this section is going to be largely descriptive. My objective here is to provide, based on fieldwork conducted between 2005 and 2011, a rapid insight into a variety of situations, profiles, and motivations that can be encountered "in the space of the people." Of course, one obvious limit of this study is that I only present cases of people reappropriating Confucian values in a conscious process and based on concrete practices—more often than not concrete self-cultivation practices based on or inspired by textual sources/ classical texts. In other words, I do not discuss the way Confucian values and mental structures may still have a determining impact on people's life in an unconscious way, a point that would be interesting to assess but that is beyond the scope of this study.

Confucianism-Inspired Groups in the PRC

Fieldwork in revivalist organizations provides clear evidence that Confucianism may again become a habit of the heart for people of extremely different social backgrounds. I illustrate this point by introducing two cases among many actually encountered in the course of ethnographic research.

The background of the first case is the city of Shenzhen and a vegetarian restaurant opened by a young lady, Mrs. D., formerly a member of the People's Liberation Army (PLA) who finally resigned to delve into business, where she became very successful. After a long period of spiritual questing that led her first to Buddhism, she finally found "inner peace and life direction" (*anshen liming* 安身立命) in Confucianism at the end of a long process that began with the discovery of the ideas of Confucian scholar and activist Wang Caigui. Now in charge of a large vegetarian restaurant, she turns it into a small "cell" dedicated to the promotion of her new faith, for example, through the organization of classics reading sessions for children or conferences for adults. Participants in this enterprise are both regular customers and employees (around eighty of them in the restaurant).[14] Among the employees, Mr. A., a young man in his early thirties, was formerly a middle-manager in a Wal-Mart supermarket in Liaoning Province. Unhappy with his work ("I couldn't stand their methods"), he resigned and came to Shenzhen, where he is now assisting Mrs. D. in the management of the restaurant. This is where he discovered the Confucian classics and especially the *Analects*, which he now reads every morning. Indeed, the reading of the *Analects* promoted by Mrs. D. has become a source of inspiration for many other members of the staff. Let us take the example of a young couple with "peasant household registration" (*hukou* 戶口): a husband (from Guangdong) and wife (from Henan) are each in their twenties and were hired as waiters in the restaurant. Both were previously workers in a shoe-producing factory in the nearby city of Dongguan. Laid off following company restructuring, they discovered Confucianism thanks Mrs. D. The husband explains:

> It is very difficult to express what I feel . . . I am totally moved. I just regret that I did not discover the *Analects* earlier. I am not

> a scholar (*xuezhe* 學者), but I am moved when I read them, I understand how great Chinese culture is. At the factory in Dongguan, people were only thinking about money, there was not mutual trust, nothing. We earn less here, but the situation is totally different.[15]

And the wife complements his words with: "My education was poor and I did not learn much. I got less during the years that I spent at school than during the months that I spent in the restaurant. I am now learning the *Analects* by heart." The couple now contemplates putting their own child in a "traditional school" (*sishu* 私塾) where he could get a proper Confucian education. This choice is also the one made by the cook of the restaurant, and his wife, originating from Sichuan. Both in their fifties, raised in a socialist context with little exposure to religion or traditional culture, they explain that they "have been fooled by the socialist discourse against superstitions"; the important thing for them, now, is to provide their children with values, with an "education about important things in life" (*shengmin de jiaoyu* 生命的教育) and not simply with utilitarian knowledge (which they associate with subjects like mathematics). Among the people that could be interviewed in this restaurant, let me also mention the case of the young accountant, a girl in her late twenties, originating from the countryside (*nongmin hukou* 農民戶口), who already knew Mrs. D. in Liaoning Province and thanks to whom she discovered the Confucian classics. For two years now, she has been reading them—especially the *Analects*—every single morning: "They provide me with a feeling of 'joy' (*kuaile* 快樂) and 'happiness' (*xingfu* 幸福); they have changed my life . . ."

A second example brings us into a completely different environment, a little Confucian society/academy[16] opened in Beijing by a university professor, Mr. Y. The latter, a man in his early forties and a disciple of Confucian scholar Jiang Qing, came late to the academic world after a solid career first as a policeman and then as an officer in charge of political work in a prison. This rich experience and the insights he could gain in the darkest recesses of society fueled his scholarly interest in Confucianism and his commitment to social action: he now runs his little Confucian academy and is also involved, along with a few friends and colleagues, in the creation of a network of rural libraries in poor areas across the country. In his academy, Mr. Y. gathers a group of well-educated young people (students and young professionals) for whom Confucianism now becomes a real spiritual resource. Together, they study ancient texts and discuss all kinds of issues. Mr. X. is one of the participants. Now an engineer, he comes from a modest peasant family in Hubei Province without any education ("there were hardly any books in our home"). His first real encounter with classical culture took place during his high-school years thanks to an inspiring teacher, and, over time, he developed a real interest in traditional culture. Studying hard, he managed to pass the university examination and went to study in Harbin. At that time, he brought with him the *Analects* of Confucius and began to read them each morning, as a self-cultivation exercise. But what he describes as a real "conversion" ("I have now come to think of myself as a Confucian") came later through a series of events: an encounter in Beijing (where he now lives) with Mr Y., who became a close friend and mentor, if not a master; a reflection on death when his father passed away ("at that time, I recalled childhood memories, sacrifices to ancestors performed with my grand-uncle; I became aware of the duties to my family"); and finally a stay at Jiang Qing's academy in Guizhou, which was one of the most important experiences of his life. Later, when he is ready, Mr. X. dreams of opening his own "academy" (*shuyuan* 書院) and having disciples. Such a clarity about what is now perceived as a "sense of mission" (*shiminggan* 使命感) is not necessarily shared by all the members of the academy. Ms. B. still has doubts about what is best for her. A young graduate in Chinese literature from a university in Beijing, now working as a journalist, she comes from a family of cadres in Hebei Province where her exposure to traditional culture was very limited. Her interest in Confucianism resulted from discussions with friends and from a number of different preoccupations: at an individual level, she was eager to find "inner peace and life direction" (*anshen liming*) and learn "how to overcome difficulties when interacting with the others" (*zenme chuli ren he ren zhijian de guanxi* 怎麼處理人和人之間的關係); at a more general level she feels that "Chinese people are now in a hurry for everything, their state of mind is really bad. There is a lack of moral strength" (*daode de liliang* 道德的力量). So far, she finds her experience at the academy fulfilling and says, "I regard Confucius as an old grandpa full of wisdom" (*wo ba Kongzi dang yi ge hen you zhihui de lao yeye* 我把孔子當一個很有智慧的老爺爺) whose teachings are for her inspirational.

Examples could be easily multiplied to provide evidence that in Confucian "cells," sprouting all across the country, forms of Confucian spirituality are now taking root. Particularly striking is the diversity of backgrounds and experiences (from the laid-off factory worker to university-graduated white-collar workers) that can be encountered. In the aforementioned examples, two well-known names appear: Wang Caigui and Jiang Qing. Both play in fact an important role in today's Confucian revival. The influence of Wang Caigui, a disciple of philosopher Mou Zongsan, is now extremely significant, and many are the people, like Mrs. D., who, after having heard records of his speeches on Confucianism and classics learning, have become his followers and, inspired by his example, themselves promote Confucianism in society. Scholarly circles mainly tend to discuss Jiang Qing's analysis of *Gongyang* studies and his positions in favor of a Confucianism-inspired refoundation of political legitimacy. But a dimension that is often overlooked is also the indirect influence of Jiang Qing through his disciples, like, in our example, Mr. Y. In both the cases of Wang and Jiang, it is interesting to note that this return of a Confucian spirituality is also accompanied by a revival of master-disciple relations, relations that may now extend over several generations (in our cases: Mou Zongsan—Wang Caigui—Mrs. D. and Jiang Qing—Mr. Y.—Mr. X.). All this being said, it is necessary to add one point: whereas, in our two cases, inspirational masters (Wang, Jiang) are prominent figures well known in academic circles, this is far from being always the case. Carrying out fieldwork in different parts of China, including in smaller provincial towns, one is struck by the importance of what we could call "local intellectuals," that is, educated people (often, but not always, teachers) who are not necessarily conducting research on Confucianism (or at least not according to the usual standards of international research) but who are very familiar with classical texts. Their role in the propagation of Confucianism is of the upmost importance. I will come back to more general considerations on the revived "habits of the heart" later on. Before that, it is necessary to emphasize the increasing popularization of Confucianism—and especially Confucian spirituality or piety—beyond specifically Confucian circles.

Other Groups and Organizations Promoting Elements of Confucian Religiosity in the "Space of the People"

Interestingly, Confucianism has again become "a habit of the heart" beyond Confucian circles. This is illustrated here with two examples: Buddhist organizations and syncretistic sectarian movements.

The first example is provided by the activities broadly promoted in China by a Taiwanese Buddhist monk, the Venerable Master Jingkong 净空 (Xu Yehong 徐業鴻), also a specialist of Pure Land Buddhism. Born in 1927, he fled to Taiwan with the Kuomintang and became a monk in 1959. From the end of the 1970s onward he began to promote Buddhism abroad in the United States, Southeast Asia, and Australia but also gradually in the PRC, where his discourses and writings were widely distributed.[17] In 2005 he opened with the support of the local authorities the Lujiang Cultural Education Center in the town of Tangchi, Anhui Province. Ji and

Dutournier, who carried out fieldwork at the center, emphasize its ambition: "It is a matter, neither more nor less, of contributing to the transformation of Chinese society by the work of collective moralization, based on the reactivation of 'tradition' and promoted by an exemplary elite."[18] One of the missions of the center is to provide selected professors from the official systems with training in moral education. The selected candidates[19] follow a six-month training course, during which they live in the community and are mainly exposed to traditional Confucian values. The main text used by the participants is the very short *Rules for Disciples* (*Dizigui* 弟子規) supposed to be, in Jingkong's words, the "root of the roots of the classics" and the best possible way toward moral practice. Participants also attend lectures, for example, on filial piety, a theme chosen, according to Ji and Dutournier, for the naturalness associated with the attitude of respect toward one's parents. Such a naturalness is to be intuitively acknowledged by the participant in the course of a training that is therefore also clearly understood as a process of practical awareness.[20]

During fieldwork carried out in 2010 in Shanxi Province, we met a group associated with Jingkong's enterprise reading collectively the *Rules for Disciples* in Taiyuan's Confucius temple (*wenmiao* 文廟). Volunteers (*yigong* 義工) in charge of the group were in fact disciples of Cai Lixu, one of the heads of the Lujiang Cultural Education Center and himself a disciple of Jingkong. The leader, a lady in her early sixties, spent some time in Lujiang. Working previously as an accountant in a local administration, she converted early to Buddhism, a faith that she still embraces along with a number of volunteers of the group.[21] While her understanding of Buddhism was largely facilitated by the books of *guoxue* master Nan Huaijin, she nevertheless always considered Buddhist sutras far too abstruse. This largely explains her enthusiasm for the self-cultivation method promoted by Jingkong on the basis of the *Dizigui*. For now more than six years, she has been involved in the promotion of this text in society, mainly through regular reading sessions in the Taiyuan *wenmiao*. Her little group is now made up of around ten volunteers and thirty regular participants with very different backgrounds and ages, from young kids to elderly people. Apart from the reading sessions themselves, participants also take part in sharing sessions often highly loaded with emotion. The emphasis is always put on the practical implementation of the text ("The *Dizigui* is a text that seems so easy! However, I have already spent six years reading it! We have to realize the real meaning of what we are learning and implement it with a serious attitude"[22]). Rote learning, though not always discarded, is considered superficial if it does not generate practical habits.

Such a promotion of the Confucian classics or core elements of Confucian ethics by Buddhist organizations is quite a widespread phenomenon in China today that is not without historical precedents. Many factors may contribute to explain it, such as the relatively simple access to some of the Confucian texts (that may pave the way for a later discovery of sutras) or the lack of barriers to fostering traditional culture (compared to religious proselytizing, which is officially forbidden). In any event, it contributes to the promotion of a Confucian ethos in society. A similar contribution is provided by syncretistic religious organizations developing nowadays in the PRC.

The case of the "Way of Pervading Unity" (Yiguandao 一貫道) is in this respect very interesting. Yiguandao is a millenarian and syncretistic religious organization often categorized as a new religious movement (NRM) or, more recently, as a redemptive society.[23] It developed very quickly in China during the Republican period, attracting millions of followers, and was severely repressed in the PRC (where it is still a forbidden organization) after 1949. In Taiwan, it was also proscribed until its legalization in 1987, and it has now become the third largest religion of the island. The first point to underscore[24] is that Confucianism and in particular Confucian classics reading sessions play a significant role in the recruitment of new adepts and largely contribute to the expansion of the movement.[25] Second, Yiguandao is a sectarian movement whose ideology is drawn from a variety of sources, including Daoism, Buddhism, the tradition of the Unborn Mother (*wusheng laomu* 無生老母), among others. However, for reasons that we have no room to discuss here, this movement underwent a gradual process of Confucianization,[26] and the Confucian classics and key Confucian concepts are now central in the self-cultivation practices of the adepts. Carrying out participatory observation during training sessions organized for "companions of the Dao" (*daoqin* 道親, the term used by the adepts to speak about themselves) based in Mainland China, I could notice the importance of texts such as the *Doctrine of the Mean* (*Zhongyong* 中庸) (understood as a scripture on ultimate reality/*bentilun* 本體論) or the *Great Learning* (*Daxue* 大學) (understood as a scripture about self-cultivation/*gongfulun* 功夫論) in the curriculum of the participants. Within the systematic training process of adepts, Confucianism constitutes a body of doctrine that is less esoteric and consequently more easily accessible than other elements incorporated in the fabric of the movement's ideology. Sociologically, it is interesting to note that the movement (currently quickly expanding in the PRC) attracts a massive following of people from simple backgrounds: workers, peasants, small enterprise employees, and merchants, office clerks, among others.[27] More often than not these people (many of them quite young) never attended university or even high school. Confucianism is not endowed for them with the negative meaning inculcated in their parents by ideological discourses of the Maoist era, and they easily embrace its values and self-cultivation ideals.

In all the cases presented here (Confucian, Buddhist, and sectarian groups), the shared emphasis is on practice and, more specifically, on non-intellectual self-cultivation practices largely based on scriptural sources. The texts are appropriated by people from the most diverse backgrounds and offer them directions for their lives. We have here some forms of reactivation of a Confucian religiosity. This religiosity is "thinner" than, say, ritual practices (be they personal or collective ones) that are again frequently encountered in China. In a way, I believe that it largely echoes one of the two dimensions associated by philosopher Tang Junyi (1909–1978) with the concepts religiosity (*zongjiaoxing* 宗教性) or religious spirit (*zongjiao jingshen* 宗教精神).[28] In an essay discussing civil religion in modern Confucianism, Thomas Fröhlich explains that, for Tang Junyi, one of the fundamental attributes of Confucian religiosity is "the religious belief that human beings are endowed with an innate cognitive capacity (*liangzhi* 良知) which can be unfolded as moral intuition in order to realize, in the double meaning of the word, Heaven (*tian* 天)."[29] For Tang, the idea of *liangzhi* is primarily regulative, "a point of reference for normative statements," and, as such, "escapes the pitfalls of Confucian moral dogmatism."[30] This kind of faith in *liangzhi* somewhat underlies many of the discourses recorded in the course of fieldwork. Of course, things are not necessarily verbalized in that way and, for example, the reference to Heaven is not often emphasized (except within the Yiguandao where references to transcendence—Heaven, Way, Unborn Mother, etc.—are much more systematic for the adepts), whereas *liangzhi*—I mean, the concept of *liangzhi*—is rarely discussed as such. However, the belief that the Confucian classics address ultimate values (as opposed to social ones) and that these values can be known and experienced by everyone by cultivating the self is a largely shared assumption within the circles of people that I could interview.

Tang Junyi attempted to analyze the role that Confucian religiosity could play in contemporary China, and Fröhlich conceives of his project as an attempt to ponder over the possibility for Confucianism to become a civil religion (even though the term "civil religion" is not used by Tang). This proposal will be discussed later. At this point, suffice it to highlight the fact that *liangzhi* appears in Tang's mind as central for the establishment of a Confucian civil religion (religiosity) in that its meaning, Tang believes, could be largely compatible with other faiths such as Buddhism and Christianity.[31] There is no room here to discuss this matter from a theoretical philosophical/theological perspective, but I just have to underline that, from the perspective of purely empirical research in social sciences, fieldwork results corroborate this point, at least for Buddhism and the sectarian tradition of the Yiguandao.

The Issue of Civil Religion

Evidence of the return of a reference to Confucianism in the mores of Chinese society having now briefly been introduced, I am going to come back in the second part of this chapter to the problematic question of a civil religion. Influenced by Durkheim, Robert Bellah reactivated this concept inherited from Rousseau in a famous 1967 essay in order to apply it to an American context,[32] thereby generating intense discussions.[33] Bellah's basic idea was that there are

> certain common elements of religious orientation that the great majority of Americans share. These have played a crucial role in the development of American institutions and still provide a religious dimension for the whole fabric of American life, including the political sphere. This public religious dimension is expressed in a set of beliefs, symbols and rituals that I am calling the American civil religion.[34]

Bellah later stopped using the term "civil religion" to avoid misunderstandings, due to a number of negative reactions of both religious believers and secularists who understood this idea as a threat, even though it was primarily rooted in the Durkheimian insight that any social group has a religious dimension.[35] However, he continued discussing this idea under different forms and the collective book *Habits of the Heart* is a result of this later development. Therefore, it might seem strange to come back to this concept today, but the fact is that the issue of civil religion has become a reactivated topic of discussion much beyond the American context. In China, it has recently been at the center of exchanges within the academic community, and several contributors to this volume have been in the forefront of the debate.[36] Considering the background where these discussions take place, that is, on the one hand, the current "Confucian revival" (a few aspects of which the present chapter briefly introduces) as well as the rise of Maoist nostalgia and anti-Confucian feelings[37] and, on the other hand, the ambiguous relation of the party-state toward traditional culture, the issue of Confucianism as a possible civil religion is a highly complex one with potential political and social implications. In the following developments I first introduce some of the positions defended in scholarly circles. Second, I emphasize the problems that a Confucian civil religion understood as a civic religion celebrating the cult of social unity could generate. Finally, I discuss briefly the possibility (or, rather, the conditions of possibility) for Confucianism to become a "common religion" or a civil religion with a primarily social orientation.

Debates in Scholarly Circles

Introducing the debate about civil religion in China, I am first going to briefly present three very different and representative positions: those of scholars Chen Ming, Ji Zhe, and Fenggang Yang.

Chen Ming was one of the first scholars to present this issue to a Chinese audience, convinced that Confucianism could become China's civil religion and thus a cultural resource contributing to solve a number of problems (cultural identity, the quest for spiritual and material peace—*shenxin andun de wenti* 身心安頓的問題) faced by China today.[38] By interpreting the concept in a broad way, Chen emphasizes that it would be possible to find in the resources of Confucianism elements that could become references for the life of the country (*guojia shenghuo* 國家生活): holy figures (Yao, Shun, Yu, Tang), sacred places (temples and altars), and rites (sacrifices to Heaven, to Ancestors), holy beliefs, and so forth. One of the characteristics of Confucianism as a religion, Chen explains, is that it could, in the past, play a linking role between the political system and the people. After the dismantling of the imperial order, it could only be found in the realm of popular beliefs, and it is just based on these popular beliefs that there is now a hope to promote it again.[39] What should the role of the state be for the realization of such a project? Chen distinguishes between "civil religion" and "political theology" (*zhengzhi shenxue* 政治神學) and explains that the first relies on a social implementation, whereas the second is established and promoted by the state.[40] Confucianism, should it become a civil religion, would be different from a national teaching" (*guojiao*) or the "union of the political and the religious" (*zhengjiao he yi* 政教合一).[41] Besides, it would potentially be compatible with a democratic regime.[42] This being said, Chen emphasizes that, as a civil religion, Confucianism would, among other functions, serve to legitimize the political authority.[43] Its symbolic institutionalization (crystallizing in holy figures, places, rites) would—even though it aims at a reactivation of this teaching "in the space of the people"—require the intervention of the authorities. As is discussed later, this is not without difficulties in the current Chinese context.

The Chinese context is precisely the main concern of Paris-based scholar Ji Zhe. In an article titled "About Civil Religion" (Lun Gongmin zongjiao 論公民宗教)[44] he begins by emphasizing that civil religion is, in general, a collective belief with a sacred dimension—he even speaks about a secular belief: *shisu xinyang* 世俗信仰—but not a religious belief.[45] Coming back to the origin of the concept in Rousseau's thought, he underlines its strong moral dimension and the fact that the provisions of civil religion, far from being ideological instruments of the state—"Would there be, he asks, anything worse than this?"—are in fact enacted by the sovereign (*le souverain*), that is, by the people. In other words, the condition of possibility of a civil religion is that political sovereignty really truly belongs to the people; therefore, a civil religion requires a democratic context.[46] Referring to Bellah's opposition to a civil religion that would become some sort of national self-idolatry, Ji insists that both for Bellah and Rousseau civil religion is not a tool of political legitimization.[47] While every person is entitled to develop his or her own particular civil religion, such a religion should fashion citizens of a "civilized society" rather than members of any national entity or race.[48]

Purdue University scholar Fenggang Yang also mentions the risk of an alienation of civil religion that, far from being only patriotic, could also turn into some nationalistic form of political religion (*zhengzhi zongjiao* 政治宗教). In his contribution to the present volume he stresses that "the suggestion to establish Confucianism as the state religion of China is not only dubious but also dangerous."[49] Discussing the American model, he emphasizes that civil religion comes from the people and is not imposed by the authorities.[50] Furthermore, civil religion even serves as a protective screen preventing mistakes from political leaders.[51] Yang believes that some form of Confucianism-based civil religion or public teaching (*gonggong zhi jiaohua* 公共之教化) could or even should be implemented in China. However, considering that Confucianism was never able to provide "inner peace and life direction" (*anshen liming*) to a large audience, beyond small circles of scholar literati, because of its "thin religiosity" (*xibo de zongjiaoxing* 稀薄的宗教性) that did not sufficiently address a number of existential questions such as those surrounding death,[52] Yang also believes that the transcendent dimension of Heaven (*tian*) should be emphasized.[53] American civil religion and its Christian roots, Yang believes, could be inspirational on that latter point. The rise of Christianity in today's China is, in fact, for Yang, the major challenge that Confucianism needs to address in the same way it addressed the one of other traditions in the past (e.g., Buddhism), and Christianity could in fact—contrary to often prevailing misunderstandings—become a resource for the renaissance of Chinese culture.[54] In the current volume, Yang goes so far as to suggest that a civil religion based on Confucianism and Christianity might be of universal (*tianxia* 天下) interest.[55]

These three very different positions about the possible role of Confucianism as a civil religion provide some good evidence that, even though the debate has been dampened in the United States, the concept remains inspirational enough to generate plenty of discussions when exported into completely different contexts. Looking at these three viewpoints, one should notice that they all rule out the possibility, contemplated by other scholars (e.g., Jiang Qing or Kang Xiaoguang) to establish Confucianism as a national teaching (*guojiao* 國教).[56] They raise two critical issues: the role of state intervention in the expression of civil religion (a problem evoked by all but particularly emphasized by Ji) and the collective expression of Confucian religiosity in the space of the people (a point that tends to be more the focus of attention of Chen and Yang).

In some respects echoing these discussions, French sociologist of religion Jean-Paul Willaime highlights two intertwined but different dimensions of the concept of civil religion. On the one hand, civil religion is "the cult of the unity of the social body, the sacrament of social unity," and such a unity needs to be constantly strengthened at a symbolic level. Civil religion appears here as a "civic religion."[57] On the other hand, he explains that civil religion also encompasses the idea of a "common religion," that is, "the diffuse set of beliefs, representations and evaluations that defines the philosophical/religious and ethical universe of a population, its ethos." In this second case, the focus is less on the institutionalization and on the political expression of the collective social feeling. Rather, the emphasis is put on the common religious culture within a population.[58] Willaime also underlines that this distinction between a "civic" and a "common" religion (at the juncture point of which the concept of civil religion lies) also reflects the distinction introduced, within an Israeli context, between a civil religion with a political orientation and a civil religion with a social orientation.[59] I discuss these two orientations in the following sections.

The Role of the State: Confucianism as a "Civil/Civic Religion"?

Speaking about a Confucian civil religion in China today is of course largely a speculative exercise. However, we have a number of concrete examples or clues—I am alluding to historical or socio-anthropological evidence—of what Confucianism could become if it were to be monitored again by the state.

The first example brings us to pre-WWII Japan. In an essay on the restoration of Confucianism in Japan and China, Nakajima Takahiro underlines that in the late 1880s modernist ideas relegated the category of religion to the private realm, whereas morality and ethics were associated with a public realm encompassing in particular State Shinto and Confucianism.[60] However, a number of scholars such as Hattori Unikochi or Inoue Tetsujiro (two supporters of the Concordia Association) insisted on the fact that Confucianism was also endowed with a dimension of religiosity. Nakajima, speaking about these scholars, explains that they advocated an amalgam of morality and religion for the legitimacy of modern Japan, and he defines this amalgam as a "Japanese civil religion."[61] Such a "Japanese civil religion" crystallized in another amalgam, the one of Confucianism and State Shinto, labeled the "Confucian Way."[62] A conference on the Confucian Way actually took place in 1935 for the reconstruction of Tokyo's Yushoma Confucian temple and followed a visit by Pu Yi, at that time puppet emperor of Manchuria.[63] In the mind of the participants, the Confucian Way, that is, this dimension of civil religion, was instrumental in supporting Japanese expansionism and nationalism. Beyond the specific case of this conference, one can emphasize that such a view was quite pervasive in circles promoting Confucianism in Japan at that time.

The second example brings us to Taiwan and to the movement of renaissance of Chinese culture (*Zhonghua wenhua fuxing yundong* 中華文化復興運動) launched in 1966 by the authorities in reaction to the PRC's Cultural Revolution. This movement, monitored by a government agency (the Committee for the Renaissance of Chinese Culture), promoted the Kuomintang's understanding of culture, largely based on the promotion of Confucian values, including filial piety and loyalty to the State and theories of the Kuomintang leaders such as Sun Yatsen's three principles of the people.[64] Kuomintang leaders were actually integrated within a long genealogy of the way (*daotong* 道統) that could be traced back to the ancestors of Chinese civilization (from Yao and Shun to Sun Yatsen and Chiang Kai-shek).[65] Two programs were implemented to promote this project of cultural renaissance among the masses: the first one was named "What Citizens Should Know about Daily Life" (*guomin shenghuo xu zhi* 國民生活須知) and the second one "Models for Citizen's Rites and Ceremonies" (*guomin liyi fanli* 國民禮儀範例). They aimed at implementing Confucian values (the "four directions" [*si wei* 四維] and eight virtues [*ba de* 八德])

while combining them, in the same spirit as the New Life movement of the Nanjing decade, with "modernization" and "rationalization." A special emphasis was put on the respect of hierarchy and frugality while daily life, in its very details, was to be ritualized and disciplined.[66] The cultural renaissance movement needs to be understood within a context of mass mobilization and anticommunism: this campaign, launched at the same time as the Cultural Revolution, reified the opposition of the CCP and the KMT in the realm of values. It was therefore an instrument supposed to strengthen the legitimacy of the KMT regime and its leadership. The whole renaissance movement was in fact purely a top-down enterprise carried out at all levels by party organs. Its intensity decreased during the 1970s.[67]

The third example is the one of today's China. The general context is a rising reference to traditional culture (not limited to Confucianism) that may sometimes translate into forms of cultural nationalism. The return of ceremonies honoring tutelary figures of Chinese culture, such as the Yellow Emperor—a case explored in depth by Térence Billeter—are good illustrations of this point.[68] The situation of Confucianism is complex. At the central level, obvious historical reasons (for example, the fact that the revolutionary tradition perpetuated by the CCP is based on the opposition to an old order largely associated with Confucianism) and anti-Confucian feelings (for example within the "red faction" instrumental in the engineering of some sort of Maoist nostalgia) explain the scarce references to Confucianism in official discourses. Episodic and symbolic nondiscursive references to Confucianism—from the scenography of the opening ceremony of the Olympic Games to the surprising apparition/disappearance of a Confucius statue on Tiananmen Square at the beginning of 2011 or the name given to the network of China's language and culture institute abroad—generate all kinds of speculations about the potential role of Confucianism in the ideological reconfiguration of the country without being able, however, to provide any solid evidence thereof.[69] One can only notice that the authorities closely follow the variety of experiments taking place in society (Confucian schools, NGOs, rituals activities, etc.) and do not discourage them.[70] Rather, they are probably waiting to assess how these phenomena develop and cleverly adapt to a rising interest for Confucianism in the population. At a local level, lots of different cases may be distinguished. Involvement of the authorities in Confucianism-related projects may be motivated by a number of reasons, including: economic local interests (e.g., tourism), the promotion of morality (e.g., with the promotion of filial piety), ideological indoctrination (I could for instance attend Confucianism-inspired interpretations of the concept of "harmonious society" to an audience of civil servants in a provincial city), the will to promote local traditions able to hinder the development of Christianity,[71] or mere Confucian "faith" of activists working in governmental offices (a frequent case). More often than not it is a number of overlapping parameters that explain why a Confucianism-related activity is carried out in a specific location. In that respect, the official Confucian ceremonies carried out in Qufu each year provide a case study (with official ceremonies totally devoid of Confucian ritual spirit, in strong contrast with *minjian* rites carried out separately at the same period of time), as does the very controversial project of creating a "symbolic city of Chinese culture" in the Qufu-Zoucheng-Jiulongshan area.[72]

The first two examples provide some evidence of what Confucianism may become when monitored to serve mainly political objectives. The third example (the PRC today) is more ambiguous: Confucianism is not necessarily invoked as such by the authorities, and, when it is (especially at the local level), a variety of possible motivations may have to be taken into account. At least, one may emphasize that they often have little to do (i.e., tourism) with the return of Confucian values "in the sphere of mores" described in the first part of this chapter. If we come back to our former reflections about civil religion and the role of the state, a possible promotion of Confucianism as a civil religion in the PRC today, as suggested by some scholars, would face the following difficulties: First, historical evidence (Japanese and Taiwanese examples) provides some clues about what could become of Confucianism in a contemporary authoritarian context. Second, considering the history of the relation of the CCP to Confucianism, one can hardly imagine that the latter could serve, at least nowadays, as "the cult of the unity of the social body, the sacrament of social unity." The fierce controversies about the "symbolic city of Chinese culture," an initiative approved at the state's highest level and that nevertheless resulted in fierce opposition among Chinese People's Political Consultative Conference (CPPCC) delegates, provides some clear evidence of this fact. More generally, anti-Confucianism remains strong in China, in spite of the "Confucian revival" (just look at some of the vehemently anti-Confucian Maoist websites). Finally, while China's current value crisis symptomized by all kinds of scandals that constantly hit the headlines may generate a demand for the reactivation of Confucian values such as *liangzhi*, this does not necessarily imply that these values need to be promoted (1) by the authorities and (2) as specifically Confucian ones. All in all, considering China's current circumstances, one might wonder whether a Confucian civil religion—at least in its civic form (Willaime) or with a political orientation—may in the end benefit Confucianism and not be totally counterproductive.

A "Common Religion"?

While Confucianism understood as a "civic religion" seems to be in the current Chinese circumstances a pretty insecure road, one can also ponder to what extent there might be room in China for the development of Confucianism as a "common religion" understood, if I come back to Willaime's aforementioned article, as "the diffuse set of beliefs, representations and evaluations that defines the philosophical/religious and ethical universe of a population, its ethos." From this perspective, the focus is primarily on the population and no longer on the state.

The first obvious thing to emphasize is that there is no such thing nowadays in China as a "common religion" that would claim a Confucian identity, even though a number of values still commonly embraced by the population were traditionally promoted by Confucianism (but more often than not, the question of their origin is not a concern). This brings us back to both our previous discussion about Tang Junyi and to fieldwork results.

Fröhlich underscores that Tang Junyi identified two important attributes of Confucian religiosity: the first one, already mentioned, is the shared belief that human beings are endowed with a capacity of innate moral knowledge; the second one is sacrificial practice and what Tang called the three ritual sacrifices (*san ji* 三祭): The sacrifice to Heaven and Earth (*tiandi* 天地), to ancestors (*zuzong* 祖宗), to saints and worthies (*shengxian* 聖賢) that are all discussed in his work *The Development of a Humanistic Chinese Spirit* (*Zhongguo renwen jingshen zhi fazhan* 中國人文精神之發展).[73] Tang highlighted the importance of these sacrifices and the necessity of their reactivation and renovation considering that the development of a Confucian spirit could not simply depend on intellectual endeavors.[74] However, it is particularly interesting to note that, for him, the promotion within society of a "spirit of rites and music" (*liyue jingshen* 禮樂精神), including the aforementioned sacrifices and, by extension, Confucian religiosity as a whole, could not be carried out by professional groups, churches, party-states, or academic congregations. Rather, "its implementation (should) start from a minority of creative individuals and, from there, it will slowly diffuse through society in a non-hierarchical manner."[75] At the time when Tang Junyi was writing about these issues,[76] he was in exile and China was undergoing a difficult period of its history. One can easily understand why he could not seriously consider any other alternative than a diffusion of Confucian values at an individual level. However, one can also have serious doubts about the possibility for Confucian religiosity to deeply diffuse into society should it only depend on "a minority of creative individuals" or "teachers and friends" (*shiyou* 師友)[77] in a completely informal way. Therefore, the question becomes the following: Considering, on the one hand, the problems incurred by state intervention within an authoritarian context (Confucian "civil religion" could become a mere political tool totally counterproductive, in the middle or long run, for the promotion of Confucian values), and, on the other hand, the likely weak impact of an action limited to "a minority of creative individuals," is there any practical road left for the future development of a Confucianism-inspired "common religion"?

In his aforementioned reflections on a "common religion" (that is, a civil religion with a primarily social—rather than political—orientation), Willaime insists on the fact that the "sacral dimension of collective identities is not necessarily the privilege of the state" and he explains that a "communitarian civil religion" (*une religion civile communautaire*) is also possible.[78] This remark is important because it enables us to point to the role of all kinds of organizations and communities active in the "space of the people" (e.g., religious or charitable organizations, but more broadly NGOs etc.). As we have previously seen in the first section of this chapter, a thin level of Confucian religiosity (that one could, for the sake of simplicity, encapsulate under the term *liangzhi* used by Tang) has nowadays become a reference point not only within openly Confucian organizations but also beyond within other religious groups; we mentioned the examples of Buddhists and sectarians. Fieldwork shows that this "thin Confucian religiosity" is in fact often easy to accept for people from all backgrounds, including the most modest ones. In other words, it is now a resource increasingly shared, transversally, by a variety of different groups. Furthermore, it is even a resource that tends to be used by some groups as a first step for the recruitment of new members. Systematic empirical research would be necessary to assess to what extent such a "thin Confucian religiosity" might spread to other groups than the ones discussed in this chapter, for example, in Christian circles, since the compatibility of Christianity and some fundamental Confucian values has been emphasized, from a more theoretical viewpoint, by numerous scholars.[79] More generally, we can posit that the present overall religious revival and, beyond, the overall countercurrent that is taking shape as a reaction against the extreme individualization of Chinese society—a countercurrent that enables the affirmation of forms of subjectivity that, in the end, recreate or reactivate collective links and values—constitute an extremely favorable ground or, in other words a very favorable "social ecology" for the development of a "thin Confucian religiosity." At the moment, phenomena that can be observed in the mores of Chinese society during fieldwork are primarily, if we borrow again the expression from *Habits of the*

Heart, "incipient changes of vision" or "new flights of the social imagination" materializing in the activities of limited and ill-structured *communitas.* Should they continue to gain momentum, they could definitely contribute to create the conditions of possibility of a Confucianism-inspired common or civil religion with a social orientation. In fact, the reappropriation in the space of the people of a Confucian ethos compatible with other forms of religiosity—a reappropriation that has already started to take place—is a prerequisite to any further reflections on Confucianism-based ritual and symbolic expressions of collective unity that would be more than mere by-products of political manipulation.

Notes

Fieldwork referred to in this chapter was made possible thanks to a grant of the Chiang Ching-kuo Foundation for a project titled "The Confucian Revival in Mainland China: Forms and Meanings of Confucian Piety Today."

1. Robert N. Bellah, Richard Madsen, William M. Sullivan, Ann Swidler, and Steven M. Tipton, *Habits of the Heart: Individualism and Commitment in American Life* (Berkeley: University of California Press, 1985), 275.

2. Yan Yunxiang, *The Individualization of Chinese Society* (London: LSE Monographs on Social Anthropology, 2009).

3. Robert N. Bellah, *The Broken Covenant: American Civil Religion in Time of Trial* (Chicago: University of Chicago Press, 1992).

4. Reinhart Koselleck, "'Erfahrungsraum' und 'Erwartungshorizont': zwei historische Kategorien," in *Vergangene Zukunft: Zur Semantik geschichtlicher Zeiten* (Frankfurt am Main: Suhrkamp, 1989), 349–375.

5. Pierre Nora, *Présent, nation, mémoire* (Paris: Gallimard, 2011), 413.

6. François Hartog, *Régimes d'historicité: Présentisme et expériences du temps* (Paris: Le Seuil, 2003).

7. Michael Szonyi, "Ming Fever: The Present's Past as the People's Republic Turns Sixty," *China Heritage Quarterly* 21 (March 2010): Web link (consulted on November 4, 2011): http://www.chinaheritagequarterly.org/articles.php?searchterm=021_mingfever.inc&issue=021.

8. See for instance the success of the CCTV program *Baijia jiangtan*.

9. Gérémie R. Barmé, *Shades of Mao: The Posthumous Cult of the Great Leader* (New York: M. E. Sharpe, 1996).

10. Sébastien Billioud and Joël Thoraval, "The Development of Contemporary Confucianism (part 1) *Jiaohua*: The Confucian Revival Today as an Educative Project," *China Perspectives* 4 (2007): 4–20; "The Development of Contemporary Confucianism (part 2) *Anshen liming* or the Religious Dimension of Confucianism," *China Perspectives* 3 (2008): 88–106; "The Development of Contemporary Confucianism (part 3) *Lijiao*: The Return of Ceremonies Honouring Confucius in

Mainland China," *China Perspectives* 4 (2009): 82–99. Sébastien Billioud, "Carrying the Confucian Torch to the Masses: The Challenge of Structuring the Confucian Revival in the People's Republic of China," *Oriens Extremus* 49 (2010): 201–224; "Confucian Revival and the Emergence of *Jiaohua* Organizations: A Case Study of the Yidan Xuetang," *Modern China* 37.3 (May 2011): 286–314. Anna Sun, "The Revival of Confucian Rites in Contemporary China," in *Confucianism and Spiritual Traditions in Modern China and Beyond*, ed. Fenggang Yang and Joseph Tamney (Leiden: Brill, 2012), 309–328; "The Religious Ecology of Confucius Temple Life," unpublished paper presented at Tokyo University, December 2010.

11. Billioud, "Carrying the Confucian Torch to the Masses."

12. Anna Sun, who conducted fieldwork on personal rites in a number of Confucian temples all over China, notices that "people who perform rituals and ask for blessings in Confucius temples do not in general consider themselves to be Confucians." Sun, "The Revival of Confucian Rites in Contemporary China," 321.

13. On the criteria of Confucian identity, see also Sun, "The Revival of Confucian Rites in Contemporary China," 312–314.

14. For a detailed analysis of the spiritual itinerary of this lady, see Billioud and Thoraval, "*Anshen liming*."

15. Fieldwork, Shenzhen, June 2007.

16. This academy has an informal dimension since it does not have a fixed location.

17. On these points and for a presentation of Jingkong, see Guillaume Dutournier and Ji Zhe, "Social Experimentation and Popular Confucianism," *China Perspectives* 4 (2009): 75–76, especially 69–70.

18. Ibid., 71.

19. In 2005 the center only accepted thirty people out of three hundred candidates. The selection was severe. Ibid., 72.

20. Ibid., 74.

21. Field observation, Taiyuan, June 2010.

22. Interview, Taiyuan, June 2010.

23. See David A. Palmer and Vincent Goossaert, *The Religious Question in Modern China, 1898–2008* (Chicago: University of Chicago Press, 2011). On the Yiguandao, see, for example: Song Guangyu, *Tiandao chuandeng: Yiguandao yu xiandai shehui*, 2 vols. (Taipei: Zhengyi shanshu chubanshe, 1996); Edward Irons, "Tian Dao: The Net of Ideology in a Chinese Religion" (PhD dissertation, UC Berkeley, 2000); David Jordan and Daniel L. Overmeyer, *The Flying Phoenix: Aspects of Chinese Sectarianism in Taiwan* (Princeton: Princeton University Press, 1986); Lu Yunfeng, *The Transformation of Yiguan Dao in Taiwan: Adapting to a Changing Religious Economy* (Lanham: Lexington Books, 2008).

24. I have conducted intensive fieldwork on the Yiguandao primarily in Hong Kong (anthropological participant observation) but also in Taiwan and the PRC between 2009 and 2011. This section builds on this fieldwork.

25. For a detailed analysis of these points, see Sébastien Billioud, "Le rôle de l'éducation dans le projet salvateur du Yiguandao," *Extrême-Orient Extrême-Occident*

(October 2011): 211–234. ("The Role of Education in Yiguandao's Salvationist Project" and "Qi jia: The Great Learning Ideal of Family Regulation in a Contemporary Syncretistic Religious Context" (Collège de France, 2015).

26. See ibid. for a presentation of the three phases of Confucianization of the organization.

27. This does not mean that there are not other people as well, but this feature was for me striking in the course of fieldwork.

28. The second dimension is ritual and will be discussed later.

29. Thomas Fröhlich, "Cultural Patriotism and Civil Religion in Modern Confucianism: A Brief Discussion on the Outlines of Tang Junyi's Political Thought," in *Guoji ruxue yanjiu* 14.2, *2005 nian guoji ruxue gaofeng luntan zhuanji*, ed. Dan Chun (Beijing: Jiuzhou chubanshe, 2005), 287–288. Tang's religious belief in *liangzhi* can be contrasted with Mou Zongsan's much more philosophical analysis of this notion.

30. Fröhlich adds that "according to Tang, the capacity to realize moral intuition did not require an individual to uncritically accept ethical values passed down by tradition; this would only cause the loss of his or her moral sensitivity." Ibid., 293.

31. Ibid., 291.

32. Robert N. Bellah, "Civil Religion in America," *Beyond Belief: Essays on Religion in a Post-Traditionalist World* (Berkeley: University of California Press, 1991), 168–189. Insights were later developed in Bellah, *The Broken Covenant.*

33. James A. Mathisen, "Twenty Years after Bellah: Whatever Happened to American Civil Religion?" *Sociological Analysis* 50.2, Thematic Issue: A Durkheimian Miscellany (Summer 1989): 129–146. Gail Gehrig, "The American Civil Religion Debate: A Source for Theory Construction," *Journal for the Scientific Study of Religion* 20.1 (March 1981): 51–63.

34. Bellah, *Beyond Belief*, 171.

35. Robert N. Bellah, "Can We Imagine a Global Civil Religion?" chap. 10 in this volume; Emile Durkheim, *Les formes élémentaires de la vie religieuse* (Paris: PUF, 2005).

36. For an overall introduction to the issue, see Joël Thoraval, "Can Confucianism Become a Modern 'Civil Religion'?" Unpublished paper.

37. See, for example, websites such as *Utopia/wu you zhi xiang* (www.wyzxsx.com).

38. Chen Ming, "Duihua huo du bai, rujiao zhi gongmin zongjiao shuo suizha," *Yuan Dao* 14 (2007): 52.

39. Ibid., 51.

40. Ibid., 56.

41. Ibid., 51.

42. Ibid., 52.

43. Ibid., 58.

44. Ji Zhe, "Lun gongmin zongjiao," *Shehuixue yanjiu* 1 (2011): 1–14.

45. Ibid., 4.

46. Ibid., 7.

47. Ibid., 8.
48. Ibid., 11.
49. Fenggang Yang, "Confucianism as Civil Religion," chap. 1 in this volume, 34.
50. Yang Fenggang, "Duiyu rujiao zhi wei jiao de shehuixue sikao," *Journal of Lanzhou University* (Social sciences) 36.3 (2008): 3.
51. Ibid., 5.
52. Ibid., 3.
53. Ibid., 5.
54. Ibid., 5.
55. Yang, "Confucianism as Civil Religion," 41–42.
56. In other words, these three discourses attempt to adapt Confucianism to modernity but do not deeply question the very paradigms of modernity as, say, Jiang Qing is doing.
57. Jean-Paul Willaime, "La religion civile à la française et ses métamorphoses," *Social Compass* 40.4 (1993): 571–572. Although Willaime's article is dedicated to the French case, his preliminary considerations about the concept of civil religion are relevant to a broader context.
58. Ibid., 572. By "common religious culture," one should of course not understand a common religion but common cultural/background references as regards religion. Willaime invokes the "religious dimensions of cultural identity."
59. Ibid., 573.
60. Takahiro Nakajima, "The Restoration of Confucianism in China and Japan: A New Source of Morality and Religion," in *Facing the 21st Century*, ed. Lam Wing-keung and Cheung Chingyuen (Nagoya: Nanzan Institute for Religion & Culture, 2009), 42.
61. Ibid., 46.
62. Ibid., 47.
63. Ibid., 46–47.
64. Paul Katz, "Religion and State in Post-War Taiwan," *The China Quarterly* 174 (2003): 402; Lin Guoxian (Kuo-hsien), *Zhonghua wenhua fuxing yundong tuixing weiyuanhui zhi yanjiu (1966–1975)* (Taipei: Daoxiang, 2005).
65. Ibid., 225.
66. Ibid., 155–156.
67. Ibid., 231.
68. Térence Billeter, *L'Empereur jaune* (Paris: Les Indes Savantes, 2007).
69. See, for instance, John Dotson, *The Confucian Revival in the Propaganda Narratives of the Chinese Government*, US-China Economic and Security Review Commission Staff Research Report, June 20, 2011.
70. Discussion with representatives of the religious authorities, Beijing, December 2010.
71. A point that I frequently noted interviewing people in the course of fieldwork.
72. Billioud and Thoraval, "*Lijiao*."

73. Fröhlich, "Cultural Patriotism and Civil Religion in Modern Confucianism," 288.

74. Tang Junyi, *Zhongguo renwen jingshen zhi fazhan* (The Development of a Chinese Humanistic Spirit) (Taipei: Xuesheng shuju, 2000), 390.

75. Fröhlich, "Cultural Patriotism," 295.

76. For instance, Tang, *Zhongguo renwen jingshen zhi fazhan*, where some of these ideas were developed, was written in 1958.

77. Tang, *Zhongguo renwen jingshen zhi fazhan*, 391.

78. Willaime, "La religion civile à la française et ses metamorphoses," 573.

79. The possible compatibility of values should not mask the potential for tensions between Confucians and Christians, a phenomenon exemplified by the "Qufu church controversy" mentioned by Anna Sun in her contribution, "The Politics of Confucianism in Contemporary China," chap. 4 in this volume.

3

Inside the Revival of Confucianism in Mainland China

The Vicissitudes of Confucian Classics in Contemporary China as an Example

GUOXIANG PENG

The topic I address in this essay is rethinking the revival of Confucianism in Mainland China. The specific approach to this issue I choose is to scrutinize the vicissitudes of the Confucian classics in a changing contemporary China. By contemporary, I mean the period from 1949 until now; by China, I mean Mainland China. By "changing," I mean not only a rapidly evolving China but also an evolution in Chinese society's treatment of the Confucian classics. The aim of this essay is to provide a personal reflection on the so-called revival of Confucianism in today's China.

Many of the contributions to this volume explore the current interest, both within and outside of China, with the possibility of taking Confucianism as a civil religion. I do not discuss this particular issue, but perceptive readers readily will infer, correctly, that I am not in favor of this proposal at least as it commonly is conceived. I am, though, deeply concerned with the current and future contribution Confucianism can make not only to Chinese culture but to world culture and specifically the roles that are and can be played by the Confucian classics and the values they convey. I firmly believe that the Confucian classics should be seen and valued as a rich moral and spiritual resource not only for the Chinese people but for all the people of the world.

My essay includes three parts: first, a retrospective on the vicissitudes of the Confucian classics in contemporary China; second, the general state of Confucian "classics education" in today's China and more particularly in China's "general education" program; and third, some personal observations on these matters. Given the limited space, my comments will be brief.

A Retrospective

Regarding the vicissitudes of the Confucian classics in contemporary China, like the fate of the Confucian tradition as a whole, it can be metaphorically but vividly expressed by two sentences from a well-known Song dynasty poem,

> Seeing mountains' climbing and rivers' curving,
> I could see no way ahead,
> Suddenly in the shade of the willows and amid shining flowers,
> A village appeared.[1]

As the verse suggests, the fate of the Confucian classics in their motherland can be divided into two sharply contrasting eras. From 1949 until the 1970s was the period of "mountains' climbing and rivers' curving," with "no way ahead" in sight. The state and situation of the Confucian tradition during that period was deplorable. The Chinese Communist Party (CCP) not only had inherited the antitraditionalism of the May Fourth movement but also carried it to an extreme. Anything Confucian became a target of attack, or, to use an expression current in the 1960s and 1970s, "a target of proletarian dictatorship" (*wuchan jieji zhuanzheng de duixiang* 無產階級專政的對象), which should be "swept into the dustbin of history" (*saojin lishi de lajidui* 掃進歷史的垃圾堆). At no level of formal education could Confucian "classics" be taught or studied at all, and during this period the term "classics" (i.e., canonical) could only refer to works of the Marx-Leninist tradition. Chinese culture in Mainland China as dominated by the Chinese Communist Party was radically uprooted from its own tradition. Fortunately, this period has now itself been "swept into the dustbin of history."

Then, "Suddenly in the shade of the willows and amid shining flowers, a village appeared"; a new way beckoned to us in the current era, which began in the 1980s. The Confucian classics could once again be studied in a new era of openness, leading many to think that Confucianism and the Confucian classics were experiencing a revival. More precisely, this period can be divided into two stages: before and after the year 2000. Between 1978 and 2000, the party and the government started to reassess Confucianism, and Confucian studies gradually became a major field in the academic world. There was even a boom in traditional scholarship, focused mainly on Confucian studies, starting with research done at Peking University in the 1990s. This phenomenon was spoken of as "the heat or fever of national learning" (*guoxue re* 國學熱) and was overplayed by the mass media (truly it was far from being a "heat or fever," *re* 熱). Only after 2000 did the aspirations of ordinary people for learning and understanding the Confucian tradition really spread throughout the country. Yet the successful promotion of the Confucian classics, as in Yu Dan's show based on the *Analects* (*Lunyu* 論語), should not be attributed to a personal engagement with the classics. Rather, it is a reflection of popular demand from ordinary Chinese people, who have felt a great vacuum in their value system after the collapse of communist ideology in the 1980s.

I can cite a revealing anecdote from my own experience, which occurred in 2003. I was in the well-known Wind Entering the Pines (*Fengrusong* 風入松) bookstore near Peking University, when a blue-collar worker asked me where he could find a biography of Confucius by Qian Mu 錢穆 (1895–1990), a great representative of traditional Chinese scholarship. After I told him where he should look, I asked, "Why do you especially want to buy a book like that?" He answered simply, "I would like to buy it for my son." At that moment, I realized the age of antitraditionalism was really gone, though a long journey still lay ahead of us if we want to restore our tradition. I do not believe that the reconstruction of a Chinese value system necessarily means reproducing another Confucian China, like the traditional China of the past. But I do believe that some Confucian values found in the Confucian classics should play an important role in any such system.

Confucianism was explored anew after the 1980s. The first indication of this was the establishment of certain institutions authorized by the party and government, for instance, the China Confucius Foundation (CCF, *Zhongguo Kongzi jijinhui* 中國孔子基金會) in 1984 and the International Confucian Association (ICA, *Guoji ruxue lianhehui* 國際儒學聯合會) in 1994.[2] The CCF was established and financially supported by the central government. The late, former vice premier Gu Mu 谷牧, a veteran and senior cadre of the CCP, was the first president of the CCF and played an important role until his death in 2009. Quite a lot of academic activities aiming at promoting the study and transmission of Confucianism, especially international conferences, have been supported by the CCF, and the periodical *Confucius Studies* (*Kongzi yanjiu* 孔子研究), the first official journal focusing on Confucianism after 1949, has been directly run by the CCF. Indeed, the CCF was a nationwide organization and exerted an influence on the development of Confucianism in China. Many overseas scholars of Confucianism have been invited to attend conferences hosted by the CCF. But right now, the CCF has gradually been transformed into a local organization and completely become an official section of the Shandong provincial party committee. Almost all the people who hold power within the organization are officials of the Shandong provincial party committee. The background and development of the ICA were very similar to those of the CCF. But the policymakers of the ICA now consist not only of retired high officials of the party but also of successful businessmen, even though many scholars who are well established in Confucian studies are members of the board of the council. Furthermore, international activities related to Confucianism are still strongly promoted by the ICA. This is different from what we find with the CCF. In any case, until now, the ICA and the CCF are still the most influential organizations supporting Confucian studies in China. But the challenge these two organizations are facing is politicization and commercialization. This involves two trends of the current development of Confucianism in Mainland China that I address in the third part of this article.

The second wave involved more academic research in Confucian studies, with Marxism no longer serving as an interpretive framework. More recently there has been a broad popularization of Confucian classics among ordinary Chinese people, and ordinary people as well as Confucian scholars have called for the incorporation of the Confucian classics into China's education system. Recently, a nine-and-a-half-meter-high statue of Confucius was set up in front of the national historical museum near Tiananmen Square. It is regarded as a strong symbol that Confucianism is promoted by the authorities. But just a couple of weeks before I began making the final proof of this essay, the statue of Confucius was moved out of Tiananmen Square. I cannot explore the meaning and significance of this inconsistent phenomenon here. Obviously, however, it reflects disaccord among the authorities and shows that Confucianism is still far from a national ideology. Many indications, various training programs in Confucianism, emerging self-proclaimed Confucian believers, increasing Confucian vocabulary in mass media, among others, all add to an impression that Confucianism is indeed coming home with official support. But through this riot of colors, can we say that Confucian values nowadays have been regained by the Chinese people? This is a very complicated issue that needs to be tackled from interrelated perspectives. But, as I mentioned at the very beginning of this essay, the perspective I am taking is to focus on encounters with the Confucian classics, especially the role that the Confucian classics play in the general education system today in Mainland China, upon which my personal remarks are based.

Confucian Classics Today and General Education

Today, the Confucian classics should be assessed in two distinct but related contexts: the Confucian classics in Chinese society and the Confucian classics as part of official university curricula. In the first category, there is seemingly a classics boom. In the second category, it seems the Confucian classics are still fighting for legitimacy.

According to a survey of the ICA in 2007, the study of the Confucian classics has been increasing. From kindergarten to middle school, there has been an explosion in the recitation of the Confucian classics with an estimated ten million children involved. This activity developed spontaneously and has enjoyed the support of twenty million parents and teachers with the rare support of the government. Some nongovernmental, volunteer organizations, such as Yidan Xuetang 一耽學堂 in Beijing and Mingde Guoxue Guan 明德國學館 in Tianjin, have played an important role in promoting the recitation of the Confucian classics. For example, the Yidan Xuetang was created by a graduate student from the Department of Philosophy of Peking University. Initially, almost all members were young college students who volunteered to promote the recitation of the Confucian classics. Now, many elderly people have joined the Yidan Xuetang and become volunteers as well.[3]

In higher education, many centers for Confucian studies or "Schools of National Learning" (*guoxueyuan* 國學院) have been established, with studies of the Confucian classics playing an important role. For example, the Chinese People's University (*Zhongguo Renmin Daxue* 中國人民大學), which had been well known for its strong adherence to communist ideology, ironically enough became the first to establish a school of Confucius studies in 2002. Other similar institutions quickly followed suit.

Now, even in business circles, there is a passion among successful businessmen for studying the Confucian classics. To meet this rising interest in the Confucian classics, new organizations, both official and popular, have rushed to provide new publications on the classics; most of them are quite popular, if not bestsellers. It is even estimated that more than one hundred modern editions and translations of the *Analects* were published in the year 2007 alone. All of this seems to indicate that the Confucian classics are flourishing.

Despite increasing popularity among the people, the Confucian classics have not been adopted into the officially sanctioned education system at any level and are not part of the general education requirements in universities. At present, there are basically two models of general education in Chinese universities. One is called Cultural Quality Education Courses (*wenhua suzhi jiaoyu ke* 文化素質教育課), which offer a range of elective courses. In the two leading universities of China, Peking University and Tsinghua University, the general education system follows this model. The model includes a foreign language (usually English), physical education and computer skills, but the main part is still two subjects (*liang ke* 兩科), namely, "Marxist theory" (*Makesi zhuyi lilun* 馬克思主義理論) and thought and moral character (*sixiang pinde* 思想品德), that is, the ideology of the Chinese Communist Party. There is still no room for the Confucian classics. At Tsinghua University, for instance, those who teach *liang ke* despite its marginal status in terms of academic research and scholarship have been buttressed by substantial financial support from both university authorities and the central government, while the support for those who teach Chinese literature, history, and philosophy has always been quite limited. Although I cannot offer concrete statistical figures as far as "general education" is concerned, the Tsinghua model is a leading and pervasive one in most Chinese universities.

But recently, hints of a new dawn have emerged. In 2005, with the establishment of Fudan College (*Fudan xueyuan* 復旦學院), another model of general education was inaugurated by Fudan University in Shanghai. Although it is basically a copy of the School of Arts and Sciences of Harvard and Yale as far as form is concerned, the Confucian classics started to be incorporated into the general education system for the first time since 1949 in China. The most striking feature of this new system that differentiates it from the prevailing one that Tsinghua represents is exactly the absence of communist ideology and the acceptance of some Confucian classics. I noticed that some Confucian classics, such as the *Book of Changes* (*Yijing* 易經), the *Analects* (*Lunyu* 論語), *Mengzi* (孟子), *Xunzi* (荀子), the *Spring and Autumn Annuals* (*Chunqiu* 春秋), and the *Book of Rites* (*Liji* 禮記) are included. Even though the *liang ke* still remain part of the curriculum, it is indeed a positive change that they have been separated from the formal general education system. Of course, even taking Fudan's new model as an example, the proportion of Confucian classics in the general education system is still very small. The total number of courses in Fudan's general education system is almost sixty, while only six courses on Confucian classics are taught. And when we scrutinize the components of this system, we still have to say it's basically a cold platter and without a clear "main course," or core. Consequently, we have to wait to see whether or not this model can be adopted by the authorities and put into effect throughout the country.

Some Personal Observations and Remarks

Finally, here are my thoughts regarding the true repossession of the Confucian classics by the Chinese people, with respect to three issues that need to be addressed.

Strictly speaking, a genuine general education program, or core curriculum, has not yet been established in China. As we know, the core of general education in American universities has for the most part been centered on the classics, while traditional Chinese education on the classics (or at least on the Confucian core) has aimed at character building and the cultivation of virtues. Indeed what the Confucian tradition did well was exactly character building and the cultivation of virtues rather than instilling specialized knowledge. Even before 1949, this remained true to some extent. It was only after 1949 that such education was thoroughly eradicated. So, even though many efforts have been made since 2000, until educators in general and high officials in the Ministry of Education in particular come up with a clearer understanding of general education as distinct from the two subjects (*liang ke*) system, it will not be possible to promote the Confucian classics seriously in higher education.

An even bigger problem today is the erosion caused by the commercialization of the Confucian classics. Though more and more people are wholehearted in their desire to learn and understand the wisdom preserved in the Confucian classics, an important issue is who is qualified to teach them? If commercialization means popularization by the mass media so that more and more ordinary people can understand the Confucian classics, then that is a good thing. But if teachers of the Confucian classics are not well trained, the mass media may promote mere opportunists just to make a profit. This would be a disaster not only for the Confucian classics but also for the unsuspecting people who are taken in. I believe many of the promoters who are advocating the classics today are sincere in devoting themselves to this great endeavor, but at the same time we must recognize that there are always some people who lack such true commitment. If the Confucian classics become fashionable as a way to gain fame and money, it will attract opportunists who will exploit the Confucian classics for their own personal gain. After a long dormancy of the Confucian tradition in particular and of traditional Chinese learning in general, it is not easy to find enough qualified teachers to meet the need of so many ordinary Chinese people. This is also one of the reasons that some charlatans are now fishing in troubled waters and masquerading as so-called Masters of National Learning (*guoxue dashi* 國學大師). But on the other hand, we have to concede that the reason those charlatans can succeed is due to a genuine, inner aspiration for Confucian values that is strongly emerging from people's hearts. It is exactly this deep aspiration inside people that constitutes a solid and wide social foundation for the popularity of the Confucian classics. In this sense, we have to recognize that there is a great opportunity for the Chinese people to regain Confucian values if only people's aspiration can be properly treated and oriented.

Beside the negative effects of commercialization, there is the danger of the politicization of Confucianism. By politicization, I mean two mutually interwoven things. One is that Confucianism may be deliberately used by proponents of narrow-minded nationalism. Another is that Confucianism may be shaped so as to oppose freedom, democracy, and human rights. In either case, it could serve nothing but to maintain the legitimacy of the present corrupt regime. For example, Yu Dan, trained in mass media rather than Confucian studies and a star of popularizing the *Analects*, was criticized for depoliticizing Confucius.[4] On the one hand, this is a fair and correct observation. But on the other hand, this apparent depoliticization is a product of current Chinese politics or serves a certain political standpoint. The politically critical spirit that has repeatedly sprung up in Chinese history, not only embodied by Confucius but also practiced by almost every Confucian master,[5] was implicitly and purposely neglected in this recent act of depoliticization, which is actually imbued with a highly political implication that drives people to a certain political orientation. As far as consequence is concerned, this depoliticization of Confucianism, that is, the neglect of the Confucian spirit of political and social critique, is in perfect alignment with the strategy of "harmony" advocated by the CCP. In this sense, this depoliticization of Confucianism per se is a kind of politicization. For instance, we cannot imagine that the flurry of overseas activities promoting Yu Dan's popular book on the *Analects* and the value of harmony that have been carried out are simply her personal business and are without the support, or at least the connivance, of the Chinese government. For instance, her meeting with the former Japanese prime minister, Yasuo Fukuda 福田康夫, deserves deep consideration. It is far from a simple cultural activity, let alone a business trip. Rather, the political implication is self-evident and should not be ignored. Recently, Yu Dan was even selected as one of the representatives of the CCP of Beijing for the Seventeenth National Congress of the CCP. Since we know that almost all representatives are high cadres of the CCP, it cannot be doubted that she is an agent of the CCP's program of politicization. This strategy of the depoliticization of Confucianism as a manifestation of politicization has two targets. Domestically, it intends to make people keep the status quo instead of thinking over the ultimate cause of all social injustice. Internationally, it seeks to convince people that China will not be an aggressive super power that will threaten other countries. Maybe people like Yu Dan are unaware of this; they just want to make their own profit. But the key is that they would be suppressed if their advocacy of Confucian values were not in line with this strategy of the CCP. Only if one promotes values that contribute to the strategy of a so-called "harmonious society" can she or he be given access to a market that is totally controlled by the government and the party. So, we can see that, unfortunately, commercialization and politicization, money and power, now are mutually reinforcing one another and in complete "harmony."

Ironically, it is now the original oppressor or terminator of Chinese culture in general and Confucian tradition in particular that claims to be upholding Confucian values. It is true that the CCP itself is undergoing some transformation, but it is reckless to think it will really give up its present domination and share power with others unless it feels some external pressure. It is naïve to think that the CCP embraces Confucian values simply because some leaders of the CCP have quoted a few words of Confucianism in their public talks. Marxism is still the national ideology, although it is actually downright dead in most, if not all, Chinese people's minds, and the head of the CCP has even strengthened this ideology since he has come to power. Two examples here, I believe, can forcefully make this point. One is a new policy about establishing a school of Marxism in every university directly affiliated with the Ministry of Higher Education. The other is the design of the Guidance of Applying for Support from the National Foundation for Humanities and Social Sciences (*Guojia sheke jijin shenqing zhinan* 國家社科基金申請指南) issued annually by a special institution, the office of the National Foundation for Humanities and Social Sciences, which is the largest financial resource for humanities and social sciences in China and directly supervised by the Publicity Department (*Zhongxuan bu* 中宣部) of the CCP. In the annual guidelines for 2009 (which are almost the same as those of 2008 and 2007), the sections about Marxism and the CCP are more than thirty pages, while those about Chinese philosophy and Western philosophy together are less than three pages.

If history can be a mirror, it shows us there have been too many dictators in Chinese history who were good at playing this double-faced deceit. To "advertise wine while selling vinegar" is their usual practice. For example, Emperor Xuandi 宣帝 of the Western Han dynasty once explicitly admonished his son, the later emperor Yuandi 元帝, that the constitution they actually follow was not the Confucian ideal that entails a humane way of politics but a blend of Confucian benevolent government in its outward appearance and Legalist dictatorship as its inner essence.[6] In the transition of China from an empire to a modern republic, Yuan Shikai 袁世凱 and some other warlords in modern China were all advocates of Confucianism and even tried once to establish Confucianism as the national religion. Similarly and obviously, what this kind of deceit eventually brings will not be a real revival of Confucianism but a complete destruction of Confucian values, which the antitraditionalism initiated by the May Fourth movement actually never accomplished.

It's a good thing that the Confucian classics can be studied and understood, and that Confucian values can start to play an important role in Chinese society once again, regardless of whether anything like a new Confucian China is to emerge from this. It would be a disaster for Confucianism, however, if it is taken advantage of by a corrupt and despotic political power. Values like freedom, democracy, and human rights are not exclusive to the Western tradition. We can find the ingredients or spirit of these values in other great traditions, Chinese as well as Indian, and so on, although the manifestations of those values are highly varied in different geographical and historical contexts. Amartya Sen has recently explored the resources within the Indian tradition for democracy conceived as public reasoning.[7] Both Yu Yingshi 余英時, a great master of Chinese history and thought, and William Theodore de Bary, who made great contributions to introducing East Asian Classics to the West, have repeatedly pointed out the dimensions of a kind of democracy and liberal tradition in the Chinese tradition.[8]

Before them, even Hu Shi 胡適, who was the most important leading figure of the New Culture movement in the 1920s and a stern critic of traditional Chinese culture, also mostly argued in his English works that there has been a tradition of fighting for freedom embodied by Confucian figures throughout Chinese history.[9] So, it would be unfortunate for Confucianism to be utilized by a corrupt and despotic establishment simply for nationalist purposes at the expense of values actually embedded in universal humanity. In that case Confucianism would not be flourishing but withering, and such politicization and commercialization would really be the kiss of death for the Confucian classics.[10] Some of the events connected with the Confucius Institutes in the United States, which showed how they were being manipulated by the Chinese government for its own political ends, should serve as a warning. Although the Confucius Institutes in the United States were not eventually shut down by the US government, the reputation of Confucius and Confucianism has already been unavoidably contaminated.

In truth, the wisdom revealed in the Confucian classics is not for the Chinese people alone but for the people of the entire world. And as Confucian values are starting to become an integral part of the consciousness of people in the West, the prospects of the Confucian classics for the emerging world would be strongly enhanced if their situation could be made more promising in the motherland itself. But whether the Confucian classics can successfully contribute to the reconstruction of the value system of the Chinese people at present and in the future depends on three interrelated conditions: first, if an educational system that focuses on the Confucian classics and includes other great books as well can be established; second, if commercialization and superficial popularization can be reined in to a certain extent, if not successfully avoided; and third, if Confucian values can be effectively promoted to transform a degenerate kind of politics without being contaminated and corrupted in the process. A real revival of Confucianism in China cannot be anticipated, and Confucianism will never authentically "come home" unless these goals can be realized. Any claim about the revival of Confucianism in Mainland China based simply upon seemingly scientific statistics, for instance, how many training programs for the Confucian classics are established, how many Confucian words are quoted by politicians, and so on, is superficial. Last but not least, I would like to say a revival of Confucianism, at least for me, will and should not mean a reconstruction of a "Confucian China." Confucian values will and should be part of a great picture of values jointly constructed by all great traditions, not only Buddhism and Daoism but Christian, Islamic, and others that flourish in an era of globalization.

It is true that Confucian values still reside within the hearts and minds of many Chinese people today, shaping their beliefs, manifested in their symbols, and informing their deliberations and actions. In this sense, Confucianism surely is one among, but only one among, the habits of the heart cherished by the Chinese people. Nevertheless, in my view, in order to be true to some of the core teachings of the Confucian tradition, it cannot remain a possession of the Chinese people alone, and so efforts to make it into our "national learning" are both misguided and in some sense a betrayal of the best parts of the tradition. I have already expressed my view on how to understand Confucianism as a religious tradition.[11] Simply put,

Confucianism can and should play an important and significant role as a source of spiritual inspiration and a tradition of living wisdom in a global context; it would, however, be a disaster if Confucianism is established as an institutional religion, especially one backed by political authority. Although the efforts that Kang Youwei 康有為 (1858–1927) and his followers put forth in order to make Confucianism into an organized religion, during the transition from the late nineteenth century to the early twentieth century, should be reevaluated and appreciated in certain ways, we can learn much more from their failures than their successes.[12] If Confucianism is or can contribute to a civil religion, in my view it should and must be the kind of global civil religion that Robert Bellah describes in his contribution to this volume.

Notes

1. 山重水複疑無路，柳暗花明又一村。The poem is entitled "Traveling to the Village to the West of the Mountain" (*You Shanxi cun* 游山西村), by Lu You 陸遊 (1125–1200). *Collected Works of Lu You* (Lu You Ji 陸遊集), vol. 1 (Beijing: Zhong hua shu ju, 1976), 29.

2. The official websites of the CCF and the ICA are, respectively, www.chinakongzi.org/bhxx and www.ica.org.cn/gjrl.php.

3. The website of Yidan Xuetang is www.yidan.net. What it has been doing is to promote the study of the Confucian classics and to purify people by Confucian values. In this sense, the role it plays is similar to a popular religious organization. But popular religious organizations are usually, if not absolutely, prohibited in Mainland China. What distinguishes the Yidan Xuetang from other popular religious organizations and makes it immune from prohibition, I assume, is the patriotism it advocates. Another organization, Mingde Guoxue Guan 明德國學館, is basically the same.

4. See Daniel A. Bell, "*Lunyu de qu zhengzhi hua: Yu Dan Lunyu xinde jianping*" 論語的去政治化——于丹《論語心得》簡評 [The Depoliticization of the *Analects*: Review of Yu Dan's *Lun yu xin de*], *Du Shu* 讀書 8 (2007): 46–55.

5. I would like to name three examples here to indicate this critical Confucian spirit. In *Analects* 14.22, when Zilu asked Kongzi how to serve the king, Kongzi said, "Don't cheat him, but you frankly remonstrate with him." In a newly excavated Confucian text, *Xing zi ming chu* 性自命出, when King Mu of Lu asked Zisi, the grandson of Kongzi, who can be called loyal ministers, Zisi answered, "Those who always point out the mistakes of the king are loyal ministers" (魯穆公問於子思曰："何如而可謂忠臣？"子思曰："恒稱其君之惡者，可謂忠臣矣。") *Newly Excavated Bamboo Slips* (*Guo Dian Chu Mu Zhu Jian* 郭店楚墓竹簡) (Beijing: Wen Wu Press, 1998), 23, 145. Fan Zhongyan 范仲淹 (989–1052), an exemplary

Confucian revered by almost all later Confucian intellectuals, was banished from the court three times because of his remonstration with the emperor. Every time he was banished, there were Confucian scholar-officials who gave him a farewell dinner and praised the three banishments as "three honors" (*san guang* 三光).

6. This story is recorded in the *Annals of Yuandi* (*Yuandi ji* 元帝紀) of the *Han Shu* 漢書.

7. See Amartya Sen, *The Argumentative India: Writings on Indian History, Culture, and Identity* (New York: Farrar, Straus and Giroux, 2005).

8. William Theodore de Bary, *The Liberal Tradition in China* (New York: Columbia University Press, 1983); *Asian Values and Human Rights: A Confucian Communitarian Perspective* (Cambridge: Harvard University Press, 1998). William Theodore de Bary and Weiming Tu, eds., *Confucianism and Human Rights* (New York: Columbia University Press, 1998).Yü, Ying-shih (Yu Yingshi 余英時), "The Idea of Democracy and the Twilight of the Elite Culture in Modern China," in *Justice and Democracy: Cross-cultural Perspectives*, ed. Ron Bontekoe and Marietta Stepaniants (Honolulu: University of Hawai'i Press, 1997), 199–215; "Democracy, Human Rights and Confucian Culture: The Fifth Huang Hsing Foundation Hsueh Chun-tu Distinguished Lecture in Asian Studies, 10 November 1998" (Oxford: Oxford University Press, 1998).

9. See Hu Shih (Hu Shi 胡適), "China's Fight for Freedom," *Life Association News* 36.2 (October 1941): 136–138, 213–215. See also Chou Chih-ping, ed., *A Collection of Hu Shih's Unpublished English Essays and Speeches / Hu Shi weikan yingwen yigao* 胡適未刊英文遺稿, (Taipei: Lianjing, 2001), 254–269.

10. I've already expressed this worry in two previously published essays. See Peng Guoxiang 彭國翔, "Ruxue fuxing de xingsi" 儒學復興的省思 (Reflections on the Revival of Confucianism), *Ershiyi shiji jingji baodao* 二十一世紀經濟報導 (21st Century Business Herald) 18.12 (2006): 35; "Rujia rentong de jueze" 儒家認同的抉擇 (The Choice of a Confucian Identity), *Zhonghua dushu bao* 中華讀書報 (China Reading Weekly) 21.1 (2009): 15.

11. See Peng Guoxiang, *Confucian Tradition: Between Religion and Humanism* (Beijing: Peking University Press, 2007).

12. As a matter of fact, contemporary new Confucian scholars such as Tang Junyi 唐君毅(1909–1978) and Mou Zongsan牟宗三 (1909–1995) already have tackled this issue to some extent. See chapter 2 of section 3 in Peng Guoxiang, *Interpretation and Examination of Confucian Tradition: From Classical Confucianism and Neo-Confucianism to Contemporary New Confucianism* (Wuhan: Wuhan University Press, 2012).

4

The Politics of Confucianism in Contemporary China*

Anna Sun

Here are three snapshots of recent events related to Confucianism that might hold the key to our understanding of the future of Confucianism in China.

The first snapshot is the latest edition of the *Annual Report on China's Religions* (2010). It is published annually by the prestigious Social Sciences Academic Press as part of an official series on the state of religion in China. Here is what the table of contents presents:

> Reports on the Major Religions:
> The Development of Buddhism and Its Dilemma in a Commercial Age Chinese Taoist Culture and Education in 2009
> A Survey of Chinese Islam in 2009
> Observations on Chinese Catholicism in 2009
> The State of Chinese Protestant Christianity in 2009
> Report on Confucianism (*rujiao*): Forms of Confucianism in Folk Culture
> The Revival of Traditions and Beliefs in Chinese Folk Religions[1]

Although this is not the first time Confucianism has been listed under "Major Religions," it is the most recent and the most noticeable. Is this a sign that Confucianism is under consideration by the Chinese state to become "a major religion," joining the other five major religions, which are all represented in the report?

The second snapshot is the thirty-one-foot bronze statue of Confucius that was erected in front of the National History Museum on Tiananmen Square in Beijing in January 2011. According to the *Economist*,

> A week before President Hu Jintao's visit to America on January 18th [2011] the appearance of a giant bronze statue of Confucius on the east side of Tiananmen Square caused a stir in the Chinese capital. He is the first non-revolutionary to be commemorated on the hallowed ground of Chinese communism. The party, having once vilified the ancient sage, now depends on him in its attempts at global rebranding. . . . During his trip to America, Mr. Hu hopes Confucius will help him connect with ordinary Americans.[2]

On April 21, 2011, however, the giant bronze statue suddenly disappeared overnight. Everyone was in shock. In an article titled "Confucius Stood Here, but Not for Very Long," the *New York Times* reported that a "spokesman for the museum, which had unveiled the statue with great fanfare, said he had no idea what had happened."[3] A day later, on April 22, *Beijing Evening News* reported that the statue had been moved inside the National Museum, where it will be displayed "along with other statues of celebrities." In the same article, a researcher at the Institute of Literature at the Chinese Academy of Social Sciences was interviewed and called the move "the right step to take": "Although Confucianism is an essential part of Chinese culture, it cannot sum up all the values and ideals that modern China represents and aspires for."[4]

The third snapshot is the so-called "Qufu Church Controversy." On December 12, 2010, Xinhua News Agency reported that a new Protestant church was about to be built in Qufu. An article titled "Jesus to Join Confucius as Qufu Plans Church" stated that this would be the first "real church" for the nearly ten thousand Christians in Qufu, since they have had only a "makeshift building," capable of seating only seven to eight hundred people. The new church would be able to hold three thousand and would cost about $3 million to build. Its foundation had already been laid in July 2010, and the planning of the building had been going on for years, with the church receiving government land use permission in 2001. Kong Xiangling, a pastor for the Qufu Protestant Church and a seventy-fifth-generation descendant of Confucius, said that "although building a church in China is nothing new, it means a lot since the Christian church is to be built in Confucius' hometown, a symbol of Chinese civilization."[5]

On December 22, 2010, ten well-known Confucian scholars, known as the Confucian Ten Scholars, published an open letter protesting the building of the church in what they called "the sacred city" of Qufu, Confucius's birthplace and home to the most majestic Confucius temple in the world. The letter was supported by ten Confucian associations and ten Confucian websites. Written in a learned half-classical, half-colloquial style, the letter stated, "When we hear that there is going to be a 40-meter-high [130 feet] church built for three thousand people near the Qufu Confucius Temple, we are shocked and dismayed as Confucian scholars and associations. We beseech you to respect this sacred land of Chinese culture, and stop the building of the Christina church at once."[6]

Two days later, there was an official response from the government in the form of an editorial from the Xinhua News Agency, which stated that there was historical precedence for the building of Christian churches in Qufu. This response did nothing to calm the gathering storm. Numerous online postings appeared, some supporting the Confucian Ten (with titles such as "Qufu Is Not Jerusalem" and "They Are Nailing Confucius on the Cross"), some supporting the Christians (with titles such as "Render unto God the Things which Are *God's* and unto Confucians the Things That Are Confucian"). Many held the position that although the church should be built, its proposed grand scale would in the end dominate the cityscape—and the fact that it could hold three thousand people was too powerful an allusion to the legend that Confucius had taught three thousand disciples—and would in effect overshadow the cherished Confucian tradition in Qufu.

Each of these events can be seen as corresponding to key issues involved in the future development of Confucianism in China. The first one might be called the "politics of epistemology," the second the "politics of the religion question," and the third the "politics of Confucian nationalism." I address each briefly before ending the discussion with an assessment of recent debates over whether Confucianism might, could, or should become the civil religion of China.

The Politics of Epistemology

Is Confucianism on its way to being classified as a "major religion" in China, as the official *Annual Report on China's Religions* seems to suggest? What is at stake in the "religion" classification for scholars of Confucianism today? As Wilfred Cantwell Smith remarked perceptively in 1963, "'Is Confucianism a religion?' is one [question] that the West has never been able to answer, and China never able to ask."[7] Do we have to answer this question today? What is at stake?

I suggest that there are at least two reasons why this question has to be addressed. First, we have to deal with the "epistemological ignorance," which is the problematic nature of the existing classifications of Chinese religious traditions. We need to examine these classifications through historical analysis as well as a critical reflection of methodologies used in social scientific studies. As we have seen in our historical case study of the birth of Confucianism as a world religion in late nineteenth-century Europe and in twentieth-century China, the normalizing force of the world religion discourse has been very much at work.

The second reason is that the institutionalization of the discourse in the popular imagination, in textbooks, in academic disciplines, and in domestic and international politics has made these classifications "real." They are real as categories in knowledge production as well as policymaking. Indeed, statistical data have become a crucial part of the statecraft of contemporary nation-states, as well as international and transnational organizations. They have become the foundation of the self-understanding and self-knowledge of modern societies.

Scholarship is always conditioned by history. And the question "Is Confucianism a religion?" has become a question to which contemporary scholars have to provide an answer. It is a question made possible by a specific set of historical conditions, and the "looping effect" of emerging historical categories through classification and knowledge production, as Ian Hacking suggests, has made it into an empirical question about social practice as well.[8] It remains to be seen whether Confucianism will eventually be classified as a "major religion" by the Chinese state, which would have significant consequences for the development of contemporary Chinese cultural and religious politics.

The Politics of Religion Question

What is at stake for the Chinese state to start calling something a religion? Why would the Chinese state be interested in classifying Confucianism as a religion in the first place? Indeed, why this sudden interest in Confucianism and Confucius, whose ideas were much maligned by the socialist ideologues for forty years until the recent rehabilitation, which did not take place until the 1990s? The appearance and disappearance of the Confucius statue on Tiananmen Square is a telling example of the complex and often ambiguous relationship the Chinese state has with Confucianism and the Sage.

There exist many contradictions within the Chinese state. Today it is ideologically atheist, politically antireligion, institutionally secular, socially increasingly tolerant toward ritual practice, culturally Han-centric (which means Confucian-centric for cultural nationalists), and ethically rooted in Confucian ethics. The pressure of conforming to the perceived norms of modernity, intensified through international comparison with Western nation-states, seems to suggest that modernity equals secularism and the separation of church and state. But how can a society be considered secular when there isn't a strong, singular, monotheistic religion to be separated from? China has been trying hard to deal with the "religion question," or perhaps the "religion complex," since the beginning of the twentieth century, and the issues are becoming more pressing.

The historian Rebecca Nedostup has detailed the uneasy and fascinating institutional and political processes through which the category of "religion"—and along with it the category of "superstition"—was introduced into Chinese life by politicians, intellectuals, and census takers during Nationalist rule in the 1920s and 1930s.[9] Is it more modern to have "religion" instead of "superstition"? Indeed, this complex situation regarding religion has informed many aspects of the politics of religion in modern China: from the Confucianity movement of the 1910s and 1920s, right after the Chinese Republican Revolution, to the establishment of the Five Major Religions classification in socialist China in the 1950s, on which basis the State Administration of Religious Affairs was founded, to today's numerous attempts to present and normalize diverse Chinese religious practices along the lines of the "norms" of major world religions.

Here is a good example of the international pressure China is experiencing today. Tony Blair wrote an essay for the *Washington Post* on April 11, 2011, titled "How Will Religion's Growth in China Impact Its Relations with the West?"

> China's growing willingness to engage with religious ideas and institutions will greatly assist East-West relations. . . . It is above all this quest for a harmonious (we would probably say fair or just) society that engages the Chinese leadership with religion. . . . The rise of interest in religious studies and their proliferation in China's universities is by-product of religious revival. Thomas Aquinas' concept of the organic society and the need for virtue fits well with aspects of Confucian ethics. There are a lot more budding Thomists in China than in Britain and a genuine intellectual excitement with themes in Christian thought. . . . So where is this all going? "Never impose on others

> what you would not choose for yourself," Confucius counseled. We may have a lot to learn from China's evolving experience of religion, just as we are learning from its spectacular purchase on the global economy.[10]

As I have shown, such strong pressure for China to engage the West in terms of the category of "religion" is nothing new; it has only intensified in recent years, as religious conflicts worsen in many parts of the world, including China itself (especially in the case of Tibetan Buddhism and Islam).

In order to present the world with a "religion" that is compatible with the political and cultural agendas of the state, China has rediscovered Confucianism, with the hope that it is something that can be used and controlled at will, a perfect cultural symbol and political tool on the international stage, with an aura of "religion" yet without any actual religious organization that the state has to deal with. After all, unlike Christianity, Islam, Buddhism, and Daoism, there is neither a clergy nor a priesthood in Confucianism. In contemporary China, it has become a diffused tradition without a core Confucian stratum fighting for its own interests. Or is this no longer the case?

The Politics of Confucian Nationalism

The so-called Qufu Church Controversy has been much discussed among Chinese intellectuals, and the staunch position taken by many well-respected scholars of Confucianism has sparked criticism of their lack of religious tolerance. This is an event that demonstrates well both the positive and negative sides of the emergence of a powerful Confucian cultural and religious identity. These Confucian activists—to use Stephen Angle's term—are now making use of Confucian tradition to forge a strong sense of self-identity and group solidarity, which could become a cause of religious conflict, as in the case of the proposed church in Qufu. Indeed, the combative and intolerant tone of many online posts is disturbing, signalling a hardening of ideological commitments of emerging cultural nationalists.

However, not all Confucian activists are Confucian nationalists. The emerging Confucian commitment to political activism could also become a source of positive political resistance and change. Indeed, as Angle remarks, "recent developments suggest a more confident attitude that is reminiscent of the traditional Confucian responsibility of intellectuals to remonstrate with superiors (be they parents or rulers) who deviate from the Way."[11]

There are several possibilities for future conflicts between Confucian activists and the state. First, there might be more tensions between the Confucian nationalists and the state. For instance, Confucian fundamentalist activists such as Jiang Qing and Kang Xiaoguang insist on the necessity of installing Confucianism as a state religion, which could become grounds for future conflicts with the state. Second, the tension between Confucianism and other religious traditions might intensify. Besides the existing conflicts between Confucian nationalist activists and Christians in China, Confucianism could also be used by the state to oppose the growth of other religious groups, which is a genuine concern long held by many Christians as well as scholars of Chinese religions.[12] Third, there is a remote possibility that the state might try to mold Confucianism into a form of "State Confucianism," like "State Shinto" in Japan, which could lead to further conflicts with Confucian activists, who would not accept the way the state makes use of Confucianism for its own political purposes.[13]

The Politics of Confucianism as a Civil Religion

The possibility of Confucianism as a civil religion has been a recurring theme among Chinese intellectuals who are interested not only in the fate of Confucianism in contemporary China but also in the fate of contemporary China itself. Many have been searching for a solution to the moral and ethical crisis in contemporary Chinese society, and Confucianism as a civil religion seems to hold great promise for a "moral reconstruction" of China, which is urgently needed at the beginning of the twenty-first century.[14]

For scholars as well as activists of Confucianism, this approach also allows them to speak of Confucianism without getting into multifarious debates over whether Confucianism is a religion. Instead they can focus on the historical and philosophical development of Confucianism and emphasize its relevance in the contemporary world as an important moral, cultural, and political force. In some ways we may say that the most pressing and relevant question about Confucianism in today's China might be moving from "Is Confucianism a religion?" to "Is Confucianism a civil religion?"

As we will see, the discussion of whether Confucianism is a civil religion has moved beyond the realm of the descriptive—how and why Confucianism has religious elements—and into the realm of the prescriptive—whether and should Confucianism be a civil religion, and whether it is compatible with democracy. This important transformation of the debate over Confucianism from issues regarding history and religion to ideas of political theory signals a shift, one that is consistent with the deep concern with politics and social order that has long been one of the fundamental elements of Confucian thought since its very beginning.

In his insightful essay "The Revival of Confucianism in the Sphere of Mores and the Reactivation of the Civil Religion Debate in China," Sébastien Billioud summarizes three main positions regarding Confucianism as a civil religion.[15] The first is represented by Chen Ming, a scholar of Confucianism and leading public intellectual who is the editor of a journal promoting "the original [Confucian] *dao*" (*yuandao*). It might be useful to call him a "cultural conservative and political liberal Confucian." He makes the distinction between civil religion and political ideology and believes that Confucianism is compatible with democracy.[16] In Billioud's analysis, Chen Ming's position is different in an important way from those of other prominent Confucian public intellectuals, Jiang Qing and Kang Xiaoguang, who want to promote a political Confucianism as the sole source of Chinese state ideology and establish Confucianism as a national religion. It might be useful to term them "cultural conservative and political nationalist Confucians," for whom it is unimportant whether Confucianism is a civil religion.

The second position is represented by Ji Zhe, a scholar of Chinese religion teaching in Paris who emphasizes civil religion as "a non-religious expression of the sacredness of modern society, and that it should be based on a rule-of-law state and a civil society. . . . According to this view, republican values should be insisted on, and national morality should be compatible with humanity's morality."[17] Billioud characterizes his position as not using civil religion as a tool of political legitimation, but "a secular belief" developed by "citizens of a 'civilized society.' "[18]

The third position is represented by Fenggang Yang, a leading sociologist of Chinese religions teaching in the United States. Billioud notes Yang's concern, based on empirical evidence, that Confucianism "could also turn into some nationalistic form of political religion." In the latest, most detailed articulation of his position, Yang speaks of his hope that

> instead of establishing Confucianism as the state religion, which would result in grave consequences, . . . it is perhaps feasible and more helpful to develop some kind of civil religion based on Confucianism, as most Chinese people share the common cultural heritage and most of the Confucian values. The Chinese notion of *tian* is so readily available for civil religion, which can be interpreted by different religions in reference to their own

> divinity, thus affirming the inclusive spirit since the ancient time of Chinese civilization.[19]

He further suggests, "a kind of civil religion based on Confucianism and Christianity, if successfully constructed or developed."[20]

It seems clear that all three scholars believe Confucianism should be the civil religion of China; where they differ seems to be how to construct or develop Confucianism as a civil religion. Here we need to return to Bellah's conception of the idea of civil religion in his 1967 essay "Civil Religion in America" as well as his later modifications of the concept in order to respond to these scholars' diverse visions.

It is a well-known fact that the idea of civil religion has long been used for different political purposes since the publication of the essay during the years of the Vietnam War. In fact, Bellah refrained from using the term "civil religion" after it was constantly misunderstood to be a concept affiliated with nationalism; he mentions in his essay "Civil Religion: Term and Concept" that the misuse would not have happened had he used more neutral terms such as "political religion," "religion of the republic," or "political piety."[21]

In his essay "Return to Durkheim: Civil Religion and the Moral Reconstruction in China," Zhe offers an excellent analysis of the Durkheimian and Rousseauian roots of Bellah's concept. It touches on two key components of the idea of civil religion: civil religion as religious collective conscience without association with a specific religion and civil religion as the political conscience of a democratic, republican society.

Here are the key aspects of these two components according to Ji's analysis, the first religious and moral, the second political:

1. As formulated by Bellah, showing great affinities with Durkheim's view on morality and society, civil religion is a generic form of moral life that expresses the sacredness of modern society, which contains essential moral ideals that hold a society together.
   a. It is not associated with specific religions, although it could come from specific existing historical religions.
   b. It is "diffused collective sentiments that express more or less explicitly the general will of a society."
   c. It resides in "habits, customs and public opinion as vehicles of simple but fundamental values."[22]

2. As formulated by Rousseau and Bellah, civil religion is "the moral content of the social contract, the sacred expression of general will, and the fundamental conscience of the Republic."
   a. Civil religion is "set by the Sovereign," and "this sovereignty is in the hands of the people."
   b. Civil religion can exist only in a democratic, republican society.
   c. Civil religion "is not aimed at legitimizing the existing government"; it judges society with moral standards, pursues civil rights, and defends civil society.[23]

If we accept Ji's formulation, how do we envision a civil religion for China? Ji ends his discussion with a call for the emergence of prophets in today's moral crisis in Chinese society, people who can forge a civil religion of universal humanity rather than a nationalistic civil religion of Chinese "traditional" values and culture. And he suggests that Confucianism, especially the moral philosophy of Mencius, might be the source we need.

There are two separate points that I would like to make regarding Ji's superb analysis. The first is normative, which is that, for all its nuance and depth, Ji's articulation of Bellah's concept of civil religion does not pay enough attention to the dynamic nature of the formation of civil religion. In order for the sacredness of morality to express itself through habits, customs, and public opinions, it must be a dynamic process of discords and reconciliations, disagreements and collaborations, actualized temporally through history. If civil religion is the fundamental conscience of the citizens of a republic, a dynamic process of democratic conflicts ought to be its modus operandi. Indeed, civil religion in Bellah's conception is not something that can be established; it has to emerge gradually and organically from the general will of the people, as with civil religion in America since the beginning of the republic, where disagreements have been constantly settled and resettled through complex historical processes of conflicts, consensus, and compromises. What we hope to see in China today is precisely the beginning of this process of the democratic emergence of civil religion. No group of people or institution can "establish" a civil religion in China, for it has to come from the sovereign power of the people.

The second point is descriptive. It seems that a more difficult, perhaps even antagonistic, path might be awaiting the rise of civil religion in China. I contend that it is not a foregone conclusion that Confucianism—or any other religious tradition—can be the single source of morality for Chinese people. And it is not a given either that the process of the emergence of a civil religion in China, which is a social, cultural, institutional, and political process, would not be an intensely contested one. Instead of peaceful dialogue and serene cooperation, what is waiting ahead might be a long process of conflict and divergence among scholars, activists, religious practitioners, many different religious and cultural institutions, and the state.

Consider the religious and moral aspect of civil religion. What does it mean to have a civil religion that expresses the sacredness of modern China, which contains the essential moral ideals that are shared by everyone in society? In the case of the United States, Christianity, more specifically Protestantism, has been the dominating source of essential ideals throughout the history of the country; no other religious tradition has seriously challenged the fact that Protestant values, symbols, and rituals are shared by most citizens of the republic. A similar case can be argued for France, replacing Protestantism with Catholicism; only in recent years has Islam been posing a challenge to the French civil religion and its sacred ideal of republican secularism (*laïcité*). What was difficult for the transformation of a specific religion to civil religion was separating the particular religious institutions from the state; what was not difficult was identifying the sources from which collective moral sentiments and moral ideals were borrowed.[23]

However, due to the pluralistic and ecological nature of Chinese religious practices and the multiple sources of Chinese moral teachings, it is not a given that Confucianism is the de facto, main source of contemporary Chinese morality. Will the moral and ethical ideals of Confucianism eventually fill the spiritual vacuum? There is conflicting evidence, and it remains to be seen whether other religious traditions, such as Christianity, Buddhism, or Daoism, might contest its claim, or whether a syncretic, truly diffused version of moral teaching might eventually emerge. As Billioud has shown in his illuminating fieldwork on Confucian-inspired organizations, many Confucian classics and ideas are in fact disseminated in Buddhist and sectarian groups. We might have to ask, "When does something cease to be Confucian and become something else?

Furthermore, in terms of ritual practice, as I have learned through my fieldwork in Confucius temples as well as survey research on religious life in China, although Confucianism does have a clear religious dimension, it is certainly not the dominant one in most ordinary people's live. People who pray to Confucius also pray to a variety of gods, and most people have a repertoire of things whose existence they believe in, including ancestral spirits, karma, the god of fortune, as well as the spirit of Confucius.[24] In such a diverse sphere of rituals and beliefs, does it still make sense for us to speak of someone being Confucian rather than Buddhist or Daoist?

The other aspect of dynamic conflict is the potential political conflict over the development of civil religion in China. If we consider the cases of the disappearing Confucius statue on Tiananmen Square and the Qufu Church Controversy, both occurring in 2011, we can see that these are emerging conflicts that might only intensify as different groups—religious, cultural, political—compete for public attention, cultural authority, economic resources, and religious legitimation, and, eventually, fight over the important role of being the leading source of a Chinese civil religion.

Pluralism is rarely about peace and consensus. But conflicts are welcome news, for one could argue that this is the essence of true pluralism and democracy. Should China become more democratic, many more conflicts will be fought openly, in the public sphere, as in the case of the Qufu Church Controversy, which made national news with its many stages of petitions and protests, unlike the case of the disappearing Confucius statue, which took place literally behind closed doors, in the darkness of the night.

We have seen how the question, "Is Confucianism a religion?" is indeed a question "the West has never been able to answer, and China never able to ask." Here is how the question, "Is Confucianism a civil religion?" is fundamentally different. This is a question that China *has been able to answer*, for the asking comes not from perplexed early comparative religionists who were unable to grasp the complexity and uniqueness of Asian traditions, but from a comparativist who understood the case of the United States through his understanding of Japan, and whose deep insights into history—as shown splendidly in *Religion in Human Evolution*, his magnum opus—allow him to speak of a grand narrative not only of the past but also of the future, which is a future of unfoldings and becomings rooted in the ethical ideals of diverse religious traditions of the axial age, the political ideals of different philosophical traditions, and the dialectical movement that is history, carrying forward the many antagonistic elements from which we can never separate our ideals—all the material, institutional, cultural, religious, as well as political forces—that constitute the very essence of modernity.

There are still uncertainties in the politics of the future of Confucianism. However, we can be sure of one thing, that Confucianism—as ritual practice, as cultural identity, as political identity, as possible foundation of morality, as possible source of civil religion—will never go away. So much has already happened in the first decade of the twenty-first century; the future of the revival of Confucianism no doubt holds for us anxiety, but also great hope.

Notes

*I thank P. J. Ivanhoe and Sungmoon Kim for making the Confucianism: A Habit of the Heart conference in Hong Kong possible and for being the most thoughtful and supportive editors. I thank Yang Xiao for being my excellent first reader. This essay was written for the conference and originally appeared in my 2013 monograph *Confucianism as a World Religion: Contested Histories and Contemporary Realities* (chapter reproduced by kind permission of Princeton University Press). My deepest thanks go to the late Robert Bellah, who generously commented on all the papers at the conference. His passionate mind was an inspiration to us all.

1. Jin Ze and Yonghui Qiu, *Zhongguo Zongjiao Baogao 2010* (Annual Report on China's Religions 2010) (Beijing: Social Sciences Academic Press, 2010).

2. "Rectification of Statues," *Economist*, January 20, 2011.

3. "Confucius Stood Here, but Not for Very Long," *New York Times*, April 23, 2011.

4. "Statue Moved Inside," *China Daily*, April 22, 2011, http://www.chinadaily.com.cn/cndy/2011-04/22/content_12373866.htm.

5. Xinhua News Agency, "Jesus to Join Confucius as Qufu Plans Church," *China Daily*, December 12, 2010, http://www.chinadaily.com.cn/china/2010-12/13/content_11695800.htm.

6. Confucian Ten Scholars, "Zunzhong Zhonghua Wenhua Shengdi, Tingjian Qufu Jejiao Jiaotang" (Respect the Sacred Ground of Chinese Culture, Stop the Building of the Christian Church in Qufu) (2010), http://www.hxwm.net/view thread.php?tid=51619. It is cosigned by the Confucian Ten Scholars, with the support of ten international and domestic Confucian cultural organizations, as well as ten Confucian websites, including Confucius2000.com and Chinarujiao.net.

7. Wilfred Cantwell Smith, *The Meaning and End of Religion* (Minneapolis: Fortress Press, 1991), 69.

8. Ian Hacking, *The Social Construction of What?* (Cambridge: Harvard University Press, 1999).

9. Rebecca Nedostup, *Superstitious Regimes: Religion and the Politics of Chinese Modernity* (Cambridge: Harvard University Press, 2009).

10. Tony Blair, "How Will Religion's Growth in China Impact Its Relations with the West?" *Washington Post*, April 11, 2011.

11. Stephen C. Angle, *Contemporary Confucian Political Philosophy* (Cambridge: Polity Press, 2012), 8.

12. Fenggang Yang, "A Sociological Perspective on Confucianism as Religion" (in Chinese), *Journal of Lanzhou University (Social Sciences)* 36.2 (2008): 2–8.

13. Helen Hardacre, *Shinto and the State, 1868–1988* (Princeton: Princeton University Press, 1989).

14. This urgency for moral reconstruction is felt strongly in China, intensified by several scandals that have enraged the nation in recent years and have signified for many the final collapse of the moral and ethical order in today's China, where

now the brute desire for profit and extreme selfishness have been justified and legitimized by China's tremendous economic success and seem to have in effect become the unspoken law of the land. The scandals include popular milk products with poisonous ingredients that led to the deaths of infants (2008), the disastrous collapse of poorly constructed school buildings in the Sichuan earthquake that led to the deaths of many young children (2008), and the death of a two-year-old year girl in car accident on a city street, in which eighteen bystanders walked past the injured child without stopping to help (2011).

15. See Sébastien Billioud, "The Revival of Confucianism in the Sphere of Mores and the Reactivation of the Civil Religion Debate in China," chap. 2 in this volume.

16. Ibid., p. 31.

17. Ji Zhe, "Return to Durkheim: Civil Religion and the Moral Reconstruction in China" (paper, Elementary Forms of Religious Life: A Dialogue between the Disciplines workshop, University of Oxford, July 2011).

18. Billioud, "Revival of Confucianism," p. 59.

19. Fenggang Yang, "Confucianism as Civil Religion," chap. 1 in this volume.

20. Ibid, p. 43.

21. Robert Bellah, "Civil Religion: Term and Concept," in *The Robert Bellah Reader*, ed. Robert N. Bellah and Steven M. Tipton (Durham: Duke University Press, 2006), 246.

22. Ji, "Return to Durkheim," 8–9, 23. According to Diana Eck's Pluralism Project, although there are a great number of religions being practiced in contemporary America, only 6 percent of the population practices non-Christian religions, that is, "diverse religious traditions within the U.S.," not counting diversity within Christianity. See The Pluralism Project, "Statistics," http://pluralism.org/resources/statistics/index.php.

23. The Horizon Spiritual Life of Chinese Residents survey, 2007.

24. Ibid.

5

Obstacles to the Globalization of Confucianism

Richard Madsen

There is no doubt that Confucianism is the source of many important East Asian habits of the heart, but the Confucian tradition has not traveled well outside of Asia, at least not in the past century. The other major East Asian religions, Buddhism and Daoism, have to a significant degree transcended their home cultures and become indigenized in North America and Europe and even parts of Africa. In both North America and Europe there are large Buddhist temples that serve non-Asian middle classes. Famous examples would be the Pacific Zen Center in California and Naropa University in Colorado, but there are smaller worship and study centers scattered throughout the United States and Europe. Buddhism—especially Zen—has had a powerful influence on American culture through the poetry of artists like Gary Snyder and Allen Ginsberg, not to mention the Zen-inspired designs of the Buddhist Steve Jobs. In South Africa, one of the most thriving philanthropic enterprises is Tzu Chi, the Taiwan-based Buddhist Compassion Relief Society, and its South African director and many of its workers are Zulus. Books by the Dalai Lama are bestsellers throughout the West, and his speeches draw massive crowds.

In theory, Confucian ideas are certainly deep enough and rich enough to contribute to a global civil religion, and they indeed might serve as a civil religion within China and other East Asian societies. But the practical difficulties that Confucianism encounters today in traveling easily and settling in comfortably outside of Asia seem to pose an obstacle to the hope that it might contribute in substantial ways to more global ethical and spiritual aspirations. In the final contribution to this anthology, Robert Bellah poses the rhetorical question, "Can We Imagine a Global Civil Religion?" One might respond "yes" one can, but in light of the concerns expressed earlier, it is more difficult to imagine Confucianism playing a significant role in a global civil religion.

Confucianism, however, has not been indigenized into non-Asian cultures. There are a few intellectuals, such as the Boston Confucians (professors of philosophy, theology, or religious studies at various universities in the Boston area), who have an almost missionary zeal for spreading Confucianism, but their efforts do not take any institutional form.[1] There is no indigenous American or European literature that utilizes Confucian themes. In popular culture, Confucianism is usually seen as something that marks Chinese identity and sets Chinese (and to some degree Koreans, Vietnamese, and Japanese) apart from Europeans—something that will eventually be worn away when Asian immigrants assimilate into Western cultures, not something that Westerners would want to absorb into their own cultures. And based on my own observations, it would seem that most Asian American students, even when they say that they have a Confucian heritage, have virtually no knowledge of the content of the Confucian tradition.

Why does Confucianism not travel as well as Buddhism or Daoism? I suggest that this is due to a combination of historical, cultural, and political factors.

Confucianism in Modern History

Before the late nineteenth century, "Confucianism" was unknown in China.[2] There was instead the "Teaching of the Scholars," a rich tradition of scholarship, based on centuries of interpretation and reinterpretation of the classics by thinkers such as Confucius and Mencius and creatively combined with Buddhism in the Song dynasty, but stagnating by the late Qing, that was used as the basis for the civil service exams. This tradition, which existed side by side and was typically interwoven with teachings of the Buddha and teachings of the Dao, was called "Confucianism" by European scholars of comparative religion.

But at the popular level at any rate, there was nothing corresponding to the twentieth century's "religions" of Buddhism and Daoism or to the supposedly secular moral traditions of Confucianism. For example, in the Ming and Qing dynasties, scholars who had gained their position by studying the Neo-Confucian classics would nonetheless call upon city gods to defend the people from Fox Spirits and upon underworld gods to determine the innocence or guilt of accused criminals. According to Sarah Schneewind, the good and bad actions of scholar-officials, "their sincerity and malfeasance, brought forth omens and portents, from double-headed grain and sweet dew to untimely snows and long droughts."[3] Among ordinary people, Buddhist bodhisattvas and Daoist immortals were worshiped together in jumbled temples along with a wide assortment of local spirits.

For Chinese modernizers, this messy undergrowth of traditional teachings had to be cleaned out if China was to meet the challenge of a scientifically superior West and to find for itself a proud position in the Westphalian order of nation-states. At the Parliament of World Religions in 1893, nation-states were represented as each having a distinctive national religion. Forced reluctantly into a world system of competing nation-states, Chinese intellectuals were being pushed to define China, against all historical precedent, as a unitary nation-state with its own distinctive religion. The Chinese ambassador to the Parliament of World Religions gave a famous speech proclaiming that China too had a national religion, and that religion was Confucianism. But if Confucianism was to be a national religion, Chinese nationalists wanted to conceive it as the most advanced form of religion.[4] According to liberal European theologians, the most advanced form of religion was a Christianity that had been stripped of its supernatural elements—an emulation of Jesus who was a wise moral teacher but did not perform miracles, was not raised from the dead, and does not sit at the right hand of God the Father. Chinese proto-nationalistic intellectuals took their Confucianism one step further: it was from the beginning just a worldly philosophy and hence superior to Christianity, which had taken many centuries to rid itself of its supernatural baggage. This was how Confucianism was presented in the early twentieth century in China.

Twentieth-century history was not kind to liberal Christianity. Stripped of all supernatural baggage, denuded of vibrant rituals, and reduced to a worldly philosophy, it was too bland and too vapid a belief system to provide consolation and hope to people facing the terrible wars, gross injustices, and intense forms of alienation of that century. Neither was the century kind to Confucianism. Shorn of a mass base and stripped down to the philosophy of a declining elite, Confucianism became a symbol of a reactionary traditionalism, an obstacle to modernization. From the May Fourth movement to the protests at Tiananmen Square in 1989, the Confucian tradition was decried as an enemy of progress. Even though the two leading revolutionary forces in China—the Nationalist and the Communist parties—were militant secularists, religious practices of many kinds flourished. In the 1930s, so-called "redemptive societies," which syncretized multiple parts of the Chinese tradition to be the basis for nationwide religious organizations, had more members than either the KMT or Communists. Vigorous Buddhist reform movements were begun.[5] And temple worship to multiple local deities flourished throughout the countryside. But although Confucianism was creatively developed by intellectuals like Qian Mu and Tang Junyi, who eventually found a home in New Asia College in Hong Kong after the Communist victory on the Mainland, it never seemed to excite popular enthusiasm, even when it was made into something of a national symbol by the KMT in Taiwan.

According to Tu Weiming, the "new Confucianism" of the twentieth century was as different from the "neo-Confucianism" of the Song Dynasty as Death of God theology to Reformation Protestantism.[6] Stripped of mystery and shorn of metaphysical elements, the twentieth-century version represented a capitulation to the Western Enlightenment project at the very time that that project was creating a spiritual void that it could not fulfill on its own terms. In China in the early twentieth century, reformed Buddhist movements and the various redemptive societies at least tried to address this void, albeit without much success.

Confucian values such as filial piety, respect for social hierarchies, a commitment to resolve disputes through social consensus, and a respect for education persisted of course, carried on partly by being embedded in Buddhist and Daoist practices, in the redemptive societies, and in the lineage and native place associations that have continued to structure the lives of ordinary Chinese, including those who migrated abroad. But under pressure from racist exclusion acts, such communities were often forced inward, with strong boundaries against contact with the outside society. The Confucian-inspired associations helped maintain the solidarities necessary to be self-sufficient in a hostile world. But this also maintained the image of Confucianism as an ethnic characteristic that was not suitable for outsiders.[7]

When the Communists assumed power in China, they replaced what remained of Confucian education with "scientific socialism." During the Cultural Revolution, Red Guards carried out vicious attacks against the "four olds," including Confucian symbols and virtues. In the last phase of the Cultural Revolution, Mao Zedong launched a campaign to "Criticize Confucius" (which was a veiled criticism of Zhou Enlai, who in his desire to mediate and compromise seemed to embody at least some remnant of the Confucian ethos). Then, as his life neared its end, Mao launched one final campaign to learn from the Qin Emperor, the brutal Legalist unifier of China, who in his day had killed the Confucian scholars and burned their books. However, after the death of Mao and under the Reform and Opening directed by Deng Xiaoping, invocations of Chinese tradition, including Confucian values, once again started to surface among aging Chinese elites. Unfortunately, these were associated with the most reactionary elites, who used Confucian tradition to justify authoritarian government. The generation of young critics who rose up in 1989 were inspired by the television series *River Elegy*, which, like the May Fourth generation, blamed China's problems on the authoritarian traditions of its Confucian past.[8] (A significant number of that movement's leaders, including the imprisoned Nobel Prize winner Liu Xiaobo, have been attracted to Christianity.)[9] After the Chinese government crushed the student movement, it began to show an increasing respect for Confucianism. Now that the Communist Party defines itself as no longer a "revolutionary party" but as a "ruling party," it is increasingly seeking to justify its rule in nationalistic terms, and this entails a celebration of Confucianism as a core part of China's "non-material cultural heritage."

Thus, somewhat similar to the KMT's attempt in the 1950s and 1960s to present itself as a preserver of traditional Confucian values (so defined as to emphasize the most authoritarian aspects of Confucianism), some elements in the Chinese Communist Party see the party as preserving a national culture based on core Confucian values, which make it superior to the declining West. In an effort to spread its "soft power" the government is sponsoring "Confucian institutes" around the world. But the connection of Confucianism with Chinese nationalism will probably continue to make Confucianism seem alien to non-Chinese.

Meanwhile, Asian forms of spiritual practice like Daoism and Buddhism, which have not been connected with nationalism and which are still rich in ritual and a sense of mystery, can become fascinating to Westerners who have become disillusioned with traditional Christianity.

Conflicts with Western Individualism

Another reason why Confucianism has not gained a solid footing in the West is its incompatibility with the dominant culture of individualism. Whatever its variants, the Confucian vision stresses the fundamentally social nature of human identity. For the Confucian, as Herbert Fingarette put it, there can be no person unless there are at least two persons.[10] The Confucian virtues are about the ways to maintain the social roles that are proper to a corporate community: child and parent, husband and wife, elder and junior, ruler and subject, and friend to friend. It is a philosophy of connection, taking its fundamental model for social relations from the most nonvoluntary of social institutions, the family, and then extending that model outward to encompass the wider social world. Western cultural life is dominated by individualism, a habit of heart that challenges the self to find meaning and purpose by separating itself from its communities of origin, defying social pressures, and choosing its own life path. In the West this hegemonic individualism is still challenged (but maybe more and more weakly) by more socially grounded visions derived from religious and civic traditions. However, these traditions do not entirely contradict individualism—indeed they bear an intimate relationship to it. Our present-day individualism, for example, owes much to the Christian emphasis on the dignity of each person. There is a family resemblance between modern individualism and Christianity, even when Christianity criticizes radical individualism by insisting on the connection of all individuals in the body of Christ. There is no such family resemblance with Confucianism. However useful a robust critique of individualism might be, when it comes from self-proclaimed Confucians, it seems to come from the outside. Just as the introduction of individualist ideology to China in the early twentieth century was seen as an imposition from outside, accepted in some circles because of the overwhelming power of the West but then often rejected when China regained some of its power, so now the introduction of a communal Confucian ideology from Asia is seen as something of an alien imposition, maybe to be taken seriously out of the necessity of competing with an economically resurgent Asia but never fully compatible with the West's values.

Somewhat in contrast, although Buddhism and Daoism are as a whole non-individualistic, they do contain elements that can actually reinforce Western individualism. Although Buddhism sees the independent self as an illusion and finds the reality of our existence in our interdependence with all beings, the practice of meditation involves a deep concentration on one's own mind and body, and, even when carried on within community, it can feel like a profoundly solitary experience. Forms of Buddhism, like Zen, that feature such meditation have thus been the forms that have caught on most widely among non-Asian populations in the West. As for Daoism, in its rejection of conventional norms it has a radically anarchistic side that can comport well with a philosophy of "doing your own thing." In fact, with its goal of relaxing into a childlike spontaneous integration of thought and feeling, body and mind, it is even more compatible with modern expressive individualism than most Western philosophy.

Thus, although neither Buddhism nor Daoism is fundamentally individualistic, certain aspects of both traditions can couple with Western individualism. This can lead to a kind of indigenization that deeply distorts the original teaching by allowing it to be seen almost entirely in individualistic terms. But it can also be the beginning of a transformation of Western culture. Once Buddhism and Daoism have gained a foothold in the West, they can begin to pull their followers into a deeper appreciation of the interconnectedness of all things. Once one goes more deeply into the practice of Buddhist meditation, for example, one can attain a mindfulness that leads to deep respect for the integrity of personal relationships and one can cultivate compassion that can lead one to shoulder responsibilities for the world.

Confucianism, though, has no such coupling points, especially in the way it has developed in the twentieth century. What used to give Chinese culture its richness was the dynamic interplay between Confucian, Daoist, and Buddhist traditions. The logic of development of Chinese religious culture was to gain breadth and depth though addition rather than subtraction. Thus, temples expand by adding more and more gods and bodhisattvas to their altars. The editing of the family genealogies that are central to ancestor worship is accompanied by sutra chanting by Buddhist monks. Chinese often seek moral cultivation through Confucian self-cultivation, health and long life through Daoist inner alchemy, and salvation after death through Buddhism. They see complementarity, not incompatibility, in the practice of several traditions at once. It is the monotheistic religions of the West, with their devotion to a jealous God, that constantly seek the purification of belief by separation from rival religions. This Western logic was brought to China by the Christian missionaries and later by secular intellectuals with the aid of Western imperialism in the nineteenth century. Under such pressure to emulate the West, Chinese intellectuals, as we have seen, attempted to purify their own traditions. Confucian tradition was turned into Confucian*ism* and distinguished from "superstitions" like Buddhism and Daoism. Meanwhile, reformers in both of those traditions tried to purify them also and reorganized them, under central government supervision, into religious congregations partly modeled after Christian denominations in the West.[11] The sum of the parts has been less than the whole, and Confucianism, which had gained some of its moral power from its connections with the other traditions, lost most of its capacity to connect to a wider social base. In the West now, one finds Buddhist temples and Daoist sanctuaries, begun through the grassroots initiative of overseas Chinese but sometimes continued through the enthusiastic participation of local citizens. But there are only Confucius Institutes, sponsored from the top down by a Chinese government eager to spread its soft power. While invoking the name of Confucius, these institutes mainly focus on teaching about Chinese language and cultural history rather than enabling any serious cultivation in Confucian virtue.

Confucianism as Political Ideology

Confucian virtues, properly understood, demand a self-sacrificing devotion to moral integrity in the face of political power. A good Confucian official should be willing to remonstrate with an unjust ruler, even at the cost of his career or his life. An example was the official Hai Rui, in the Ming dynasty, who was dismissed by the emperor after he had protested policies that were oppressing the poor. In 1964, the playwright and Beijing deputy mayor Wu Han wrote a play about Hai Rui, which was seen by Mao Zedong as a veiled support of party officials who had followed their consciences in criticizing Mao. In his fury at this play, Mao then launched the Cultural Revolution.

As in every society, righteous officials who endanger themselves to remonstrate in the name of morality against unjust power are rare. More common are those who turn moral traditions into an ideological mask in support of power. When this is done too often, it can certainly discredit the moral tradition. This has been done too often by advocates of Confucianism in the twentieth century. The conversion of Confucianism into political ideology started during the KMT's New Life movement in the 1930s. Partly modeled after European fascist movements, this attempted to mobilize the Chinese people to support the regime in the name of Confucian values.[12] (The movement did not emphasize the need for good Confucians to remonstrate against tyrannical rule.) While severely restricting most forms of Chinese popular religion, during the 1950s and 1960s in Taiwan, the KMT also promoted itself as the creator of a cultural renaissance that would restore the best of the Confucian tradition, namely, those parts that emphasize obedience to authority. This tradition was picked up and elaborated by Lee Kwan-yu in Singapore in the 1980s. Through the development of Confucian textbooks and many other writings promoting its version of "Asian values," Singapore became widely identified as the world's most successful embodiment of a Confucian culture (even though 25 percent of its population consists of Muslims and Hindus). Meanwhile the Singaporean Internal Security Department (ISD) was arresting, beating, and imprisoning without trial journalists, politicians, labor leaders, and Christian justice and peace workers who dared to question Prime Minister Lee's pro-business one-party rule.

In the 1980s, some Chinese intellectuals were advocating a "new authoritarianism" based on the Singapore model, even as cultural critics who supported the Tiananmen movements in 1989 complained bitterly against cultural traditions that supported authoritarianism. Now, with Marxist ideology having largely collapsed, some leaders in the Chinese Communist Party are looking with favor on the Confucian tradition as a justification for the party's attempts to create a "harmonious society." The old rites to venerate Confucius were revived in Beijing in 2010. Some prominent voices want to make Confucianism a new state religion. Even those who would not go this far still support the promotion of the values of social harmony. Meanwhile, the state security apparatus continues to arrest and torture dissidents. As far as I know, those who, sometimes at great danger to themselves, try to resist this have never claimed that they are taking their inspiration from the best of Confucian traditions. Indeed, the so-called "rights lawyers," and social critics like the Nobel laureate Liu Xiaobo, are much more likely to be Christians.

In China and in other parts of Asia, Confucianism has thus been transformed into a political ideology for authoritarian governments, who increasingly argue that their version of order-producing Asian values is superior to the democratic values of the West. One can certainly make a case that the best of the Confucian tradition can support genuinely democratic institutions, and in any case that it does not support the brutalities of dictatorial rule. In societies like Taiwan or South Korea, which have made a transition to democracy, a freely developing Confucianism has made important contributions toward supporting a vibrant, socially responsible civil society. But the ideological use of Confucianism by powerful and assertive political actors like the PRC regime has given Confucianism its primary global image. In 2011, the winner of China's Confucian Peace Prize (an effort by some Chinese entrepreneurs to invent a competitor to the Nobel Peace Prize) went to Vladimir Putin for his conduct of "righteous wars for unification of the country," especially the war in Chechnya. According to the citation, "His iron hand and toughness revealed in this war has impressed the Russians a lot, and he was regarded as bringing safety and stability to Russia. He became the number one anti-terrorist, and national hero."[13] This may affect perception of the Confucian brand more than a multitude of high-minded and accurate scholarly disquisitions.

Such a brand image makes Confucianism attractive to all the wrong people: Western business leaders who praise the suppression of labor unions in Asian developmentalist states; their political and academic allies who argue that Western support for human rights amounts to a kind of cultural imperialist disrespect for Asian values; even those who praise the driven, authoritarian parenting of "tiger moms" as an example of Confucian values worth emulating. Those on the other side of contemporary political and social struggles will become wary when they hear talk of promoting Confucianism.

Besides becoming a political ideology, Confucianism can be turned into a gender ideology. The second of the five basic principles of relationships according to Mencius is that between husbands and wives there should be "difference" (*bie* 別). The basic meaning seems to be that husbands and wives should play different roles in marriage while mutually supporting one another. But in history, this has usually been taken to mean that husbands should have authority over their wives. In the Ming dynasty, this was summarized in the "three obediences" (*sancong* 三從): a woman should obey her father, her husband, and her grown sons. Reformers in the twentieth century sharply criticized this patriarchal ideology, and the critique was an important reason for the rejection of Confucianism by May Fourth intellectuals. In response some Confucian intellectuals have gone to considerable lengths to argue that the modern quest for female equality is compatible with Confucian traditions, rightly understood.

Those who advocate this feminist-friendly interpretation of Confucianism, however, often seem defensive, as if they have to labor hard to overturn a mountain of tradition.[14] And whatever the robustness of their intellectual arguments, it is rhetorically difficult to maintain their credibility in face of the gender bias that is still pervasive in Chinese culture, bias manifested in the preference for sons (even to the point of frequent abortion of female fetuses in the PRC). In most Confucian Asian societies, there are few women in high echelons of government, academia, or business, with the partial exception of Taiwan and Hong Kong. Moreover, men often invoke cultural traditions as the reason for keeping women in a subordinate position. This history of gender subordination naturally makes Western women reluctant to give Confucianism careful consideration.

Although it might be reasonably argued that gender bias in Asian societies is supported by many cultural forces in addition to Confucianism, the fact is that prominent Asian governments have proudly proclaimed an ideologized Confucianism as their core value, to which other traditions like Buddhism and Daoism are subordinate. Confucianism then comes to bear the burden of all the modern deficiencies of their polities and culture, as well as to take some credit for their successes.

Paths to Globalization?

We have offered some possible reasons why Confucianism has difficulty in becoming transplanted to non-Chinese cultures. The reason is not simply an anti-Asian prejudice—other Asian spiritual traditions like Buddhism and

Daoism have become indigenized in cultures around the world. One reason for their success lies in what they are not. They are not ruling class ideologies. They are not entirely incompatible with individualism. They have not been stripped of ritual and myth in the course of the twentieth century. Yet they assuage some degree of spiritual hunger created by the moral emptiness of radical individualism in association with neoliberal capitalism. Confucianism might do this if it disassociates itself from political power, comes to terms with the rights and freedoms that Western Enlightenment liberalism has made possible, and re-embeds itself to some degree in the myths and rituals that give meaning to ordinary life.

How might it do this? Disassociating itself from political power is probably the most difficult challenge. Confucianism is after all a political philosophy. It is a guide to cultivating elites who will be fit to govern. It aims to create "superior men" (*junzi* 君子) who are better than ordinary people and therefore qualified to lead them. The temptation is strong for a ruling party to claim the mantle of Confucian virtue even when it is mostly composed of thugs and thieves. It can especially do this if it can intimidate, censor, or co-opt people who would accuse it of hypocrisy. One way to disconnect Confucianism from a too-close subservience to political power is to institute democratic reforms that make a government accountable to all sectors of a society and to let citizens debate freely what kind of moral norms they want their government to uphold. In countries with a strong Confucian tradition, the ensuing debates will bring about both criticism and renewal of that tradition. Such has happened in Taiwan and South Korea. Such public debates also serve to bring Confucianism closer to the masses. The Confucians historically tried to cultivate an educated ruling elite at a time when education could only be available to a few. Now with mass literacy and mass communication, ordinary people rightly feel that they would like to become cultivated themselves and that they ought not to defer to people who have traditionally claimed higher cultivation. The Confucianism that is developed from the ground up in such locations will be more credible globally than that promoted from the top down.

Such Confucianism developed from the ground up is also more likely to become adapted to the necessities of a mobile modern life. Modern occupations demand personal initiative and creativity, some of the best qualities of individualism. Urbanization often brings about kinds of geographical and social mobility that separate people from the day-to-day connections with family and friends that have been central to a Confucian way of life. People who want to maintain what is most beautiful in the Confucian tradition will want to find a way to reconcile it realistically with the personal agency and the interpersonal distance that much of modern life entails, all the while humanizing that life by striving to make it conform with those ideals.

Finally, Confucianism has to become more than an academic philosophy. It needs to become enlivened by the most appealing myths and rituals of the Chinese tradition. Some of this has already happened through popular culture. At the rural level in China, the local operas that are a staple of all temple festivals feature stories of heroes and heroines who embody Confucian virtue. The immensely popular novels of Hong Kong–based Jin Yong present young and old readers with a rich fund of common myths of Confucianism in action. Some of this sensibility has become conveyed to the West by talented filmmakers such as Ang Lee and Hou Hsiau-hsien. The rituals of Asian martial arts, like Aikido and Taiji, with the importance given to the student's relation to his master and the cultivation of moral wisdom to contain bodily strength, all provide partial models of Confucianism in action.

If Confucianism does indeed become globalized, its major carriers in the twenty-first century may indeed be Asian artists and storytellers rather than scholars and politicians. Another set of carriers may be humanistic Buddhist and Daoist associations such as those that have recently developed in Taiwan and now offer compassionate relief for the poor and afflicted around the world. Though their religious vision derives from Buddhism and Daoism, their social ethic is heavily Confucian. This embedded Confucianism may have a better chance of spreading than a separated, purified version.

In any case, the globalization of Confucianism and other Asian spiritual and moral traditions will probably more likely take place in a relaxed confluence of cultures rather than a fearfully politicized one. Proponents of Confucianism may best spread this habit of the heart by sincerely and effectively promoting peace among nations.

Notes

1. John Berthrong, "From Beijing to Boston: The Future Contributions of the Globalization of New Confucianism," in *Confucianism and Spiritual Traditions in Modern China and Beyond*, ed. Fenggang Yang and Joseph Tamney (Leiden: Brill, 2012), 131–147.

2. "Confucianism" is a Western name, first coined by the Jesuit missionaries of the seventeenth century to refer to the intellectual traditions of those scholar-officials the Chinese called the *ru*, who considered Confucius to be their preeminent sage. But European scholars of comparative religion in the nineteenth century further refined the term to refer to a systematic body of doctrines—an "-ism" supposedly comparable to what these European scholars took to be the "-isms" of other "world religions.

3. Sarah Schneewind, "'The Honor of Officials Depends on the People': Shrines to Living Officials in Imperial China," paper presented at the American History Association Annual Meeting, San Diego, January 2010. See also, Sarah Schneewind, *A Tale of Two Melons: Emperor and Subject in Ming China* (Indianapolis: Hackett, 2006), 30–35.

4. Hsi-yuan Chen, "At the Threshold of the Pantheon of Religions: Confucianism and the Emerging Religious Discourse at the Turn of the Twentieth Century," paper presented at the International Conference on Religion, Modernity, and the State in China and Taiwan, University of California at Santa Barbara, 2005. See also Hsi-yuan Chen, *Confucian Encounters with Religion: Rejections, Appropriations, and Transformations* (London: Taylor and Francis, 2006). See also Ya-pei Kuo, "Redeploying Confucius: The Imperial State Dreams of the Nation, 1902–1911," in *Chinese Religiosities*, ed. Mayfair Meihui Yang (Berkeley: University of California Press, 2009), 65–84.

5. David Palmer and Vincent Goossaert, *The Religious Question in Modern China* (Chicago: University of Chicago Press, 2011), 132–137.

6. Tu Weiming, "Multiple Modernities: Implications of the Rise of 'Confucian' East Asia" in *Chinese Ethics in a Global Context: Moral Bases of Contemporary Societies*, ed. Karl-Heinz Pohl and Anselm W. Muller (Leiden: Brill, 2002), 55.

7. Richard Madsen and Elijah Siegler, "The Globalization of Chinese Religions and Traditions," in *Chinese Religious Life*, ed. David A. Palmer, Glenn Shive, and Philip L. Wickeri (New York: Oxford University Press, 2011), 227–240.

8. Su Xiaokang and Wang Luxiang, *Deathsong of the River: A Reader's Guide to the Chinese TV Series Heshang*, ed. and trans. Richard W. Bodman and Pin P. Wan (Ithaca: Cornell East Asia Series, 1991).

9. Gerda Wielander, "Bridging the Gap? Intellectual House Church Activities in Beijing and Their Potential Role in China's Democratization," *The Journal of Contemporary China* 18.62 (November 2009): 849–864.

10. Herbert Fingarette, "The Music of Humanity in the Conversations of Confucius," *Journal of Chinese Philosophy* 10 (1983), as quoted in Henry Rosemont, "Commentary and Addenda on Nosco's 'Confucian Perspectives on Civil Society and Government,'" in *Civil Society and Government*, ed. Nancy L. Rosenblum and Robert C. Post (Princeton: Princeton University Press, 2002), 365.

11. Vincent Goossaert, "Republican Church Engineering: The National Religious Associations in 1912 China," in *Chinese Religiosities*, ed. Mayfair Meihui Yang (Berkeley: University of California Press, 2008), 209–231.

12. James Claude Thomson, *While China Faced West: American Reformers in Nationalist China, 1927–1937* (Cambridge: Harvard University Press, 1969).

13. *New York Times*, November 16, 2011.

14. See Joseph Chan, "Confucian Attitudes towards Ethical Pluralism," in *The Many and the One: Religious and Secular Perspectives on Ethical Pluralism in the Modern World*, ed. Richard Madsen and Tracy B. Strong (Princeton: Princeton University Press, 2003), 142–145.

6

Beyond a Disciplinary Society

Reimagining Confucian Democracy in South Korea

Sungmoon Kim

In the past decade, Confucianism, long considered the single greatest stumbling block on the road to modernization, has made a heroic comeback to the mainstream of political discourse and political theorization in China and pan-Chinese communities of the East Asian region. Scholars of China, once dwarfed by the communist authoritarian regime that completely demolished Confucianism during the Cultural Revolution by calling it the relic of feudalism, now boldly assert that Confucianism can save the Chinese people from the cultural and political crisis they currently are experiencing in the post–Cold War era. For instance, a good number of scholars are engaging in serious discussion about how to reform China's constitutional structure and the political institutions that undergird it in light of Confucianism, the central philosophical assumptions and ethical precepts of which they believe are incompatible with the rights-based liberalism of the West.[1] These scholars are largely convinced that Confucianism supports a kind of political meritocracy—in Daniel Bell's expression, a rule by the best and the brightest elites[2]—and Confucian meritocratic elitism can be a realistic political alternative to an individual rights-centered liberal democracy in greater China. A more radical group of Confucian scholars even attempts to restore the political and religious orthodoxy of Confucianism by advocating it as a national religion.

The recent valorization of Confucianism is not limited to the anti-democratic camp. While being equally critical of the wholesale Western liberalization of Confucian East Asia, many Confucian-minded scholars based in Hong Kong, Singapore, and Taiwan are vigorously exploring a democratic government and civil society that are grounded in Confucian ethics and philosophy.[3] Even Western scholars such as David Hall and Roger Ames are convinced that Confucian ritual (*li* 禮)–constituted democracy can offer a powerful alternative to Weberian claims concerning the inevitable rationalization and "disenchantment" of the modern world.[4] Despite ongoing debates on what constitutes the central tenets of Confucian democracy, scholars in this camp maintain that Confucian democracy is a sort of communitarian social practice in which individual and government as well as civil society and the state are in a mutually constituting relationship rather than in stark opposition.

Of course, whether the suggestions of Confucian constitutionalism and Confucian democracy advanced thus far are theoretically robust and politically practicable in a particular East Asian society is an entirely different question. But given that constitutionalism and democracy are not only about institutional political power but are also deeply concerned with the collective life of the people (i.e., collective self-determination), it is quite natural that many scholars in East Asia are immersed in the search for a mode of political life that is best suited for East Asia's Confucian social context.

South Korea (hereafter, Korea), however, is one critical exception to this trend. Not only is it difficult to find a Korean scholar who is actively engaged in the international academic debate about Confucian democracy and constitutionalism, but, more importantly, there seems to be no viable scholarly or public debate about this topic among Korean intellectual communities or Korean citizens. Scholars studying Korean democracy rarely pay attention to Korea's Confucian societal culture, which, albeit arguably, played a significant role in facilitating the democratic transition and consolidation of Korean society.[5] They evidently express no interest in the question of how to make Korean democracy work better in the given societal context and, if necessary, how to modify it. They seem to believe that a genuine democracy in Korea will be attained only after the existing Confucian societal culture has faded. For them, the democracy to be consolidated in Korea is a Western-style liberal democracy, and therefore what is urgently needed is a cognitive, affective, and attitudinal transformation of individual Korean citizens and thus Korean society.[6]

This Korean aberration is counterintuitive given that not only was Korean society thoroughly Confucianized during the Chosŏn dynasty (1392–1910),[7] contemporary Koreans are still deeply saturated with Confucian habits and mores in their daily social life.[8] After all, Koreans never actively disowned Confucianism as the Chinese did during the Cultural

Revolution. Then, why is there such nonchalance toward Confucian democracy in Korea?

Various answers can be given to this question, but I believe one of the primary reasons for the virtual lack of interest in Confucian democracy in today's Korea has a great deal to do with Korean citizens' disillusionment with "New Confucianism," a view that combines Confucian democracy and Confucian capitalism, which a group of Korean scholars eagerly presented in the late 1990s and early 2000s. These scholars—mainly consisting of social scientists who received their PhDs from distinguished American universities—drove what can be called a "New Confucian movement" by, among other things, publishing a quarterly magazine called *Tradition and Modernity* (*Jeontong-gwa Hyeondae* 전통과 현대) (published from 1997 to 2002), promoting Confucianism in various media outlets and offering courses on Confucian democracy and Confucian capitalism in major Korean universities.[9]

In a nutshell, there seems to be no major difference between what these Korean New Confucians did and what Chinese scholars are now doing, except that none of the Korean scholars presented themselves as an opponent of democracy: they found fault with rights-based liberalism, upheld Confucian relational virtues and familialism, and supported a good government led by meritorious elites.[10] Then the question arises: What went wrong with this movement? Why did this movement fail to generate a more serious and enduring discussion about the character of Korean democracy during its period of consolidation? More importantly, why did it fail to resonate with the general Korean public (especially young Koreans), who still remain deeply Confucian in practice, if not in faith, and eventually made them turn away from Confucian democracy?[11]

In this chapter, I attempt to explicate the sudden disappearance of the discourse of Confucian democracy in Korean academia and civil society in the early 2000s and the general Korean nonchalance to it since then by critically examining the core claims made by Korean new Confucians, particularly Hahm Chaibong, who spearheaded the New Confucian movement with an articulate political theorization of what he calls "postmodern Confucianism."[12] My central argument is that though Hahm's poignant epistemological critique of Western modernity was intellectually stimulating, his overemphasis on self-discipline, which he singled out as the core ethical and cultural element of Confucianism, made his vision of Confucian democracy less politically robust as a democratic theory and more governability oriented, thus failing to come to terms with the active participatory citizenship and strong democratic civil society that were increasingly characterizing Korean politics in the postdemocratic context.

Furthermore, I argue that while Korean Confucian democrats such as Hahm envisioned the ideal Confucian state in terms of a disciplinary state, a state mainly concerned with economic development and the production of docile subjects, Korean citizens then were actively reappropriating Confucian familialism as the critical source for participatory citizenship and democratic justice. In short, Korean Confucian democrats failed to consider, much less engage with, the evolving habits of the Confucian heart in postdemocratic Korean society.[13]

Postmodern Confucianism: The Epistemological Foundation

Although largely unknown to scholars outside Korean academia, among Confucian democrats of late, Hahm Chaibong presents one of the most philosophically sophisticated and theoretically rigorous justifications for Confucian democracy. Trained in modern epistemology and postmodern political theory, Hahm begins his search for a Confucian democracy that he roughly defines as "a non-liberal democracy that is grounded in Confucianism, which, however, neither violates universal suffrage nor oppresses certain social classes," by critiquing the epistemological foundation of modern (liberal democratic) political theory.[14]

Drawing attention to the inextricable intertwinement of modern epistemology and modern political theory, and reminding us of Frederick Mote's observation that epistemological concerns "remained peripheral to the concerns and values of China's major philosophical schools,"[15] Hahm points to Descartes, who, being primarily a philosopher, never formally offered what we now call modern political theory, as the one who originated modern political theory. Hahm says,

> Descartes' self-assigned task became the discovery of a new ground for "certain knowledge." . . . That is, he turned to himself, to the cognitive capacity of man, to find the foundation of knowledge. As a result, he arrived at the now famous conclusion that it is only the *cogito* that can provide the basis for certain knowledge. In this system, a clear distinction is drawn between the subject, which contains the "consciousness," and the object, or outside world. The result is that the subject came to be viewed as a radically self-sufficient being independent of all things external to it, including other human beings. This view of subjectivity clearly enforced the idea of radical human freedom.[16]

According to Hahm, Descartes's contribution to modern political theory lies in his invention of the idea of an "absolute individual."[17] Epistemologically, the absolute individual refers to a man who is skeptical of custom, tradition, example, faith, or anything that preexists before the self or anything that is unexamined by the critical mind, which is pure self-consciousness—in other words, one who solely relies on his clear and certain knowledge of existence. Ontologically, the absolute individual is a model modern man who is completely deracinated from all external institutions or social customs that would otherwise give him an identity as a member of a particular moral, cultural, or political community. Reconstructed as a pure mind or radical subjectivity, then, the modern absolute individual turns his onto-epistemological anxiety into a source of freedom, thus transvaluating the very meaning of freedom: what used to be considered isolation into which man was accidentally or punitively thrown—by rebellion, ostracism, uprooting, exile, noble hubris, or other cataclysms—is now simply called freedom, the defining characteristic of modern man.[18] It is quite natural that modern political theory regards negative freedom as the only meaningful notion of freedom because it understands government, state, custom, tradition, or culture as something that fundamentally oppresses or distorts individual freedom, thereby obstructing one's self-determination or autonomy.[19] The radical dichotomy between absolute knowledge (*epistēmē*) and whatever prevents it, namely, politics as the epitome of worldly affairs (*doxa*), gives rise to the core liberal antitheses between "individual versus society," "individual versus state," and "individual versus culture."[20]

The modern political theory of the absolute individual is crystallized in modern social contract theory. Hahm says,

> Social contract theory stipulates that man is in essence a pre-social and pre-political creature, a perfectly self-sufficient being before the creation of political community. Political community is a necessary evil that individuals are forced to create solely in order to maximize their own self-interests. Social contractarians such as Hobbes and Locke and (continental) philosophers such as Montesquieu . . . identified the core of the self-identity of such individuals in terms of basic instinct and desire. For them, nature meant to be man's basic instinct or desire. Social contract is a mechanism through which the state of nature is turned into (political) community. It is for this reason that these early modern thinkers understood society as a place where man's desire for self-preservation or self-love (Hobbes), possession or prop-

> erty (Locke), self-interest (Montesquieu) is respected, protected, and even actively cultivated. This affirmation of man's instinct and desire was part of their endeavor to liberate man from the authority of the medieval church or Christian morality and [this endeavor] paved the philosophical foundation of modern liberalism and capitalism.[21]

Whether Hahm's understanding of modern social contract theory is accurate is open for debate. In my view, Hahm, like many other Confucian democrats, misinterprets the political implications of the social contract by confounding social contract and what it sets out to overcome, that is, what Charles Taylor calls "atomism."[22] According to Hahm's account, social contract denotes a mere numerical aggregate of atomistic individuals devoid of any organic reality or vision, or merely a hostility-repressed mechanical social tie that forms a *Gesellschaft*.[23] As I have shown elsewhere, it is for this type of (mis)understanding of the social contract that John Dewey criticized Henry Maine, emphasizing that the essence of social contract lies in the creation of a social organism, which gives rise to democratic citizenship.[24] As Benjamin Barber says, the purpose of social contract is political, namely, to reclaim the original meaning of freedom, a solemn declaration that man is free only in society, only when he is in association with others.[25] What is central to social contract, therefore, is not so much the libertarian protection of one's archaic desire, passion, or untrammeled self-interest but sociality in which passion calms down, desire is articulated, and self-interest is moderated.

What is important in the current context, however, is *why* Hahm (and other Korean Confucian democrats who were strongly influenced by his work) is dissatisfied with liberal democracy, the political theory that is premised on modern social contract theory, and, ultimately, how he justifies Confucian democracy as an alternative to liberal democracy.

Hahm's greatest problem with modern political theory (and liberal democracy as its most prominent heir) is that its epistemological foundation is absurd. The Cartesian separations between mind and body, self and world, and between fact and value not only portray the ontology of human existence incorrectly, which Hahm, following Charles Taylor, understands as *intersubjective*, but, more problematically, they create an equally absurd world-image in which man, now valorized as the absolute individual, is pitted against other human beings and society. In Hahm's understanding, social contract can in no way resolve these modern antimonies; it only exacerbates them because it is premised on the assumption of a highly idiosyncratic and ontologically absurd description of man. Since modern political theory is founded on modern epistemology, Hahm argues, we only have to prove modern epistemology wrong in order to refute modern political theory. Thus understood, the real issue is not so much politics but what man really is. In any case, the modern *man*—be it *cogito*, ego, self, or individual—should not be the foundation of politics of any kind.

For Hahm, therefore, the following statement by Michel Foucault is not merely about the archaeology of the human sciences; it has profound implications for politics. That is, it is about the absurdity of modern politics, of which liberal democracy, with its foundational idea of the liberal *man*, is the most dominant offspring.

> One thing in any case is certain: man is neither the oldest nor the most constant problem that has been posed for human knowledge. . . . In fact, among all the mutations that have affected the knowledge of things and their order, the knowledge of identities, differences, characters, equivalences, words—in short, in the midst of all the episodes of that profound history of the Same—only one, that which began a century and a half ago and is now perhaps drawing to a close, has made it possible for the figure of man to appear. And that appearance was not the liberation of an old anxiety, the transition into luminous consciousness of an age-old concern, the entry into objectivity of something that had long remained trapped within beliefs and philosophies: it was the effect of a change in the fundamental arrangements of knowledge. As the archaeology of our thought easily shows, man is an invention of recent date. And one perhaps nearing its end.[26]

In short, Hahm concludes that modern political theory is founded on the philosophy of *man*, namely, atomism. Once realizing that the idea of man is a modern scientific invention, hence having almost nothing to do with the "original character of the being of human life itself,"[27] Hahm then turns to Martin Heidegger and the later Wittgenstein, who each in his own way posed one of the most poignant criticisms of modern epistemology and logical positivism and emphasized the intersubjective nature of human existence.[28] Again, Hahm's most eminent concern is to rescue the real man from the modern scientific artifact and place him into the real human condition (*Lebenswelt*), that is, into the *postmodern* condition.

For instance, Hahm articulates the "postmodernity" of Heidegger's hermeneutics by saying:

> Heidegger's analysis thus freed understanding (understood as "the original form of the realization of There-being, which is being-in-the-world") from the traditional epistemological problematic based on the subject/object dichotomy and the problem of the other mind. [. . .] Heidegger's analysis completely reformulates the idea of objectivity by showing the hermeneutic understanding of objectivity to be the more general and prior mode, while showing the natural scientific notion of objectivity to be the particular, derivative case.[29]

Then, finally, Hahm relates his discussion of Heidegger to Confucianism, Neo-Confucianism in particular, which profoundly shaped and is still deeply influencing the Korean way of life.

> Heidegger's is an account of the act of understanding strikingly similar to the Neo-Confucian conception. While for the Neo-Confucians the essential moment in the "investigation of things" is "sincerity in thought," for Heidegger it is "concernful being-in-the-world." The world is not an "object" or an "entity" which is "outside" the *cogito*. Rather, "Self and the world belong together in the single entity, *Dasein* . . ." (Heidegger, 1982, p. 297). And once the subject/object dichotomy of modern epistemology is overthrown, man is seen as an intersubjective being, "being-in-the-world," whose fundamental mode of a "being" in the world is through "concernful circumspection."[30]

Hahm's so-called "postmodern Confucianism" is a premodern Neo-Confucianism rediscovered in light of the Heideggerian postmodern hermeneutics—postmodern in the sense of critiquing, if not completely departing from, modernity—and as will be discussed shortly, from the perspective of the Foucauldian deconstruction of modern political theory, which Hahm, following Foucault, understands as *liberational* or fanciful.[31] The central claim of Hahm's postmodern Confucianism is that the monistic ontological and epistemological assumptions premised in premodern Neo-Confucianism defy modernity's problematic separations between mind and body, self and world, fact and value, and ethics and politics, thus making a surprising rendezvous with postmodernism.[32]

Postmodern Confucianism has two central theses—the ontology of *ingan* 人間 (*renjian* in Chinese) and the inextricable entwinement of knowledge and self-discipline. First, Hahm presents the *ingan* ontology thesis as the Confucian and postmodern (hence, postmodern Confucian) antithesis of the modern onto-epistemology of the absolute individual.

> The Confucian worldview is completely opposed to that assumed in Western modern political theory. First, ontologically, not only does Confucianism not presuppose an "absolute individual" but [more fundamentally] there is no discourse in Confucianism, with which we can imagine such a human type. *Ingan* is fundamentally an intersubjective being and [in the idea of *ingan*] one's humanity is attained only in relation with others. The "Three Bonds and Five Relationships" (*samgang oryun* 三綱五倫), which embody the essence of traditional Confucian ethics, clearly demonstrate the ontology of intersubjectivity. Family is the basic and most important social unit where one learns human intersubjectivity.[33]

In the idea (or ideal) of *ingan*, value, *Sollen* (the imperative to be), and morals are all integrated. Though Neo-Confucian epistemology supports the idea of "subjectivity," it is in fact intersubjectivity.[34] Modern political theory stipulates that the rights of man are respected and protected by destroying social hierarchy, separating morals from politics, and minimizing the intervention of social and political authority in the private affairs of civil society. By contrast, in Confucianism, man (i.e., *ingan*) is best respected in the context of social hierarchy, morals, and authority.[35] There can be no denial of or way out from this fundamental human condition—hence, anti-*liberational*! What is needed is to simplify a variety of human relationships into a few core or cardinal ones, moralize them, and sustain them faithfully.

Family is the place where cardinal human relationships are preserved, educated, and reproduced. Unlike the Western political tradition, which holds a bias against the family—"a bias that regards family as a lesser realm, a realm of menial labor, or a biological construct at best," in Confucianism "family has a *telos* of its own, a *telos* at least coequal to that of the state."[36] If civil society and the modern state are two institutional pillars to underpin the ontology of the absolute man, it is the family that offers the institution for the *ingan* ontology.[37] Though Hahm does not say this explicitly, given his valorization of Confucian familialism, we are led to believe that the state possesses its ethical meaning only if it is a family-state, what Koreans call the *kukka* (*guojia* 國家 in Chinese).

As the *ingan* is not schizophrenically polarized into body and mind and man is an integrated whole of *Sein* and *Sollen*, knowledge in Confucianism is not acquired through the *perception* of the external world.

Instead, "it is attained through one's relentless self-cultivation (K. *sushin*/C. *xiushen* 修身), self-overcoming (K. *geukgi*/C. *keji* 克己), and self-discipline (K. *hunryeon* /C. *xunlian* 訓練). Put differently, the ontology of the *ingan* presupposes *Sollen* and the recognition and realization of *Sollen* is possible only through self-discipline."[38]

Thus far, I have examined the epistemological foundation of Hahm's postmodern Confucianism, a Confucianism reaffirmed through postmodern insights. The reason that Hahm's argument captivated many Korean intellectuals and citizens in the late 1990s and early 2000s is not difficult to understand. Until then, virtually no modern Korean intellectual had presented Confucianism in an intellectually interesting and philosophically intelligible way, which allowed Koreans to see Confucianism not as an archaic relic of a shameful past but as their beloved tradition that possesses a robust ethical theory as well as a plausible, even charming, epistemology and ontology, comparable, or even superior, to modern epistemology and political theory. At the very least, Hahm's works enabled Koreans (especially intellectuals and college students) to see Confucianism with an impartial eye and view it as on a par with liberalism. Most importantly, Hahm's work helped Koreans make sense of why there had always been a cacophony between their liberal democratic institutions and their ordinary way of life and thought. Though offering no alternative political institutions to replace or complement existing liberal democratic institutions, Hahm encouraged Koreans to entertain the possibility of a Confucian democracy, a democracy that is grounded in Confucian epistemology, ontology, and ethics—but is not necessarily antiliberal.

How then do we explain the sudden disappearance of academic and public interest in postmodern Confucianism and Confucian democracy? I now turn to Hahm's idea of Confucian democracy.

A Tough Road from Postmodern Confucianism to Confucian Democracy

The idea of postmodern Confucianism sounds fascinating because it presents premodern Confucianism as a postmodern philosophy, a philosophical system that can overcome the modern epistemological and political predicaments. However, because of such a fascinating rendezvous between premodernity and postmodernity, postmodern Confucianism looked to many people like a chimera rather than a coherent ethical, philosophical, and political system that is practicable in a modern democratic and increasingly pluralized Korea. Let us return to why Hahm calls traditional Neo-Confucianism postmodern Confucianism.

> Speaking about postmodernism in the post-Confucian context is perhaps another instance in which the postmodern discourse has freed what Michel Foucault calls "subjugated knowledge." That is, the renewed interest in Confucianism can be viewed as part of the "post-colonial" discourse in which previously "subjugated" peoples such as women, various ethnic groups, and religious groups (e.g., Islam and Hinduism) have found the means to reaffirm their cultural heritage and identity. . . . What is required, then, is the ability and willingness to affirm "Confucianism" over and against "Modernity" but, in the final analysis, to overcome modernity by embracing some of its central political tenets within the context of Neo-Confucianism.[39]

In practice, what postmodern Confucianism delivers is a postmodern redescription of premodern Confucianism. There has been no philosophical, ethical, or political reconstruction of premodern Confucianism in reformulating Confucianism in postmodern terms. In other words, premodern Confucianism remains intact in postmodern Confucianism. This raises (as it did in Korea) a fundamental question for all interested audiences—so what? How does the fact that premodern Confucianism is equipped with mesmerizingly complex moral cosmology, compelling onto-epistemology, and rigorous ethical teachings make a difference in practice in Korea's postdemocratic and pluralist societal context? Does this mean that Koreans should recommit themselves, as their Confucian ancestors did during the Chosŏn dynasty, to Neo-Confucianism in order to live their "postmodern" lives better? Hahm's postmodern Confucianism is premised on the "monistic" Neo-Confucian moral cosmology and political metaphysics that defies the separations (even distinctions) not only between fact and value, and ethics and politics, but also between private and public and between civil society and the state.[40] But how can Koreans accept this Neo-Confucian holism given the way their contemporary social and political life is structured? Furthermore, given the increasing significance of one's private life and the value of civil society as the bastion of public freedom, how can Koreans, as Hahm wishes, establish their liberal democratic social and political institutions on Neo-Confucian soil?

Hahm, however, does not seem to think this is a problem. His concern is not so much ethical monism but ethical pluralism, which he thinks is likely (if not necessary) to generate a dangerous politics of culture, which often characterizes, even defines, postmodern politics.[41] Ironically, Hahm, who upholds a postmodern epistemology, calls for a (modern?) democratic politics precisely because of the dangers of postmodern politics.

> How can a reaffirmation of Confucianism through postmodern insights be prevented from sliding into a crude politics of culture? At least one precondition for a balanced consideration of postmodernism in the post-Confucian context is the affirmation of democratic politics. That is, it should be made clear that any talk of postmodernism, especially its political aspects, is meaningless unless it is prefaced by a serious consideration of the ideals of "rights," "equality," and "political participation." The postmodern critique of modernity should in no way be viewed as condoning authoritarianism or limitations on political participation.[42]

Therefore, in a nutshell, the kind of Confucian democracy that Hahm advocates is a democratic politics predicated on Neo-Confucian epistemology and moral cosmology. Unfortunately, however, Hahm does not embark on what I consider the most difficult task, that is, to construct a *political theory* of Confucian democracy, in which Neo-Confucian epistemology and moral cosmology is coherently interlocked with democratic practices and institutions. In Hahm's work, political questions such as how to protect a citizen's civil, political, or economic rights, how to respect political and economic equality, or how to promote political participation, are simply put aside. In fact, it is highly dubious that Confucian democracy can intelligently make sense of individual rights, as long as it is pivoted around the idea of postmodern Confucianism, grounded in the postmodern critique of the modern construct of man and his freedom. This is not to deny the possibility of Confucian democratic rights. My point is that Hahm does not articulate how rights are justified in his idea of Confucian democracy and what they actually look like in the context of postmodern democracy.

Instead, Hahm's postmodern Confucianism supports Confucian democracy in a counterintuitive and arguably self-contradicting way. The most controversial part of Hahm's idea of Confucian democracy is his reappropriation of Michel Foucault's notion of discipline to justify the modern "authoritative" state.[43]

Foucault's study of modern society as a "disciplinary society" is well known. Central to his argument is that in modern society power no longer works as an indomitable force wielded by an identifiable power-holder and targeted at one's physical pain or the brutal end of one's life. Rather, it works through one's body, not in the sense of causing pain but by socially disciplining the body in everyday social institutions that appear liberal and democratic.

> Not only did the monarchies of the Classical period develop great state apparatuses (the army, the police and fiscal administration), but above all there was established at this period what one might call a new "economy" of power, that is to say procedures which allowed the effects of power to circulate in a manner at once continuous, uninterrupted, adapted and "individualized" throughout the entire social body. These new techniques are both much more efficient and much less wasteful (less costly economically, less risky in the results, less open to loopholes and resistances) than the techniques previously employed which were based on a mixture of more or less forced tolerances (from recognized privileges to endemic criminality) and costly ostentation (spectacular and discontinuous intervention of power, the most violent form of which was the "exemplary," because exceptional, punishment.[44]

What is important is Hahm's interpretation of Foucault's argument. Drawing from Foucault, Hahm turns the conventional wisdom that sees modernity and discipline *or* authority in oppositional terms upside down. He says,

> One of the most innovative parts in Foucault's study [of power] is [his observation] that modern individuality was possible only after the creation of a disciplinary society and therefore the modern disciplinary society and the modern individual that enjoys rights and freedoms are the two sides of the same coin. Throughout his work, Foucault shows that the modern individual and the modern disciplinary society are mutually constitutive.[45]

Hahm then concludes that in practice the modern individual is not so much a man who enjoys absolute (negative) freedom, as modern social contract theory portrays, but one who is highly disciplined, thus so-called *well normalized*.[46]

In Hahm's view, Foucault's genealogical study of modern society shows us that modern man is not someone who is absolutely free from the community. Modern man, whose individuality is formed by being situated and disciplined in various social institutions such as school, army, hospital, or prison, does not exist prior to the creation of a society. Therefore, Hahm argues that

> the common belief that in the Western political tradition, individuality, which had been repressed throughout the ancient and medieval times, was fully liberated only with the advent of modernity should be reexamined. Quite contrarily, a modern individual is living in a highly disciplinary society, to which no ancient or medieval society in the West can possibly compare in terms of complexity and thoroughness of social disciplines.[47]

There is nothing special about Hahm's understanding of Foucault's idea of a modern disciplinary society. In fact, considering Hahm's postmodern penchant, one may think it is quite natural that Hahm echoes and reiterates Foucault's critique of modern liberal society that in reality turns out to be more oppressive and alienating precisely because of its constitutive power of the individual self than, say, Max Weber's "iron cage." Hahm, however, moves in the completely opposite direction. Quite surprisingly, he affirms the modern democratic and capitalistic state *because* it is predicated on a disciplinary society.

> Discipline and order are the precondition of capitalism and democracy and this conclusion is supported by Gerhard Oestreich's and Michel Foucault's works. Oestreich's and Foucault's shared conclusion is that democratization, like economic development, is possible only if individuals are disciplined and ordered, and only if there is a spiritual, ethical, and psychological transformation [in an individual] that puts the interest of the entire society [before self-interest]. That is, although it may sound paradoxical, as Oestreich shows, democracy can be sustained [only] by citizens who are highly disciplined and ordered, and only by focusing on individual merits such as sincerity, responsibility, and diligence instead of feudal privilege or any authoritarian legacy. Thus understood, democratization does not merely refer to the social expansion of rights because it simultaneously requires a high degree of self-discipline. If we examine the historical formation of a modern capitalistic and democratic society, our Confucian tradition, with its emphasis on self-cultivation, self-discipline, and social order, turns out to be quite modern rather than premodern.

> In this respect, it is hardly surprising that newly industrialized East Asian countries that have the Confucian tradition in common are all enjoying remarkable economic development. . . . What is certain is that it can be no longer sustained that Confucianism is a premodern system of thought simply because it emphasizes authority and discipline. Even if discipline and authority may not provide a sufficient condition for modernization, at least it offers modernity's necessary condition.[48]

Here Hahm arrives at an odd conclusion from both the Foucauldian and his own postmodern Confucian perspectives. First of all, Hahm utilizes Foucault's postmodern critique of a modern disciplinary society in order to affirm the modern society and, more problematically, the developmental states in East Asia, most of which are only "democratic" in a minimal sense (as of 1998). The reason for this self-defeating conclusion results from Hahm's idiosyncratic understanding of Foucault's idea of the mutual constitution of modern individual and modern disciplinary society. While Foucault's intent with this idea is to launch a *political* critique of the inauthenticity of modern individuality, Hahm understands it as an *epistemological* and *historical* claim that modern individuality, which he now finds quite attractive because of the economic productivity with which it allegedly is associated, was (and is) possible only under a modern disciplinary society.

George Kateb, however, criticizes the thesis that sees society in terms of discipline in the Foucauldian spirit, the view that the state exists to transform superfluous or otherwise ungovernable masses into docile and productive creatures. He says,

> [Central to this idea] is what Foucault refers to as the problem of the modern plebs, the solution to which is the creation of order by the training and enlistment of energies that threaten gross disorder. Indeed, the overwhelming passion in [this idea] is a passion for order, for stillness, for regularity, for predictability, for a coherence that can exist only as the result of a drastic purification of human inclinations and actions, and a continued exercise of fundamentally undemocratic authority in every area of society.[49]

This is not to argue that we must embrace Kateb's normative argument that democracy must be a liberal democracy predicated on the idea of strong and authentic individuality (what he calls *democratic individuality*). At issue here is to explicate Hahm's unexpected affirmation of a modern disciplinary society through a Foucauldian postmodern critique of modernity.

Hahm's conclusion, even from his own idea of postmodern Confucianism, is also odd. As we have seen, for Hahm, premodern Confucianism possessed profound postmodern implications because of its intersubjective nature, and his critique of modernity was centered, almost singularly, on the idea of the absolute individual. In his conclusion, however, he is arguing that the absolute individual does not exist in reality and modern individuals are "modern" because they are radically situated in a variety of liberal institutions that form them into governable citizens by socially disciplining and normalizing them. There is no objection to the claim that there is no absolute individual, sociologically speaking. As a matter of fact, and contra Robert Nozick's libertarian depiction of John Locke's state of nature, no early modern social contractarians understood the state of nature and man's radical freedom in a sociological sense.[50] What is puzzling is, first, if modern man is not an absolute individual but a socially disciplined intersubjective being, then, there seems to have been no need for the postmodern critique of modernity; all we had to do was simply point out the apparent discrepancy between liberal democratic practices that are in reality *not* operating on or operate independently from the idea of the absolute man and the liberal onto-epistemology that is a mere scientific construct.

However, from the postmodern Confucian (or just Confucian) standpoint, what is more problematic is Hahm's failure to distinguish between Foucauldian self-discipline and Confucian self-cultivation (*xiushen* 修身). In *Discipline and Punish*, Foucault's most prominent concern was to deconstruct the idea of the modern man, whose individuality is formed through the normalizing processes in variegated social institutions, by revealing and critiquing the inauthenticity of individuality and sociality thus created. In Foucault's viewpoint, the liberal civility that modern society valorizes was in truth docility, and it was docile bodies that buttressed modern governmentality and political economy.[51]

Confucian self-cultivation aims at the exact opposite. The gist of Confucian self-cultivation lies in one's moral development and the achievement of sagehood. Most tellingly, in *Analects* 12:1, Confucius illustrates what Confucian self-cultivation involves:

> Yan Hui inquired about *ren* 仁 [Confucian virtue par excellence, often translated in English into benevolence or human-heartedness]. Confucius replied, "Through self-overcoming (*keji* 克己) and observing ritual propriety (*fuli* 復禮) one becomes

> *ren* in one's conduct. If for the space of a day one were able to accomplish this, the whole empire would return to *ren*. Becoming *ren* in one's conduct is self-originating (*youji* 由己)—how could it originate with others?"[52]

According to Confucius, Confucian self-cultivation consists of two parts: self-overcoming and observing ritual propriety. What Confucius actually meant by self-overcoming is a matter of some debate, but Neo-Confucians (such as Zhu Xi), on whom Hahm draws extensively on other occasions, understood it to mean overcoming one's selfish desires or self-centeredness.[53] Apparently, the modern disciplines that Foucault was highly critical of are not focused on the overcoming of selfish desires or self-centeredness, nor are they conducive to the formation of citizenship as Hahm argues. They only help *normalize* the self by depriving every individual's inner sphere, erasing individual distinctiveness, and transforming her into a docile subject. The result is not so much democratic citizenship as social conformism.

There have been more controversies regarding how to interpret the meaning of "observing ritual propriety"—self-effacing ritualism or a moral practice that involves a critical moral agency such as reflexivity and flexibility.[54] Without delving into a sophisticated scholarly debate on this issue, let me draw attention to Confucius's remark, which is directly relevant in our context, that "becoming *ren* in one's conduct is self-originating." Confucius's point is that Confucian self-cultivation is concerned with the authentic formation of the self and its continuous moral development in association with others. Self-originated, Confucian civility is, therefore, qualitatively different or even starkly opposed to institution-originated Foucauldian docility in which there is no room for individual moral agency and self-identity. Foucauldian docility involves no soulcraft, only a suffocation of the soul. By contrast, Confucian self-cultivation is concentrated precisely on soulcraft, though Confucians had a different understanding of the soul than that held by their Western counterparts.[55]

In the end, Hahm's postmodern Confucianism abandons its postmodern critical edge and his Confucian democracy turns out to be closely related to, almost analogous to, Confucian capitalism, for the success of which the governability of individual subjects is of critical importance.[56] The following statement presents Hahm's Confucian capitalist-democratic vision most succinctly and in a strikingly disillusioning tone.

> It is here that Korean traditional Confucianism can be presented as an alternative [to Western modern ontology and

> epistemology]. Korea is said to be a society that still operates on the basis of school, blood, and regional connections. And many intellectuals say that only when such premodern ways of thinking are abolished can a genuine liberal democracy prosper in Korea. . . . However, the worst problems or antinomies in modern political thought stem from the dissolution of "human relations." If the ideal society we picture in our minds is a more "humane" one, relationships based on school, blood, and regional origin must not be subject to blind demolition.[57]

In this understanding of Confucian capitalist-democracy, what is important is neither Confucian ethics nor democratic values, even though Hahm never actively disowns them. The only thing that remains in Hahm's postmodern Confucian democratic vision is a defense of the cronyism that undergirded Korea's developmental state and allegedly boosted the Korean economy during the 1970s and 1980s. Cronyism, often blamed as the premodern way of governance, is now valorized as a kind of ethical human relationship, rationalized in terms of postmodern Confucianism and Confucian democracy.[58] As Confucianism allows no liberating way out of existing social relations, in Hahm's ideal Confucian democratic society, citizens are expected to actively transform themselves into disciplined role-players. It is doubtful, however, whether there is any vision of, let alone a call for, a robust democratic citizenship in Hahm's political proposal. After all, premodern Confucianism never envisaged the sixth relationship, namely, the relationship among citizens, or civic relationships. While some Confucian democrats take pains to contrive and articulate this sixth relationship,[59] Hahm evidently does not seem to be troubled by its critical absence in his postmodern Confucian democracy.

Toward Confucian Democratic Citizenship

Those who were initially fascinated by Hahm Chaibong's postmodern and Confucian critique of modern epistemological and political theory were later frustrated by his failure to articulate a political theory of postmodern Confucianism and his active defense of East Asian developmentalism.[60] For many, it was far from clear how Hahm's idea of Confucian democracy is truly democratic and how the Confucian civilities that Hahm espoused could in practice be prevented from deteriorating into docility, democracy's worst enemy according to Alexis de Tocqueville. That is, while Hahm's postmodern

Confucianism seemed to provide an alternative conceptual framework to make sense of the Confucian capitalistic elements in economic developmentalism under the previous authoritarian regime, it could hardly help Koreans to come to terms with Korea's democratic development that began in the mid-1980s, characterized by one of the most socially vibrant and politically contentious civil societies among the new democracies after the third wave of democratization.[61] In short, Hahm's postmodern Confucianism was retrospectively evaluative but hardly prospectively in a democratic-political sense.

However, as many scholars have observed, Korean democratic civil society during and after democratization was galvanized not only by left political ideologies or doctrines, as commonly noted, but just as equally, perhaps even more so, by Confucian civic virtues, the virtues that enabled both intellectuals and ordinary citizens to boldly confront the authoritarian forces of the regime and force a drastic political reform.[62] Hardly educated in democratic theories and mostly unaware of what would eventually result from their "democratic" struggle (as we now call it), Koreans "aimed less to implement an abstract democratic ideal than to remedy evils experienced in consequence of prior political institutions."[63] Intellectuals, like their Neo-Confucian predecessors, saw themselves as representing public opinion (*gongnon/gonglun* 公論) and considered it their moral mission to rectify (*jeong/zheng* 正) the political leaders that had gone astray, which is the very definition of government (*jeong/zheng* 政) in traditional Confucian politics. Likewise, ordinary people took to the streets not necessarily in order to achieve a liberal democracy—most of them did not understand what liberal democracy means or what it consists of practically—but to pull down the autocratic government that brutally injured and even murdered university students whom they considered their own sons and daughters.

In short, the vitalizing energy of Korean democratization largely came from the Korean people's civic reappropriation of Confucian familialism. Though Koreans never consciously refuted the traditional Confucian idea that the state is the family-state, in their public mind, the state should no longer remain a hierarchical political entity in which a father-like ruler is supposed to take care of the children-like subjects. The traditional idea that government is the ruler's exclusive business was fundamentally revamped. What prevailed during and after democratization was the idea that government is the people's business and political leaders (particularly the president) must be elected by the people and should be held politically accountable to them throughout their tenure. Put differently, during this period, Koreans actively transformed themselves from people (*min* 民) who were once passive beneficiaries of the government's care into democratic citizens who govern themselves. Civil society emerged as a new home for Confucian familialism, now democratically reimagined: while still seeing themselves in Confucian familial terms, Koreans have learned that they are politically equal and free as citizens who share a common political fate.[64]

In this political milieu, Hahm's Confucian capitalistic justification for East Asian developmentalism did not sound so compelling to many, especially young, Korean democratic citizens, as they came to the realization that what is more important than economic growth is a free and equal democratic citizenship (or democratic self-determination) and democratic justice.

Hahm and company were right when they argued that the democracy to be consolidated in Korea should not necessarily be a liberal individualistic democracy but a Confucian democracy, a democracy that is grounded in and has respect for Korea's traditional Confucian culture, in which Koreans are still deeply soaked. After all, as John Dewey reminds us, democracy is profoundly concerned with the way of the collective/public life and as a way of life it cannot be established in a societal vacuum. This, however, does not mean that Confucian democracy must be predicated on traditional Neo-Confucian epistemology and moral cosmology as Hahm suggests, which is no longer tenable in the modern Korean democratic societal context. Not only are Koreans not "Confucian" in any strong traditional sense but, furthermore, Neo-Confucian epistemological and ethical monism does not seem to be able to come to terms with pluralism, which is increasingly characterizing social life in Korea. Therefore, if Confucian democracy were to have any meaning for Korean citizens, it must be able to generate and support a social practice in which democracy and Confucianism are mutually constraining, thus dialectically transforming, each other. In such a case, Confucianism must be reconstructed from what John Rawls calls a comprehensive moral doctrine into a set of civic virtues that are concerned with the sustenance of the democratic regime and the public freedom of the Korean citizenry. In other words, Korean democracy must be grounded in the Confucian habits of the heart of the Korean people, which are never static but constantly evolving and contestable.

In no case, however, can Confucian democracy be just another name for Confucian capitalism. For it to have public support, Confucian democracy must be centered on a robust democratic citizenship. Unfortunately, however, this was not the prominent concern of participants in the New Confucian movement in Korea. It is our turn and challenge to reimagine a Confucian democracy that is culturally relevant and politically practicable in Korea's postdemocratic context.

Notes

Sungmoon Kim is a professor in the Department of Public Policy, City University of Hong Kong, 83 Tat Chee Avenue, Kowloon, Hong Kong, Email:sungmkim@cityu.edu.hk. The author is grateful to P. J. Ivanhoe, Sung Ho Kim, and Doohwan Ahn for their comments on the earlier version of this chapter. The research for this chapter was supported by the National Research Foundation of Korea Grant funded by the Korean government (NRF-2014S1A3A2043763).

1. See Kang Xiaogang, *Renzheng: Zhongguo zhengzhi fazhan de disantiao daolu* (*Benevolent Rule: The Third Way for Chinese Political Development*) (Singapore: Global, 2005) and Jiang Qing, *Zhengzhi ruxue* (*Political Confucianism*) (Beijing: Sanlian shudian, 2003). Also see Daniel A. Bell, *Beyond Liberal Democracy: Political Thinking for an East Asian Context* (Princeton: Princeton University Press, 2006). For useful surveys of various constitutional reform suggestions by Confucian-minded scholars in greater China, see Albert H. Y. Chen, "Is Confucianism Compatible with Liberal Constitutional Democracy?" *Journal of Chinese Philosophy* 34 (2007): 195–216; and Peng Chengyi, "The New 'Romance of Three Kingdoms': The Competition of Three Constitutional Discourse for 21st Century China," PhD Dissertation, City University of Hong Kong, 2011, 72–87.

2. Bell, *Beyond Liberal Democracy*, 154.

3. Joseph Chan, "Moral Autonomy, Civil Liberties, and Confucianism," *Philosophy East and West* 52.3 (2002): 281–310; Sor-hoon Tan, *Confucian Democracy: A Deweyan Reconstruction* (Albany: State University of New York Press, 2004); Li Minghui, *Dangdai Ruxue zhi Ziwo Zhuanhua* (The Self-Transformation of Contemporary Confucianism) (Taipei: Academia Sinca, Wenzhesuo, 1994).

4. David L. Hall and Roger T. Ames, "A Pragmatist Understanding of Confucian Democracy," *Confucianism for the Modern World*, ed. Hahm Chaibong and Daniel A. Bell (Cambridge: Cambridge University Press, 2003), 143. Also see their *Democracy of the Dead: Dewey, Confucius, and the Hope for Democracy in China* (La Salle: Open Court, 1999).

5. On the Confucian contribution to Korean democratization and democratic consolidation, see Geir Helgesen, *Democracy and Authority in Korea* (Surrey: Curzon, 1998); Cho Hein, "The Historical Origin of Civil Society in Korea," *Korea Journal* 37.2 (1997): 24–41; Namhee Lee, *The Making of Minjung: Democracy and the Politics of Representation in South Korea* (Ithaca: Cornell University Press, 2007).

6. Doh Chull Shin and Chong-Min Park, "The Mass Public and Democratic Politics in South Korea: Exploring the Subjective World of Democratization in Flux," in *How East Asians View Democracy*, ed. Yun-han Chu, Larry Diamond, Andrew J. Nathan, and Doh Chull Shin (New York: Columbia University Press, 2008), 39–60.

7. Martina Deuchler, *The Confucian Transformation of Korea: A Study of Society and Ideology* (Cambridge: Harvard University Press, 1992).

8. Koh Byung-ik, "Confucianism in Contemporary Korea," in *Confucian Traditions in East Asian Modernity*, ed. Tu Weiming (Cambridge: Harvard University Press, 1996), 191–201.

9. These Korean New Confucians include Hahm Chaibong, Lew Seok-choon, Song Bok, Jang Hyeon-geun, and Kim Seok-geun, among others.

10. See, for instance, Lew Seok-choon, Chang Mi-hye, and Kim Tae-eun, "Affective Networks and Modernity: The Case of Korea," in *Confucianism for the Modern World*, 201–217.

11. See C. Fred Alford, *Think No Evil: Korean Values in the Age of Globalization* (Ithaca: Cornell University Press, 1999).

12. Hahm was the editor-in-chief of *Jeontong-gwa Hyeondae*. Hahm's idea of postmodern Confucianism is articulated in his *Talgeundae-wa Yugyo: Hangukjeong-chidamnon-ui mosaek* (Postmodernity and Confucianism: In Search of Korean Political Discourse) (Seoul: Nanamchulpan, 1998). The core argument of this book is recapitulated in English in Chaibong Hahm, "Postmodernism in the Post-Confucian Context: Epistemological and Political Considerations," *Human Studies* 24 (2001): 29–44.

13. This is not to say that Hahm represents the entire group of Confucian democrats. For instance, scholars such as Lee Seung-hwan, though also standing on the editorial board of *Jeontong-gwa Hyeondae*, strongly disagreed with Hahm's (and other Korean Confucians') rightist rendition and advocacy of Confucian democracy. See Lee's *Yugasasang-ui Sahoecheolhak-jeok jaejomyeong* (A Social Philosophical Reexamination of Confucian Thought) (Seoul: Korea University Press, 1998). In his subsequent work, Lee clearly distinguished himself from Hahm and company by calling his own Confucianism a "progressive Confucianism." See Lee Seung-hwan, *Yugyodamnon-ui Jihyeonghak* (A Typology of Confucian Discourse) (Seoul: Pureunsup, 2004).

14. Hahm Chaibong, *Yugyo, Jabonjuui, Minjujuui* (Confucianism, Capitalism, Democracy) (Seoul: Jeontong-gwa Hyeondae, 2000), 120.

15. Frederick Mote, *The Intellectual Foundations of China* (New York: Alfred A. Knopf, 1971), 94, quoted in Hahm, "Postmodernism in the Post-Confucian Context," 30.

16. Hahm, "Postmodernism in the Post-Confucian Context," 31.

17. The term "absolute individual" is originally coined by Alasdair MacIntyre. See his *A Short History of Ethics* (London: Routledge & Kegan Paul, 1967).

18. See Benjamin R. Barber, *Strong Democracy: Participatory Politics for a New Age*, twentieth anniversary ed. (Berkeley: University of California Press, 2003), 70.

19. Hahm, *Talgeundae-wa Yugyo*, 57.

20. Ibid., 109.

21. Ibid., 54.

22. See, for instance, Hall and Ames, *The Democracy of the Dead*, 216. On atomism, see Charles Taylor, "Atomism," in *Philosophy and the Human Sciences: Philosophical Papers 2* (Cambridge: Cambridge University Press, 1985), 187–210.

23. Ferdinand Tőnnies, *Community and Civil Society*, ed. Jose Harris, trans. Jose Harris and Margaret Hollis (Cambridge: Cambridge University Press, 2001), 52–91.

24. See Sungmoon Kim, "The Anatomy of Confucian Communitarianism: The Confucian Social Self and Its Discontent," *Philosophical Forum* 42.2 (2010): 118–119.

25. Benjamin R. Barber, *Fear's Empire: War, Terrorism, and Democracy* (New York: Norton, 2003), 88–91.

26. Michel Foucault, *The Order of Things: An Archaeology of the Human Sciences* (New York: Vintage Books, 1994), 386–397. The fuller version of this passage is quoted in Hahm, *Talgeundae-wa Yugyo*, 42.

27. Hans-Georg Gadamer, *Truth and Method* (New York: Crossroad, 1982), 230, quoted in Hahm, "Postmodernism in the Post-Confucian Context," 40.

28. See chapter 1 of Hahm's *Talgeundae-wa Yugyo*, titled "Postmodeoniseum-gwa Geundae jeongchi sasang" (Postmodernism and Modern Political Thought).

29. Hahm, "Postmodernism in the Post-Confucian Context," 40.

30. Ibid., 41. The reference to Heidegger is from Martin Heidegger, *Basic Problems of Phenomenology*, trans. Albert Hofstadter (Bloomington: Indiana University Press, 1982).

31. Hahm, *Talgeundae-wa Yugyo*, 52.

32. Ibid., 258.

33. Ibid., 260.

34. Hahm, "Postmodernism in the Post-Confucian Context," 36. A similar argument is found in Hwa Yol Jung, "Confucianism as Political Philosophy: A Postmodern Perspective," *Human Studies* 16 (1993): 213–230.

35. Hahm, *Talgeundae-wa Yugyo*, 261.

36. Hahm Chaibong, "Family versus the Individual: The Politics of Marriage Laws in Korea," in *Confucianism for the Modern World*, 358. Please note that this is Hahm's claim and I do not intend to say that this view is a generalizable truth. Most tellingly, John Stuart Mill's *The Subjection of Women* and Susan M. Okin's *Justice, Gender, and the Family* strongly vindicate liberalism's strong moral commitment to the family. In his critique of the Western "bias" on the family, however, Hahm largely glosses over the liberal-feminist reconceptualization of the family in modern and contemporary Western political theory and merely focuses on classical and modern-contractarian views of the family that liberal feminists equally criticize.

37. Hahm Chaibong, "Ga-ui Inyeom-gwa Cheje" (The Ideal and Institution of the Confucian Family), *Jeontong-gwa Hyeondae* 14 (2000): 73–114. Also see Hahm Chaibong, "The Ironies of Confucianism," *Journal of Democracy* 15.3 (2004): 98–102.

38. Hahm, *Talgeundae-wa Yugyo*, 268.

39. Hahm, "Postmodernism in the Post-Confucian Context," 43.

40. In various places, Hahm emphasizes the monistic nature of Neo-Confucianism and its postmodern implications. See Hahm, *Talgeundae-wa Yugyo*, 261–269;

"Postmodernism in the Post-Confucian Context," 33–37; "The Confucian Political Discourse and the Politics of Reform in Korea," *Korea Journal* 37.4 (1997): 69–72.

41. Certainly, Hahm does not dismiss the value of ethical pluralism, but it remains a puzzle how Neo-Confucian monism can accommodate ethical pluralism, without undergoing a substantive internal reconstruction. It should be remembered that during the late Chosŏn dynasty, the heyday of Neo-Confucianism in Korea, those who upheld values different from the Neo-Confucian Dao were blamed as the despoilers of the Way and often persecuted. See Martina Deuchler, "Despoilers of the Way—Insulters of the Sages: Controversies over the Classics in Seventeenth-Century Korea," in *Culture and the State in Late Chosŏn Korea*, ed. JaHyun Kim Haboush and Martina Deuchler (Cambridge: Harvard University Asia Center, 1999), 91–113.

42. Hahm, "Postmodernism in the Post-Confucian Context," 43.

43. In Hahm's understanding, the authoritarian state is the state that arbitrarily or undemocratically yields power. He clearly opposes such a state. Instead, Hahm, drawing on the Oakeshottian and Arendtian distinction between power and authority, supports what can be called an "authoritative state," a state that has a moral authority. For him, the Confucian state under a virtuous ruler offers a paradigmatic case of the authoritative state. See Hahm, *Talgeundae-wa Yugyo*, 299–319.

44. Michel Foucault, "Truth and Power," in *Power/Knowledge: Selected Interviews & Other Writings, 1972–1977*, ed. Colin Gordon (New York: Pantheon Books, 1980), 119, quoted in Hahm, *Talgeundae-wa Yugyo*, 291.

45. Hahm, *Talgeundae-wa Yugyo*, 290.

46. Ibid., 293.

47. Ibid., 294 (a bit paraphrased when translated into English).

48. Ibid., 298. For reference to Gerhard Oestreich, see his *Neostoicism and the Early Modern State*, ed. Brigitta Oestreich and H. G. Koenigsberger, trans. David McLintock (Cambridge: Cambridge University Press, 1982).

49. George Kateb, *The Inner Ocean: Individualism and Democratic Culture* (Ithaca: Cornell University Press, 1992), 125.

50. Put differently, for them, the state of nature held a normative meaning. On this point, see John Dunn, *The Political Thought of John Locke: An Historical Account of the Argument of the "Two Treatises of Government"* (Cambridge: Cambridge University Press, 1969) and Jeremy Waldron, *God, Locke, and Equality: Christian Foundations in Locke's Political Thought* (Cambridge: Cambridge University Press, 2002).

51. Michel Foucault, "Governmentality," in *The Foucault Effect: Studies in Governmentality*, ed. Graham Burchell, Colin Gordon, and Peter Miller (Chicago: University of Chicago Press, 1991), 87–104.

52. For the English translation, I referred to Roger T. Ames and Henry Rosemont, *The Analects of Confucius: A Philosophical Translation* (New York: Ballantine Books, 1998), but I have made some modifications.

53. Daniel K. Gardner, *Zhu Xi's Reading of the* Analects: *Canon, Commentary, and the Classical Tradition* (New York: Columbia University Press, 2003), 79–80.

54. The former position (i.e., self-effacing ritualism) is presented most famously by Herbert Fingarette in his *Confucius: The Secular as Sacred* (New York: Harper, 1972). Recently, however, an increasing number of scholars are subscribing to the latter position. See, for instance, Kwong-loi Shun, "*Jen* and *Li* in the *Analects*," *Philosophy East and West* 43.3 (1993): 457–479; Sin Yee Chan, "The Confucian Notion of *Jing* 敬 (Respect)," *Philosophy East and West* 56.2 (2006): 229–252; Karyn Lai, "*Li* in the *Analects*: Training in Moral Competence and the Question of Flexibility," *Philosophy East and West* 56.1 (2006): 69–83.

55. In his later works such as *The Care of the Self* (New York: Vintage Books, 1986), Foucault explored an alternative mode of self-discipline that involves soulcraft by thoroughly examining the ancient Greco-Roman technologies of the self. Relying on these works and Foucault's later interviews, Hahm argues that there is a great parallel between Confucian self-cultivation and ancient Greco-Roman technology of the self. See his "Confucian Rituals and the Technology of the Self: A Foucaultian Interpretation," *Philosophy East and West* 51.3 (2001): 315–324. I think this is a plausible claim that deserves a more serious comparative philosophical investigation. There are two problems with Hahm's thesis: first, Hahm fails to differentiate between the modern discipline that Foucault critiqued in his early works and the ancient discipline in which he saw an ethical alternative to a modern individuality; and second, Hahm misinterprets Confucian self-cultivation as involving no soulcraft by misunderstanding that Confucian ritual practice is solely concerned with one's body (*shen* 身) but not one's soul (so-called *xin* 心 in Confucian moral-psychological terminology). Surprisingly, though upholding his postmodern Confucianism by reiterating Neo-Confucian epistemology and moral cosmology, Hahm completely dismisses the moral individualism integral to Neo-Confucian ethics and moral psychology. On moral individualism in Neo-Confucianism, see William Theodore de Bary, *The Liberal Tradition in China* (New York: Columbia University Press, 1983).

56. Also see Son Byong-hae, *Yugyomunhwa-wa Dongasia Gyeongje* (Confucian Culture and East Asian Economy) (Deagu: Kyungpook National University Press, 2006).

57. Hahm, *Talgeundae-wa Yugyo*, 275. The English translation is consulted with Seong Hwan Cha, "Myth and Reality in the Discourse of Confucian Capitalism in Korea," *Asian Survey* 43.3 (2003): 499.

58. For a further discussion of the cronyism-based Confucian democracy by Korean New Confucians, see Lew Seok-choon, "Dongasi 'Yugyo Jabonjuui' Jaehaeseok (East Asian 'Confucian Capitalism' Revisited), *Jeontong-gwa Hyundae* 3 (1997): 124–145.

59. See Fred R. Dallmayr, "Confucianism and the Public Sphere: Five Relationships Plus One?" in *The Politics of Affective Relations: East Asia and Beyond*, ed. Hahm Chaihark and Daniel A. Bell (Lanham: Lexington Books, 2004); Sungmoon

Kim, "Beyond Liberal Civil Society: Confucian Familialism and Relational Strangership," *Philosophy East and West* 60.4, (2010): 476–498.

60. Hahm's active defense of East Asian economic developmentalism is found in "Asia-jeok Gachinonjaeng-ui Gukjecheongchihak" (The International Politics of the Asian Values Debate), in *Yugyo, Jabonjuui, Minjujuui*, 65–115.

61. For an empirical study supporting this claim, see Sunhyuk Kim, "South Korea: Confrontational Legacy and Democratic Contributions," in *Civil Society and Political Change in Asia: Expanding and Contracting Democratic Space*, ed. Muthiah Alagappa (Stanford: Stanford University Press, 2004), 138–163.

62. In addition to the works cited in note 5, see my "Confucianism in Contestation: The May Struggle of 1991 in South Korean and Its Lesson," *New Political Science* 31.1 (2009): 49–68.

63. This quotation is from Ian Shapiro, *Democratic Justice* (New Haven: Yale University Press, 1999), 2.

64. For a more detailed discussion of the Confucian nature of the post-democratic civil society in Korea, see my "On Korean Dual Civil Society: Thinking through Tocqueville and Confucius," *Contemporary Political Theory* 9.4 (2010): 434–457.

7

The Experience of Village Leaders during the *Saemaul* Movement in the 1970s

Focusing on the Lives of the Male Leaders

Do-Hyun Han

The *Saemaul* (New Village or New Community) movement was a social and economic initiative developed and implemented by South Korean president Park Chung-Hee on April 22, 1970. The program was inspired and partially based upon the model of the *hyang'yak* (Community Compact), a written agreement enforced by local scholars and officials that afforded a degree of local autonomy and functioned as informal common law in traditional Korean society. This historical connection, which often is completely unknown or overlooked, is important for appreciating the degree to which this modernization movement was modeled and depended upon traditional, largely Confucian values, orientations, and practices.

The primary aim of the *Saemaul* movement was to improve life in the countryside by developing local infrastructure, raising the standard of living, and instilling a spirit of entrepreneurial independence, local solidarity, cooperation, and pride among rural villagers. While initially aimed exclusively at rural development, the movement was successful, leading to its expansion into industrial and urban contexts and its transformation into a comprehensive national modernization campaign. This essay explores this important Korean social movement from the first-person perspective of village leaders who participated in it during the 1970s. It illustrates the extent to which the underlying structure and subsequent success of the *Saemaul* movement depended directly and critically upon the underlying traditional Confucian beliefs, commitments, and practices of those who carried it forward. The

Confucian orientation and values of those who participated in the *Saemaul* movement provided both the initial motivation and sustaining perseverance required to implement this large-scale and dramatic social initiative. These Confucian habits of the heart also guided the approach and style not only of those who planned the movement but the activities of those who carried it out.

Forefathers of the *Saemaul* movement were compared to the Pilgrim fathers of New England. Although *Saemaul* leaders worked for the economic betterment of themselves and their villagers, their sacrifice and devotion remind those who read about their contributions of the religious dimension of this national campaign. This distinctively Korean religious dimension, which can be found throughout the national campaign of the *Saemaul* movement, comes from Confucianism. In the campaign and records of *Saemaul* leaders, phrases such as the Promised Land, New Jerusalem, Chosen People, among others, which are like those found in American civil religion,[1] are not to be missed. Those expressions appear without their original Christian connotations but in Confucian terms and as expressions of developmentalism. Confucian traditions still work in various ways both in rural and urban Korea. According to a survey from 1999, even young radicals in South Korea surprisingly are favorable to essential elements of Confucian traditions.[2] Another survey of 2013 concludes that even people of their twenties and thirties say "traditional values are important for Korean social development."[3] Without this Confucian civil religion, it would be almost impossible to understand the sacrifice and wholehearted commitment of village leaders for the national goal of rural transformation.

Without the village leaders, the *Saemaul* movement would likely have been nothing more than a government slogan or short-term campaign. They were first cultivated as "a best farmer" and then as "a transformational leader"[4] who transformed their fellow villagers and revolutionized rural Korea. These ideas, of the need for self-transformation and the profound transformational influence proper leaders have upon those around them, are characteristically Confucian in nature. *Saemaul* leaders were charged with creating faith in developmentalism and carrying out corresponding projects as a sort of "entrepreneur."[5] They, however, were not just the machinery of modern developmentalism. Instead, they knew the habits of heart that motivated their villages and transformed these into forms appropriate for a modern age.

Although many recognize the significance of the *Saemaul* leaders, there is little scholarly research to reflect this in reality. Regarding research on individual roles in the movement, there is Jin-Hwan Park[6] as well as Se-

Yeong Lee's autobiography.[7] There is also the research of Jeong-Mi Yoo; Seung-Mi Han; Mi-Kyung Chang; Byeong-Yong Yu, Bong-Dae Choi, and Yoo-Seok Oh; Dae-Young Kim; Won Koh; among others, but none provide a comprehensive image of the *Saemaul* leaders.[8]

Research regarding the *Saemaul* leaders is still in its infant stages. Only Yoo-Seok Oh's team has stepped forward to take charge of the collective effort to construct a *Saemaul* movement archive, to which the collection of oral testaments of *Saemaul* leaders will likely make a major contribution in the future.[9]

Research Method and Data

Since there were one male and one female leader per village, one can estimate that there were about seventy thousand *Saemaul* leaders operating at one time. In principle, these leaders were elected annually at the village assembly, but since tenure lasted about three years,[10] there would have been more than two hundred thousand village leaders during the 1970s in Korea.

As Yang-Bu Choi points out, the majority of existing research concerning *Saemaul* leaders is socio-technological.[11] For example, Sun-Gyu Kim and colleagues emphasize the necessity to build *Saemaul* leaders into an elite, while discussing how to instill them with a sense of duty and fervor.[12] Jong-Seop Kim and colleagues also provide a similar context.[13] Since a *Saemaul* leadership position was unpaid, these scholars stressed the need to earnestly consider a system for promoting a fighting spirit, while proposing an alternative motivation policy involving both internal (values, intensity of attitudes) and external motivations (strengthening of social acknowledgment, payment system). Scholars working in such fields as the science of public administration or the discourse over farm village leadership employ the same way of thinking.

Mobilizing social science and women studies theory in order to analyze the character, education, and other qualities of *Saemaul* leaders is a relatively recent phenomenon. Among others, the research of Jeong-Mi Yoo, Mi-Kyung Chang, Byeong-Yong Yu and colleagues, Seung-Mi Han, Do-Hyun Han, and Yeong-Mi Kim best represent this trend.[14] Their research has largely utilized memoirs and oral accounts. Oral history is a record of people's memories, permeated by the experiences of the unique lives therein, making it a living, breathing history.[15] More than policy and socioeconomic analysis, in order to understand the firsthand experience of the participants, oral materials possess a major advantage.

Although this essay employs oral history, allowing for costs and time, it has selected only ten *Saemaul* village leaders as subjects. In order to select these participants, primary sources stored at the History Hall in the Central *Saemaul* Undong Training Institute, such as listed success cases and the registry of reward recipients, were examined. During the process of selecting oral subjects, Vice President Kab-Jin Jeong of the *Saemaul* Undong Central Training Institute (retired in 2008), as well as former *Saemaul* training institute instructor Mr. Ki-Myeong Kim, were a great help.

For the sake of logistics, former *Saemaul* leaders in Gyeonggi and Chungcheong provinces were selected for interviews. Thus, since among the hundreds of thousands of former leaders existing all over the country only ten were interviewed from the Gyeonggi and Chungcheong regions, this research cannot claim to rely upon the kind of representative sampling typically demanded of sociological surveys. Moreover, since this research deals only with leaders involved in successful *Saemaul* projects, it does not account for the experiences of those who were not.

Outside the ten participants listed here, this essay also employs the testimony of Sa-Yong Ha. His testament is located in the archives of the National Institute of Korean History and was recorded in 2004. All other oral materials were recorded over the period of October to November in 2008.

Transformational Leadership: The Leadership Qualities of *Saemaul* Leaders

As the figures engaging in face-to-face interaction with villagers most affected by the *Saemaul* movement, along with the traditional village heads, the *Saemaul* leaders could be called ground-level leaders. A "ground-level leader" or grassroots leader is an exemplary and devoted leader who lives among the people. As demonstrated by the likes of Se-Yeong Lee, Yeong-Mo Yu, Jae-Yong Lee, and Sa-Yong Ha before the *Saemaul* movement was fully under way in the 1970s, a considerable number of *Saemaul* leaders were already acting as leaders in rural modernization projects, or at the very least providing the foundations for their implementation.[16] Thus, as Yeong-Mi Kim asserts, the fact that these elected leaders existed at the outset of the movement and continually led the way thenceforth was a major contribution to the ultimate success of the *Saemaul* movement.[17] However, although prior to the *Saemaul* movement these leaders excelled in farming, most of village leaders of thirty-five thousand villages were intensively educated and

Table 7.1. Background Information on the Interviewees

Alias (year of birth)	*Education*	*Administrative Area*	*Major Work Experience*	*Medals*
X-Gi Choi (1935)	Elementary	OO Village, Gongdo Township, Anseong County, Gyeonggi Province	Village Head, County Chair of Agricultural Cooperative	Effort Award
X-Il Hong (1933)	Elementary	OO Village, Namsa Township, Yongin County, Gyeonggi Province	Village Head, Township Mayor	Self-Help Award
X-Mok Lim (1934)	High School	OO Village, Daehoji Township, Dangjin County, South Chungcheong Province	Township Official (temporary)	Effort Award
X-Geun Han (1927)	Elementary	OO Village, Seokmun Township, Dangjin County, South Chungcheong Province	Village Head	Diligence Award
X-Gyu Jeon (1929)	Elementary	OO Village, Yugu Township Gongju County, South Chungcheong Province	Korea Young Men's Association, Village Head	Cooperation Award
X-Heon Yun (1930)	Elementary	OO Village, Yeonsan Township, Nonsan County, South Chungcheong Province	Rural Volunteer Leader (County Chairman)	*Saemaul* Award
X-Sun Lim (1926)	University	OO Village, Dongi Township, Okcheon County, North Chungcheong Province	Chairman of *Saemaul* Movement Associations of Okcheon County	*Saemaul* Award

continued on next page

Table 7.1. *(continued)*

Alias (year of birth)	*Education*	*Administrative Area*	*Major Work Experience*	*Medals*
X-Ryeon Kim (1943)	High School	OO Village, Boeun Township, Boeun County, North Chungcheong Province	County Official	Effort Award
0-Mo Yu (1942)	University	OO Village, Cheongpung Township, Jaecheon County, North Chungcheong Province	Chair, Cooperative Agriculture (Icheon, Gyeonggi Province), Regional Director at the Central *Saemaul* Undong Training Institute	Effort Award
X-Weon Lee (1950)	University	OO Village, Gonggeun Township, Hwengseong County, Gangweon Province	High School Teacher, Employee of Korean Federation of Livestock Cooperatives	Effort Award

trained during the *Saemaul* movement. It was through this education that these existing leaders strengthened their leadership qualities. Those leaders sacrificed themselves for the development of their villages and the welfare of their fellow villagers. In them the habit of heart, spirit of community, could be best found.[18]

If one were to meet these key players in the success stories of the 1970s, one would certainly have trouble calling them typical leaders. Rather, one might perceive them as simple country folk. Indeed, ground-level leadership in other countries shares this trait as well.[19] However, it was this very approachability and humility that was the *Saemaul* leaders' greatest strength. They looked upon their achievements as "nothing special" or "insignificant," always careful not to display unnecessary pride.[20] The attitude of being "nothing special" is an important asset for leaders of a community. As Seung-Mi Han described, this kind of leadership was well suited to the egalitarian rural polices proposed by President Park Chung-Hee.[21] The leaders did not have to be extraordinary but simply those already living among the rural folk. Thus, by selecting from among the rural villagers for its *Saemaul* leaders, the government was able to instill the spirit of the *Saemaul* movement within the very roots of society. Under the ordering principle of "better living," the habits of heart such as diligence, self-help, and cooperation were the key elements of the spirit of the *Saemaul* movement. Furthermore, this strategy of choosing ordinary farmers provided flexibility to meet the unique challenges of each village. As Anderson points out, within each village, and within each venture, since the characteristics therein were unique, the leadership of the village "had to be continually redefined to meet changing contexts."[22]

Participating in the movement, the *Saemaul* leaders each experienced a self-transformation and became the proselytizers of this phenomenon in turn. After receiving their preparatory training and education, some *Saemaul* leaders would claim things like, "This has had the deepest and most unforgettable impact on my life," as well as, "There is a throbbing sense of duty in my chest," before returning home to their villages.[23] Clearly, the *Saemaul* education was not a simple conveyance of knowledge but a solemn process whereby those involved were so deeply connected that, during the lectures, some among them would be moved to tears.[24] In sum, "When one claims that the *Saemaul* movement was something that created new people, it means that it created people with new values, new ways of thinking, and a new code by which to live, so as to completely remodel oneself."[25]

It was not only the leaders that were transformed but the people as well. This process is reflected in the phrase "teaching and learning to grow together" (K. *Kyohaksangjang*; C. *jiao xue xiang zhang* 敎學相長), which indicates the demand for relationships to be dialectical, mutual interactions. This interactive process entailed a drastic change in the behavior and values of those involved. Burns labeled this phenomenon "transformational leadership"; the elevation of motives and ethics to a higher level is the particular characteristic of transformational leadership.[26] Holding the goal of village development in mind, *Saemaul* leaders used transformational leadership to transform the attitudes or value orientation of the villagers. It is the expression of one of the four principles of the community compact, that is, the mutual encouragement of virtuous acts. Thus, these leaders surely did not simply exist to passively enforce policies in the village handed down by the government.

The Realm of Experience of Transformational Leaders

Becoming Leaders by Saemaul *Education*

At the outset of the *Saemaul* movement, there existed traditional leaders within the villages, such as the village administrative heads or local people of influence. As the movement progressed, a portion of these traditional leaders also became *Saemaul* leaders, though many leaders were recruited from common ranks as well. The traditional village head was a representative of the administration located on the frontline, providing a link between the local government and the people. Although these leaders received a regular salary, in contrast, *Saemaul* leaders were unpaid volunteers. The concept of having an unpaid volunteer leader was quite innovative. Furthermore, traditional village leaders, that is, village administrative heads, had never received any kind of formal leadership training, and their plan for organization management was not well defined. *Saemaul* leaders, on the other hand, would receive systematic leadership training, as well as training concerning the establishment of a clear vision for organization management and goal achievement. In other words, taking into consideration that the *Saemaul* leaders learned the "science of organizational management" to become "organization leaders," they could easily be differentiated from the traditional administrative village leaders of the past. Nevertheless, despite these modern additions, the training of *Saemaul* leaders built upon deep and long-standing conceptions and practices drawn from the Confucian tradition. The *Saemaul* volunteers saw themselves as engaged in a modern form of moral self-cultivation that was aimed at developing them into leaders who would transform their local communities and society as a whole into a new and flourishing order. From the start and throughout, the *Saemaul* movement was a moral enterprise aimed at enhancing the common good; those who volunteered to be its leaders were regarded as the vanguard of this enterprise. Like traditional Confucian "gentlemen," *Saemaul* leaders were not only to instruct but inspire, by deed, word, and personal example, a larger social transformation.

The education of *Saemaul* leaders took place at the Central *Saemaul* Leaders Training Institute, as well as extensively at the county and provincial levels. Over the course of the 1970s, over six hundred thousand leadership figures, coming from all walks of life, received education at the training institute.[27] If one intended to enter the *Saemaul* Leaders Training institute, one first had to be selected as the leader of an outstandingly successful village within a particular county.[28] Thus, by completing training at the Central *Saemaul* Training Institute and becoming a *Saemaul* leader, one would occupy a considerably honorable position whereby one could receive priority when financial assistance for *Saemaul* projects was distributed. In his book entitled *The* Saemaul *Movement of Pungdeok Village*, Se-Yeong Lee boasted, "Word came from the county office on September 29th that I was nominated for *Saemaul* leadership education at the Central *Saemaul* Leaders Training Institute,"[29] and "shortly after returning home on October 11th, on October 13th, I bragged about the training process I had undergone at the training institute to fellow villagers as well as to the Village Development Committee."[30]

In order to modernize rural areas, President Park recognized the need for leadership at the village level. Stressing this necessity, President Park Chung-Hee ventured so far as to say that if there were even as little as one highly effective leader per county, the ripple effect would create radical change in the structure of rural society.[31]

X-Ryeon Kim described his experience at the *Saemaul* Leaders Training Institute as a trainee of the second session in 1972:

> There was never anything like that education before. It was like being in the military, getting up every morning on the double. But there were rewards too. When noble women such as the wives of the ministers, vice ministers, and their entourage came to prepare meals for us trainees, it was very rewarding. Since the orders came from President Park at the Blue House, those ladies came to cook for us. It was really honorable.[32]

Those who received education at the *Saemaul* Leaders Training Institute praised the content of the education they received. X-Gyu Jeon described what this education meant to him:

> If anybody wants to be engaged in the *Saemaul* movement, he has to be educated at the *Saemaul* Leaders Training Institute. Only through the education at the *Saemaul* Leaders Training Institute can he be a true *Saemaul* leader. That's what I think.[33]
>
> During the education process I've had a lot of feelings. It's like a blast furnace, but with people instead of iron. The *Saemaul* Leaders Training Institute is a kind of blast furnace where we're reborn.[34]

As the vice governor of his county put him on the list of trainees at the *Saemaul* Leaders Training Institute without his consent, X-Weon Lee complained, "I was forced to go." Thus, though at first he reluctantly entered the *Saemaul* Leaders Training Institute, after attending classes, he remarked, "I sat down and right way I was totally absorbed."[35] Among the leaders of the early 1970s, compared to other *Saemaul* leaders, X-Weon Lee was a highly educated person, and although he had majored in agriculture at university, the *Saemaul* training was so impressive as to command his complete and full attention. Following his completion of the program, he promised, "Now that I've finally completed my education, as long as I live in the countryside, for the sake of our nation, I'll participate in this kind of valuable, meaningful work."[36]

At first, the *Saemaul* Leaders Training program was two weeks long, but starting from the eighth session in July of 1973 and lasting until the eighty-sixth session of December 1979, it was reduced to ten days and eleven nights.[37] The curriculum was composed of subjects like agricultural technology, agricultural cooperatives, *Saemaul* projects, *Saemaul* spiritual education, success stories, and group discussion, with trainees showing particular interest in the success stories, *Saemaul* spiritual education, and group discussion classes.[38] Through these subjects, *Saemaul* leaders became proficient in various useful organizational skills, involving cooperative organization, techniques for leading farmers, how to be a leader, and the spiritual revolution of cooperative work. During the group discussion class, trainees dealt with a number of subjects concerning organization management, including how to create desirable leadership, how to instill in people a sense of community involvement, how to create a *Saemaul* movement execution plan, and how to maintain the vitality of this plan.[39] Moreover, with practical skills like how to raise income, how to engage in environmental improvement, and how to manage village funds, subjects such as organization management showed participants how to display leadership as well. Thus, by learning organization management, leaders acquired the skills necessary to mobilize the participation of their fellow villagers in the *Saemaul* project, as well as to mediate conflicts therein.[40] In short, the trainees cultivated the kind of organization management skills that meant "[they] were no longer individuals, but a group branded to begin new lives as leaders."[41]

The group discussion class was particularly helpful because it encompassed practical management issues, helping *Saemaul* leaders confront the realities of organization management. The class would concentrate on discussions concerning solving problems encountered in the process of executing *Saemaul* projects, proceeding with discussions concerning an overarching theme, a subtheme, and on to reasons for choosing the subtheme to be discussed under the overarching theme, defining problems to be solved (diagnosis of phenomena), an execution plan, and finally a conclusion.[42]

The group discussion class of the twenty-first session of the *Saemaul* Leaders Training course of October of 1974 is worth examining in detail. Here, in the second discussion class of the session, the instructor was Ki-Myeong Kim, the class president was Chun-Man Lee, the secretary was Weon-Sang Lim, and the total number of trainees was seventeen. The overarching theme was that of creating a development plan for sustainable *Saemaul* projects, while the subtheme concerned what kind of leader might best increase villagers' income. The discussion proceeded in stages. First, the characteristics of a leader conducive to increasing rural income were critically examined. Next, identifying six foreseeable problems, the specifics of each of these problems were further divided four to seven ways. In this manner, the participants came up with solutions for the specific problems presented. Finally, they finished by writing a final conclusion. This particular class's conclusion read, "Up until now, we believed that village leaders had performed their duties in a proud and worthy manner, but through our education at the leadership training institute, we have discovered their many deficiencies."[43] Looking at the record of this particular class, it is apparent how members intended to diagnose and create concrete and critically examined solutions, as well as how the process provided an opportunity to allow them to reflect on themselves and learn from each other. The method of education was not by ideological indoctrination or one-sided lecturing but by mutual learning and self-reflection. Mutual learning and self-reflection is well expressed in the practices of the Community Compact: mutual correcting of wrongdoings. This process was so effective that the firsthand experience of the graduates from this group discussion class later appeared in letters sent to the director of the *Saemaul* Leaders Training Institute by *Saemaul* leaders. For instance, Sang-Gil Lee, from Chungmu County in Gyeongnam Province and a graduate of the twenty-fifth session, declared, "There were many days when we went past midnight in the group discussion class, but it was a spirited education that made me feel reborn."[44]

The education of the *Saemaul* leaders did not finish with training received at the *Saemaul* Leaders Training Institute but was complemented by guidance in the form of follow-up and correspondence and coexisted with education at the city, county, and provincial levels. Within the *Saemaul* leader education program, leaders from exemplary villages would become lecturers, traveling from village to village presenting the success stories of the *Saemaul* movement. These exceptionally successful characters became inspirational mentors to their fellow farmers. Meanwhile, visits to successful villages by graduates were continuous as well. Located in Anseong, Gyeonggi Province, X-Gi Choi's village was designated as exemplary by the Minister of Home Affairs, and as such, graduates would, "finish their education and hop on the training bus," coming in droves, where during a single month as many as 1,200 people visited.[45] These visitors would come to see the conditions conducive to success, with comments like: "Although I've thought of myself as a leader, I haven't accomplished anything like this," as they reflected on their own efforts.[46]

The Planning and Realization of Village Development

Proposing a Vision: A Village of Progress

The *Saemaul* leaders were resolute to improve their villages. The improvement of village life was the goal of the Community Compact. *Saemaul* leaders actively proposed a new vision in their villages for the development of villagers' welfare.

Although it was true that from the colonial era the rural areas had undergone great changes with the penetration of modern capital and bureaucracy,[47] through the *Saemaul* movement, transformation took place at a more qualitative level. The *Saemaul* movement was based on principles of developmentalism like "better living" and increasing non-farm cash income. Clearly, these kinds of goals were not meant as an escape from the market economy but as a mechanism of expansive development of the market economy. This is what differentiates the *Saemaul* movement from the romantic agrarianism or anti-urbanism of the "agriculture first" principle.[48]

If we refer to 1970s Korea as a developmental state, then we might also refer to the villages of the *Saemaul* movement as "developmental villages."

The ones working on the scene in these developmental villages, putting plans into motion, were none other than the *Saemaul* leaders.

> When we no longer farm simply to survive, but to create surplus income, we can no longer refer to that as farming for survival. It's agricultural enterprise. If one engages in agricultural enterprise, one can earn more money and live better. That's why I was saying we needed to engage in agricultural enterprise, not "farming." That's what I'd been saying since the 1960s. But finally in the 1970s, while participating in the *Saemaul* movement, I could give lectures about this on a grand scale.[49]

This quotation is taken from the testimony of the enormously popular and legendary figure of the *Saemaul* movement, Sa-Yong Ha. Although he had not received a modern education, he was acutely aware of which direction to take rural development, as well as agricultural enterprise. Trailblazers like Mr. Ha existed in Korea during the 1960s,[50] and many of them later became the leaders of the *Saemaul* movement in the 1970s. As these pioneers united in the national *Saemaul* movement campaign, armed with the will to escape hardship and overthrow poverty, they undoubtedly rendered the *Saemaul* movement more than just a simple slogan.

X-Gyu Jeon stated, "Agricultural enterprise is a high-income venture on a new horizon." Planning to establish a "high-income venture" in his own village, Jeon even set out to investigate other "first-rate villages" for inspiration. At first, as recommended by a head of the *Saemaul* department in his county, he explored poultry farming. However, the foul odor was unbearable and he soon gave that up to focus on dairy farming instead. While the Ministry of Agriculture authorized two cows for every five hectares of grassland, as Jeon's village lay in the mountains, it could not receive dairy farming assistance. Thus, the villagers dug up all the mulberry trees meant for silkworm farming and planted corn. Then, Jeon met with the county governor, the vice county governor, and the provincial governor, persuading them to provide assistance. In addition, the village received aid from the Ministry of Agriculture-Forestry-Fisheries as well, allowing them to build fifty stables in the village and eventually rear five hundred cattle. X-Gyu Jeon comments, "For the nation to be rich and powerful, the people must live well. If the people live poorly, that is not a rich and powerful nation. Therefore, we have to live well. The first thing we have to do is live well. That's essential."[51]

After successfully introducing dairy farming, X-Gyu Jeon did not stop there, moving on to establish a deer ranch as well as a shiitake mushroom farm. Regarding this pioneering process, Jeon stated, "People must be in a complete state of frenzy for the *Saemaul* movement to work."[52]

After X-Ryeon Kim presented a successful story of the *Saemaul* project of his village at the Monthly Economic Trend Briefing held at the Blue House (Presidential Office), he was to receive a truck as a reward but insisted vehemently that the government build him a greenhouse instead. The request was granted, and in Kim's village, a 1,500 *pyeong* (4,958.7 sq. meters) greenhouse for farming chili peppers was constructed. Eventually, the village "made a fortune" selling chili pepper seedlings. Kim claimed that in the early 1970s, "There was no other place where one could get chili pepper seedlings."[53] Additionally, he declared that his was the first village to use a greenhouse for farming chili peppers as well. Bearing these achievements in mind, one might ascertain just how visionary a leader Kim was. Nevertheless, other leaders demonstrated similar successes. X-Mo Yu also raised chili peppers as a cash crop, to the extent that he toured the country giving lectures as an expert in the field.[54] X-Sun Lim increased his village's income through grape farming. Then there was X-Weon Lee, who established a "hop seedlings" class in his town, in order to "increase profits tremendously," which ended up a great benefit to the villagers. These cases, involving the likes of X-Weon Lee, X-Sun Lim, X-Gyu Jeon, and X-Ryeon Kim, never demonstrated "traditional farming for survival" but put forth a vision of "agricultural enterprise for good living" and succeeded. It was this clearly proposed vision that led to the success of not only these particular men but countless other successful *Saemaul* leaders as well. In their visions, the *Saemaul* leaders emphasize the economic welfare of the individual villagers, not benefits of the community or the country. By focusing on the economic welfare of individual villagers, the movement was able to avoid being the tool of political campaigns. In the Confucian tradition, "feeding the people" or the economic welfare of people was emphasized.[55]

Persuasion and Cooperation

The *Saemaul* leaders existed to communicate a vision to the villagers. Toward this end, the leader must first propose his vision. However, for its realization, participation of the villagers must be assured. While there were times when the people actively participated, there were also many times when they did not. Here, a leader must ceaselessly utilize his powers of persuasion and conflict management.

For the success of the *Saemaul* projects in his village, X-Gyu Jeon recognized the urgent necessity for road expansion. While most villages began with roof improvements, Jeon's was one of the few to first start with road expansion. Eventually, they expanded the farm road to a width of five meters and the village road to a width of four and a half meters. While this was quite a commendable expansion, the process was not without complication. That is, the need for capital for road expansion caused much conflict. First of all, the government did not have the money to purchase the land required for road expansion, which was owned by private individuals. While research existed claiming that land donations were a part of the "village community tradition" of the *Saemaul* movement, in reality, it was a difficult process that needed the tireless effort of persuasion. Jeon says:

> Even when they claimed not to oppose it, that was a lie. I would visit once, twice . . . twenty times until they would agree. Villagers would say things like, "You're just like a leech that won't let go." . . . I'd start with the land of owners who had move into the city. After observing the donation of former villagers in cities, villagers finally joined this donation drive.[56]

This quotation is loaded with examples of how Jeon exercised powers of persuasion to secure land donations from the people. First, Jeon received land from former villagers living in cities so as to build momentum. However, though ceaselessly working to persuade villagers to donate some of their land, some steadfastly refused. In these cases, Jeon would continue the road construction around them until they were "the only ones left," and they would finally give in out of guilt. Some old people living in the village would say to Jeon, "Do you think I gave up my land for nothing? I gave in because you worked so hard to persuade me."[57] To that extent, Jeon's persistent persuasion moved the hearts of the people. Regarding the power of persuasion, Jeon remarked that magnanimity was the essential element.

> For having friendly relationship with villagers, I frequently visited villagers and helped them make a fire for heating. Sometimes, I would say to them, "Hey, I'd like to have breakfast at your home here." It wasn't because I didn't have my own food, but because I wanted to mingle with and be close to them. And the villagers understood that.[58]

The *Saemaul* leader's ability to forge friendly relationships with the people was not only his essential virtue but his essential strategy as well.

For instance, since X-Mo Yu was quite a capable Go-Stop (Korean card game) player, he would gather up his pennies and teach the game to the locals, so as to get them on his side. Particularly, young people in their twenties and thirties were attracted by the game. In fact, it was the catalyst strengthening bonds between them, allowing Yu to create a core leadership team: "We would buy some liquor, meat, and tofu for an evening snack and sit down to learn the game. Eventually, we'd get to talking about successful *Saemaul* projects too. . . . As we bonded, I was able to persuade them of the importance of working together to improve our lives."[59]

After X-Mo Yu bonded with the young people over a game of Go-Stop, he would communicate to them his impressions of the National Convention of *Saemaul* Leaders or the lessons of successful villages, and then the young people would bond with the *Saemaul* movement as well. Using persuasion, he secured the unity of the young generation and was able to carry out roof improvement almost entirely without any coercion. Moreover, using the straw they had gleaned from thatched roofs for compost, that year saw a rich yield in chili pepper farming. Eventually, they improved the roofs, they widened the road, and the chili pepper farming went well, of which Yu remarks, "If I told them to jump they would ask how high."[60] Yu was an able leader who successfully mobilized his persuasion skills, civil engineering techniques, and chili pepper farming technology altogether. Furthermore, he also worked to persuade the village to get rid of a problematic local tavern. In this instance, he again put his wit into practice. First, he invited members of the village women's *Saemaul* association to a village meeting. He planned to use women's power to pressure men in the meeting. Knowing that people were uncomfortable raising their hands at meetings, he asked, "Those that oppose the removal of the tavern please raise your hands," and the majority of male attendees present were too ashamed to do so. Moreover, some male participants that did raise their hands, intuiting the cold disapproving glare of the village women, soon quietly put them down. In this manner, Yu acquired unanimous approval for getting rid of the problematic tavern. Finally, Yu utilized mechanisms of cooperation in the village to establish a pine mushroom cooperative organization, which led to an increase in agricultural income.[61]

Just as X-Mo Yu first forged strong bonds with young people in order to build a leadership team, X-Weon Lee did not at once gather all the people of the village together but worked to form a core leadership team first. Moreover, requiring the cooperation of the development committee, he did not attempt to face the seven members all at once but one at a time, "sitting down over a nice cup of *Makgeollie* (rice wine)."

> By building trust with a committee member, it would make him feel special. Then, I would sit down with the next one and do the same thing. I would ask them, "Do you care only for yourself? You should help others, shouldn't you?" In this way I had a man-to-man talk with each of the members before holding a general meeting with all of them together.[62]

In this manner, Lee employed a strategy of "defeating one by one" to persuade the members of the development committee.

What made this persuasion and cooperation possible was the traditional structure of Korean villages. Through the practices of the Confucian virtue of cooperation and community participation, villagers have cherished the solidarity among them. This sense of community was conducive to the donation of their private land for the improvement of their villages.

> The advent of the 1970s *Saemaul* movement marked the point at which farmers' eyes were opened. It was unbelievable. In the 1970s, everyone was completely self-motivated. With a shovel or a pick in hand they would come alive for the sake of the village. They got in high spirits. They widened the village roads by themselves. If the villagers wanted to do something for a better life, a village road wide enough for a power-tiller was needed. Then, if we needed to tear down the wall by my house to widen the road, so be it. So, I would donate this plot of my land for widening the village roads. I did it. These were not things we did because the government told us to. We did it for ourselves.[63]

The desire to make one's village better than the next one spread like wildfire among the people.

> The executives of the village development committee would make their donation toward the village *Saemaul* collection, and the villagers would gather in the village hall and engage in amicable debate regarding how to implement *Saemaul* projects. In any case, everybody agreed we had to stay ahead of the neighboring villages.[64]
>
> A message came from Jungwon County saying that the new phases in Yeonpung Township in Goesan County would likely be featured in the Monthly Economic Trend Briefing of May 1973. . . . Hearing about this news, villagers and members of

> the Women's *Saemaul* Association worked all the more enthusiastically to see through their own *Saemaul* projects.[65]

Of course, cooperation and persuasion were not always achieved without difficulty. In one case, a villager came at X-Geun Han, shouting, "I'll kill you!" While this is an extreme example, X-Muk Lim, X-Sun Lim, and X-Ryeon Lee all testify to the difficulty of persuading people. As X-Muk Lim describes, "When nothing else worked, I resorted to bullying, fighting, or whatever I could do. I would use a little coercion. I had no other choice."[66] In order to persuade people, X-Sun Lim sometimes had to hold a meeting concerning a single item on the agenda as much as thirty times, and even then there were times when town officials or the county governor had to be called in to compel agreement. Even in that extreme case, persuasion was widely mobilized.

Becoming Mentors of the *Saemaul* Movement

As the *Saemaul* leaders led village development, not only were they business leaders but mentors influencing other leaders as well. This was because successfully developed villages served as dynamic educational case studies. Sometimes, the stories were even made into movies or published in other mediums and disseminated throughout the nation. Furthermore, some of the successful villages provided an on-site training ground for leaders from lagging villages and acted as the site of field trips during *Saemaul* education. The leaders in these successful villages became mentors to the visiting trainees. As noted earlier, the *Saemaul* leaders not only instructed but inspired those around them, thereby apprising, in modern guise, the role of a traditional Confucian teacher, one who not only transmits information but cultivates the character of his disciples and leads them by his own inspiring ethical example.

The Presentation of Success Stories

There was much talk about what led to success within the *Saemaul* movement, because that in turn led to the creation of more success. Thus, success stories from all over the country were shared. The magazine entitled Saemaul *Movement*, published by the Ministry of Home Affairs, introduced as many as 178 successful cases. Among these, some were presented at the National Convention of *Saemaul* Leaders and received medals of commendation from the president himself. Furthermore, some were also presented at the Monthly Economic Trend Briefing held at the Blue House, where representatives of these cases also presented in front of the president and received medals and bounties.

Aside from receiving medals at the National Convention of *Saemaul* Leaders and the Monthly Economic Briefing, successful villages, as well as the leaders therein, were eligible for all kinds of assistance. Moreover, partnership opportunities with sister institutions involving Koreans in Japan, public institutions, and private companies were available. As well, successful villages received field visits from the likes of foreign dignitaries, presidents, prime ministers, ministers, and governors, much to their pride. Finally, the improved image of these villages would be featured in newspapers and on television,[67] providing an opportunity for these small villages to display their successes on the national stage. As leaders became known nationwide, they became the teachers of *Saemaul* education on a grand scale, serving to modernize the nation.

"Without even using notes, by just presenting the success stories as they were, not only were the *Saemaul* leaders able to capture the hearts of their fellow leaders but the social elites as well."[68] Therefore, the success stories were the most important facet of the *Saemaul* movement education. The core leadership lecturing on success stories at the *Saemaul* Leaders Training Institute consisted of fifty-six men, while a trainee admitted to the institute listened to an average of ten success stories during their training period.[69] The leaders lecturing on these success stories soon became lecturers to the nation. Among these successful cases, particularly dynamic ones were even turned into movies or television dramas. For example, the famous movie *The Light in a Prairie* (K. *chowon-ui bulbit*) was based on a legendary figure of the *Saemaul* movement, Sa-Yong Ha.

During the early stages of the *Saemaul* movement, tasks like environment and roof improvement were emphasized, but these were not the goals of the movement in and of themselves. In reality, the goal of the *Saemaul* movement was for poor villages to become "prosperous villages." Thus, Sa-Yong Ha's success story, "getting rich," became a national success story. The story of a poor farmer achieving prosperity or a poor village becoming a profitable one were examples of stories that became inextricable from the *Saemaul* movement.

As well, being no more than elementary school graduates did not stop the likes of X-Gyu Jeon and X-Geun Han from lecturing on success stories, nor did it stop them from becoming teachers and mentors to those *Saemaul* leaders seeking out their guidance.[70] Ki-Myeong Kim, an instructor at the institute, stated of these lectures, "These were not the transformational words of great scholars but words exchanged between comrades." This remark reminds us of the mutual encouragement of virtuous achievements emphasized in the Community Compact. In this sense, storytelling of the successful cases by the *Saemaul* leaders is an outstanding example of the community of practice.

The Field Training of Leaders from Lagging Villages

Among the educational techniques adopted during the *Saemaul* movement, for those leaders from lagging villages, there was that of the field-training program. During the *Saemaul* movement, village development was classified into three stages, consisting of "basic villages," "self-help villages," and "self-reliant villages." Villages where the *Saemaul* project had failed to move forward were known as basic villages. For the leaders of these villages, the training program consisted of several stages. During the first week of training, they would receive proscribed education at the *Saemaul* Leaders Training Institute from leaders of self-reliant villages. Then, during the second week, they would stay in one of the twenty self-reliant villages over three nights and four days. This was known as field training.[71] In other words, the leaders from basic villages would travel to self-reliant villages where they could directly experience and study the *Saemaul* movement,[72] and in groups of about six to ten, they would receive room and board at the homes of the self-reliant village leaders;[73] thus, host wives made tremendous sacrifices too. Self-reliant village leaders would engage in the field training according to a schedule determined by the *Saemaul* Leaders Training Institute.

To increase the effectiveness of field education, leaders from exemplary villages would employ creative methods particular to their own style. For example, although during the duration of the training program the consumption of alcohol was prohibited, some outstanding village instructors would drink late into the morning, working to understand the basic village leaders.

> Sure, we'd have a drink. We'd drink our fill. We'd discuss and complain, say this and that about the *Saemaul* education, about each other's villages and lives, and the night would pass before we knew it. That's where you can really get to know a person: that person's heart of hearts and such and such. We all think

> we're too busy with our own lives to help others and this kind of thing. But spending time like that together, they came to see things from a different point of view. And just like that within four days we'd become quite close.[74]

During the night the leaders would hold candid conversations, and during the day they would engage in serious training. While moving about the village, the basic village leader would ask the exemplary leader, "What did you do to produce these kinds of results?" Here, a leader remembers the fruits reaped through on-site education: "Well, even when we were making simple straw bags, the trainees would be looking on so intently. Are they idiots? (Not at all.) They would be with the village people all the time, asking them about everything. . . . If you spend a week like that, you really learn something."[75]

The field training program consisted of a follow-up stage as well. After the basic village leaders had finished their training and returned to their villages to apply what they had learned, self-reliant leaders would later pay a visit so as to evaluate their progress. Upon one such occasion, it's reported that the wife of a basic village leader even performed a ceremonial bow to a self-reliant leader, so as to signify her great respect.[76] This shows how successful farmer-teachers were in teaching *Saemaul* projects; they were good at listening to their fellow students and helped their students learn by themselves. Finally they evaluated the progress of their students by visiting the villages of the fellow students. This educational method is much different from bureaucratic and massive modern education but similar to the spirit of Confucian education.

Identifying with the President of the Nation

Saemaul village leaders tended to connect the cause of their commitment and sacrifice to the supportive leadership of President Park Chung-Hee. Even though they lived and worked in a village, they were not confined to their village only. Their vision went beyond their village to the nation, which resembles the Confucian expansion from self-cultivation through governing the family to governing the nation and bringing harmony on the earth (*Great Learning*, *Da Xue*).

It is said that the *Saemaul* leaders were so fond of President Park that they considered him a "comrade."[77] They were grateful that President

Park had loved them and granted them significant authority within their own jurisdiction. It's said that, even though they did not receive any salary, since these leaders represented the president, there were none that defied their authority.[78] Leaders such as X-Geun Han and X-Muk Lim remember how the president actively aided and supported them and carefully listened to their words. According to X-Geun Han, when a village pastor named X-Hwa Lee met with President Park, he mentioned his village's need for a phone. When the phone arrived the next day, it went a long way toward lending credibility to the village leader.[79] The quick and efficient execution of a request made by a village leader was made possible by the instructions of President Park.

X-Weon Lee describes how, when President Park toured Gangweon Province, he would often be invited along.[80] To that extent, President Park demonstrated a deep concern for the *Saemaul* village leaders. X-Sun Lim, of Wokcheon County, remembers how Park was "spiritually connected with" and "loved" the *Saemaul* leaders.[81] X-Ryeon Kim, who presented a success story at the Monthly Economic Trend Briefing at the Blue House, remembers how, "if the *Saemaul* leaders were lacking in strength, the president would lend support and assistance," making sure the *Saemaul* leaders had the strength to see through their projects.[82]

Of course, there were a great number of village leaders across the nation that never had the opportunity to meet President Park. However, they came into indirect contact with him through bounties and gifts. X-Il Hong of Yongin County claimed that *Saemaul* leaders were greatly touched by the fact that President Park sent his secretary Park Jin-Hwan to deliver the president's gift to exemplary village leaders. After receiving the personal gifts from President Park, they strived all the more to fulfill the goals of the *Saemaul* movement.

> Those *Saemaul* leaders couldn't help but go into a frenzy. It was President Park's philosophy . . . I don't even know whether to call it a political philosophy or what. It was just unbelievable. When I was doing field training with leaders from lagging villages, President Park would send me a bounty twice a year. It wasn't conveyed through the provincial governor or the county governor either. Rather, Park Jin-Hwan, the president's special economic secretary, came directly to my house dozens of times. . . . He would come and encourage me. So, in the vitality of youth, one couldn't help but go into a frenzy.[83]

Famous for the land reclamation project he and his villagers succeeded in without any support of the government, the leader X-Muk Lim remarks, "Because [he] was involved in *Saemaul*," he could meet the likes of powerful people like President Park. These words emphasize that it was the *Saemaul* movement that made his meeting with the president possible. Lim continues, "I could die now without regrets."[84]

X-Mo Yu describes how he met President Park at the National Convention of *Saemaul* Leaders held in Gwangju, saying, "One was powerless against the charisma of this man."[85] Within his career, upon receiving a medal from the president at the Blue House, he mused, "Am I really worthy of being here? What have I done to deserve to shake hands with the president? As long as I am alive, I'll have to get along with my fellow men."[86] Statements such as these testify to another powerful Confucian source motivating and sustaining the *Saemaul* movement. President Park was widely regarded as a hard-working and benevolent leader, and this accorded him the moral charisma or "virtue" of the ideal Confucian ruler. This perception inspired and motivated the volunteers and kept them loyally dedicated to the movement throughout the long and difficult years in which it unfolded.

These presidential rewards, along with other medals of commendation, were presented at the Monthly Economic Trend Briefing or the National Convention of *Saemaul* Leaders.[87] At the Monthly Economic Briefing held at the Blue House from 1971 to September 1979, more than 150 *Saemaul* leaders presented success stories before the president.[88]

As the leaders presented their stories at the Monthly Economic Trend Briefing, President Park would ask them, "What project do you most desire to see undertaken in your village? What is your dream project?" Then, he would pledge to aid the proposed project.[89] The meetings at the Monthly Economic Briefing demonstrated the deep bond between the *Saemaul* leaders and President Park. That is, by meeting with the president in the Blue House and receiving awards, the authority of the *Saemaul* village leaders became greater than it had ever been before.

The *Saemaul* leaders considered President Park an ally. While in the past township or county governors, or other positions of leadership, had been considered as sources of much fear and anxiety, as the *Saemaul* movement steadily moved forward, those in positions of power simply became means for *Saemaul* leaders to utilize toward their own ends. Moreover, while previously farmers had been the subjects of regulation and domination, the *Saemaul* movement changed this.

Conclusion: A Korean Type of Transformational Leadership

In the 1970s, there were an unbelievable number of *Saemaul* village leaders, with a male and female leader in each village, and over thirty-five thousand villages altogether. Those leaders were unpaid leaders, more importantly, regular farmers. Considering the amazing sacrifices they made for their villages, these regular farmer-leaders could be defined as incarnations of the spirit of community or priests of the Korean civil religion. Their spirit of community, however, was not just for a great cause or the country but for visible improvement of the economic livings of their fellow villagers. In this sense, their spirit of community was a very modern one, or the spirit of economic development-oriented community.

Although village leaders preceded the *Saemaul* movement, the *Saemaul* program was systematically composed of education and training targeting this very group. Moreover, not only was the content systematically composed, it was effectively communicated within ten to fifteen days. Thus, although the university graduates X-Weon Lee and X-Mo Yu investigated in this chapter are BA degree holders, they have emphasized the fact that, through their education at the *Saemaul* Leaders Training Institute, they certainly developed as leaders. Indeed, though one can acquire technical skills at a college of agriculture, the skills required for organization management and constructing a vision for rural development, such as goal management, conflict management, and the ability to persuade, are all taught as a part of the *Saemaul* Leaders Training program. Thus, the leaders referenced in this essay have all ceaselessly recognized the importance of this education. Most *Saemaul* leaders remember this training institute as a furnace of their rebirth. The largely unstated, underlying moral principles and ideals that made such a program and such transformation possible are quite similar to the expression of a civil religion described by Robert Bellah. After "conversion," they became preachers and were ready to be "martyrs." Not only could a leader personally grow through his or her education, by conveying their personal stories of success, they contributed to the growth of their colleagues as well. Moreover, through the education of leaders from lagging villages, they developed as teachers too. Indeed, a farmer becoming a national lecturer and addressing the likes of the "social elite" was unprecedented. Moreover, since the very material by which these people lectured was their own personal stories of success, they could speak freely without preparing lecture notes of any kind.

Since the *Saemaul* movement of the 1970s reflected the strong will of President Park Chung-Hee, the participating *Saemaul* leaders essentially equated him with it. They believed that the aid of their great leader was the very mechanism by which they could actively work in the villages. As well, they were deeply grateful for the support and concern he displayed.

With incomes rising through *Saemaul* projects, all of the villagers became *Saemaul* leaders as well.[90] By observing this fact, one can detect the powerful influence of transformational leadership. These were leaders sharing a common vision with the villagers, compelling not just personal transformations but a revolution in values too. As such, these were transformational leaders. Moreover, considering that these transformational leaders were discovered and developed through strong government assistance, they exemplified a uniquely Korean characteristic: grassroots leadership with the synergy of government and village. That is, the authoritarian government of the 1970s advanced the rural modernization program of the *Saemaul* movement as an essential national policy, allocating it as an important indicator of the performance of local government and particularly the civil service. Thus, within the context of the *Saemaul* movement, the close productive relationship and partnership between business and government that Evans has emphasized was also clearly manifest in the relationship between the government and the village leaders.[91] In a uniquely Korean style, this characteristic forged transformational leaders in countless villages across the nation, creating the success stories therein. Even while the government aggressively propelled *Saemaul* movement policies, since the leaders within the villages were entrusted with the tasks of problem solving, persuasion of the villagers, and conflict management, the "productive partnership" between the government and the leaders was clear. In cultivating this grassroots leadership, cultivating virtue was emphasized; spiritual revolution or mental reform was always emphasized. Capacity building through virtue education comes from the Confucian tradition.

From this, the author would conclude that the village leaders in 1970s rural Korea show that the spirit of community is very dynamic, not just a static cultural element. Village leaders and the government were very successful in forging a new version of the spirit of the community or reinventing the tradition of the Community Compact. The village leaders and the government were very responsive to the dream of a better life for villagers and suggest a new vision. The spirit of community was very effective for the economic improvement of individual farmers and villages.

Repeated surveys show that most Koreans are proud of the *Saemaul* movement, and the *Saemaul* movement has enabled the Korean people to have a can-do spirit. This spirit surprised the world in 1997 when the South Korean people launched a national campaign for collecting gold to save the country from the Financial Crisis of 1997. People donated their gold to save the country by selling the gold that was collected. This campaign of collecting gold was initiated by the nationwide organization of the *Saemaul* movement. Again, the campaign was similar to a crusade in secular form under a civil religion.

Notes

This essay was first published in Korean in *Society and History* (*Sahoewa Yeoksa*) 88 (2010): 267–305. An English version was presented at the workshop History as Social Process in Leiden University, 28–29 October, 2011.

1. Robert N. Bellah, "Civil Religion in America," reprinted in *The Robert Bellah Reader*, ed. Robert N. Bellah and Steven M. Tipton (Durham: Duke University Press, 2006), 225–245.

2. Sang-Jin Han and Ki-Soo Eun, "Value Orientation of the Reform-Oriented Middle Class and Building Participatory Trust Society," Policy Report, Ministry of Education and the Academy of Korean Studies, 1999.

3. Kyun-Yeol Park, Dong-Jun Park, Kyu-Seon Seo, and Byung-Ki Park, "A Survey on Civic Value Consciousness in Current Korean Society" (Seongnamsi: The Academy of Korean Studies, 2013).

4. James M. Burns, *Leadership* (New York: Harper & Row, 1978).

5. Do-Hyun Han, "President Park Chung-Hee and The Saemaul Movement," in *Revisiting the Period of Park Chung-Hee*, ed. Lee Ji-Su (Seoul: Seonin, 2010), 53–58.

6. Jin-Hwan Park, "The Case of Best Farmer Sa-Yang Ha's Success and the 1970 Saemaul Movement" (Goyang, Gyeonggi Province: Institute of Rural Development in the College of Agricultural Cooperatives, 2001).

7. Se-Yeong Lee, *The Saemaul Movement in Pungdeok-ri: Biography of Saemaul Award Recipient Se-Young Lee* (Seoul: Munhwa Printing, 2003).

8. Jeong-Mi Yoo, "An Analysis of the Experience of Women Who Participated in State-Led Development: Focusing on the Example of Female Saemaul Leaders," MA thesis in Women's Studies, Ehwa Women's University, 2001; Seung-Mi Han, "The New Community Movement: Park Chung-Hee and the Making of State Populism in Korea," *Pacific Affairs* 77.1 (Spring 2004): 69–93; Mi-Kyung Chang, "The Formulation and Change of Identity of Saemaul Women Leaders in the Developmental State Period: Focusing on the Successful Cases or Essays of Saemaul Women Leaders," *Social Sciences Review* (Sogang University) 16.1 (2008): 426–461; Byeong-Yong Yu, Bong-Dae Choi, and Yoo-Seok Oh, *Modernization and the Saemaul Movement* (Seoul: Baeksan Seodang, 2001); Dae-Young Kim, "The Mechanism of Park Chung-Hee Regime's State-Mobilization: Focused on the New Community Movement," *Economy and Society* 61 (2004): 172–207; Won Koh, "Saemaul Move-

ment in the Era of Park Chung-Hee Regime and 'Making the Nation,'" *Economy and Society* 69 (Spring 2006): 178–201.

9. Research Institute of Democracy in Seonggonghwe University, "The Systematic Establishment and Foundation of the Research of the Saemaul Movement Archive of Historical Materials on the History of Local and Daily Affairs during the Park Chung-Hee Era," http://saemaul70.or.kr/lab_task.htm; Yoo-Seok Oh, ed., *Saemaul Movement in the Era of Park Chung-Hee: Modernization, Tradition, and Subject* (Seoul: Hanul Academy, 2014).

10. In-Jeong Hwang, *Integrated Rural Development in Korea: Evaluation of the Rural Saemaul Undong and its Perspective* (Seoul: Korean Rural Economic Institute, 1980).

11. Yang-Bu Choi, "A Social Scientific Study of the Rural Saemaul Movement," *Rural Society* 1.1 (1973): 34.

12. Sun-Kyu Kim, Myeong-Gil Lee, and Chung-Sin Lim, "Suggestions for Improving the Morale of the Saemaul Leaders (Ⅱ)," *Collected Papers of the Saemaul Movement*, vol. 1 (Seoul: Research Association of the Saemaul Movement, 1975).

13. Jong-Seob Kim, Jeong-Bin Lee, and Jong-Yeol Han, "Suggestions for Improving the Morale of the Saemaul Leaders (I)," *Collected Papers of the Saemaul Movement*, vol. 1 (Research Association of the Saemaul Movement, 1975), 352–358.

14. Yoo, "An Analysis of the Experience of Women Who Participated in State-Led Development"; Mi-Kyung Chang, "The Formulation and Change of Identity of Saemaul Women Leaders"; Byeong-Yong Yu et al., *Modernization and the* Saemaul *Movement*; Seung-Mi Han, "The New Community Movement"; Do-Hyun Han, "The Spirit of Community in Confucian Social Theory," *Korean Religion and Cultural Values* (Korean and Korean American Studies Bulletin) 14.1, 2 (2004); Do-Hyun Han, "President Park Chung-Hee and the Saemaul Movement"; Yeong-Mi Kim, *The Saemaul Movement of Theirs* (Seoul: Purunyeoksa, 2009).

15. Taek-Lim Yun and Han-Hee Ham, *Research Methodology of Oral History for Alternative Historiography* (Seoul: Arke, 2006).

16. Se-Yeong Lee, *Saemaul Movement in Pungdeok-ri*; Yeong-Mi Kim, *The Saemaul Movement of Theirs*; Jin-Hwan Park, "The Case of Best Farmer Sa-Yang Ha's Success."

17. Yeong-Mi Kim, *The Saemaul Movement of Theirs*, 358, 368, and 373.

18. Robert N. Bellah, Richard Madsen, William M. Sullivan, Ann Swidler, Steven M. Tipton, *Habits of the Heart: Individualism and Commitment in American Life* (Berkeley: University of California Press, 1985).

19. Lisa Anderson, Pauline O'Loughlin, and Annette Salt, "Community Leadership Programs for NSW" (Sydney: University of Technology Sydney, 2002).

20. Yeong-Mi Kim, *The Saemaul Movement of Theirs*, 364.

21. Seung-Mi Han, "The New Community Movement."

22. Anderson et al., "Community Leadership Programs for NSW," 10.

23. Saemaul Leaders Training Institute (1982), 327–328.

24. Ibid., 331.

25. Ibid., 20.

26. Burns, *Leadership*, 20; Do-Hyun Han, "President Park Chung-Hee and the Saemaul Movement."

27. Gap-Jin Jeong, "The Experiences of the Korean Saemaul Undong of the 1970s," *KDI* (2009): 123.

28. Saemaul Leaders Training Institute (1982), 150.

29. Se-Yeong Lee, *The Saemaul Movement in Pungdeok-ri*, 321.

30. Ibid., 323.

31. Jin-Hwan Park, "The Case of Best Farmer Sa-Yang Ha's Success," 138.

32. X-Ryeon Kim, unpublished transcripts of oral interviews conducted by and available from the author, 2008, 16.

33. X-Gyu Jeon, ibid., 16.

34. Ibid., 18.

35. X-Weon Lee, ibid., 6.

36. Ibid., 7.

37. Saemaul Leaders Training Institute (1982), 151.

38. Jin-Hwan Park, "The Case of Best Farmer Sa-yang Ha's Success," 147.

39. Saemaul Leaders Training Institute (1982), 158.

40. Do-Hyun Han, "President Park Chung-Hee and the Saemaul Movement," 54.

41. X-Mo Yu, unpublished transcripts of oral interviews conducted by and available from the author, 2008, 29.

42. Saemaul Leaders Training Institute (1982), 473–479.

43. "Results of 1974 Group Discussion" (Seongnam: Saemaul Undong Central Training Institute, 1974), 11–22.

44. Receipt Number 1292, "Saemaul Leader Sang-Gil Lee's Letter" (Seongnam: Saemaul Undong Central Training Institute, 1975), 12, 15.

45. X-Gi Choi, unpublished transcripts of oral interviews conducted by and available from the author, 2008, 4.

46. X-Il Hong, ibid., 13.

47. Sub Park and Heng Lee, "State and Farmers in Modern Korea: An Analysis of New Village Movement," *Korea Political Science Review* 31.3 (1997); Yeong-Mi Kim, *President Park Chung-Hee's Modernization of the Korean Economy and the Saemaul Movement* (Seoul: The Association of Commemoration of President Park Chung-Hee, 2005), 73.

48. Do-Hyun Han, "President Park Chung-Hee and the Saemaul Movement," 44–52.

49. Sa-Yong Ha, unpublished transcripts of oral interviews, The National Institute of Korean History, 2004, 62.

50. Yeong-Mi Kim, unpublished transcripts of oral interviews conducted by and available from the author, 2009, 373.

51. X-Gyu Jeon, unpublished transcripts of oral interviews conducted by and available from the author, 2008, 7.

52. X-Gyu Jeon, ibid., 9.

53. X-Ryeon Kim, ibid., 3.

54. X-Mo Yu, ibid., 10.

55. Sang-Joon Kim, "Let There Be No Starving Persons in the Whole Country: The Confucian Theory of Feeding the People and Relief Work," in *The Power of Confucianism Which Supported the Community for Five Hundred Years*, ed. Han Hyeong-Jo, Kim Yong-Hwan, Oh Hang-Nyeong, Jeong Jin-Young, No Kwan-Beom, Kim Sang-Joon, Park Won-Jae, Han Do-Hyun, Lee Eun-Seon (Seoul: Geulhangari, 2013), 183–219.

56. X-Gyu Jeon, unpublished transcripts of oral interviews conducted by and available from the author, 2008, 15–16.

57. Ibid., 16.

58. Ibid., 17.

59. X-Mo Yu, unpublished transcripts of oral interviews conducted by and available from the author, 2008, 5–6.

60. Ibid., 7–8.

61. Ibid., 34–35.

62. X-Weon Lee, unpublished transcripts of oral interviews conducted by and available from the author, 2008, 17.

63. Sa-Yong Ha, unpublished transcripts of oral interviews, The National Institute of Korean History, 2004, 77.

64. Se-Yeong Lee, *The Saemaul Movement in Pungdeok-ri*, 290.

65. Ibid., 305.

66. X-Muk Lim, unpublished transcripts of oral interviews conducted by and available from the author, 2008, 22.

67. On December 27, 1973, Se-Yeong Lee and Ja-Ho Lee were each featured in the broadcast by KBS in which Pungdeok village was recommended as a contestant for the National Saemaul Competition. See Se-Yeong Lee, *The Saemaul Movement in Pungdeok-ri*, 333.

68. X-Muk Lim, unpublished transcripts of oral interviews conducted by and available from the author, 2008, 9.

69. Jin-Hwan Park, "The Case of Best Farmer Sa-Yang Ha's Success," 161–167.

70. X-Gi Choi, unpublished transcripts of oral interviews conducted by and available from the author, 2008, 20; X-Gyu Jeon, ibid., 26; X-Geun Han, ibid., 10.

71. X-Mok Lim, ibid., 11.

72. Jin-Hwan Park, "The Case of Best Farmer Sa-Yang Ha's Success," 169.

73. X-Mok Lim, unpublished transcripts of oral interviews conducted by and available from the author, 2008; X-Weon Lee, ibid.

74. Ibid., 12.

75. X-Weon Lee, unpublished transcripts of oral interviews conducted by and available from the author, 2008, 15.

76. X-Geun Han, ibid., 8.

77. Jin-Hwan Park, "The Case of Best Farmer Sa-Yang Ha's Success," 172.

78. X-Sun Lim, unpublished transcripts of oral interviews conducted by and available from the author, 2008, 8.

79. X-Geun Han, ibid., 4.
80. X-Weon Lee, ibid., 21.
81. X-Sun Lim, ibid., 7.
82. X-Ryeon Kim, ibid., 14.
83. X-Il Hong, ibid., 4–5.
84. X-Muk Lim, ibid., 35.
85. X-Mo Yu, ibid., 1.
86. Ibid., 20–21.
87. X-Weon Lee, ibid., 25.
88. Jin-Hwan Park, "The Case of Best Farmer Sa-Yang Ha's Success," 60; Do-Hyun Han, "President Park Chung-Hee and the Saemaul Movement," 73.
89. X-Geun Han, unpublished transcripts of oral interviews conducted by and available from the author, 2008, 4; X-Ryeon Kim, ibid., 22.
90. X-Mo Yu, ibid., 33.
91. Peter Evans, *Embedded Autonomy: State and Industrial Transformation* (Princeton: Princeton University Press, 1995).

8

Contemporary Japanese Confucianism from a Genealogical Perspective

Takahiro Nakajima

The Confucian Boom in Japan

In recent years, the widespread phenomenon of a Confucian boom has appeared not only in China but also in Japan. What is interesting about the Confucian boom in Japan is that it limits itself to praising the spirit of Confucius and his teachings as represented in the *Analects*, while Confucian ritual practices are neglected and other Confucian scholars such as Mencius, Xunzi, and Zhu Xi are almost wholly excluded.

Behind and motivating this broad movement is a widely held belief in the existence of a pure Confucian spirit that can and must be extracted from the text of the *Analects* and internalized within each person to serve as an unwavering moral compass and offering a way to recover a profound sense of spirituality. The different thinkers whose works we explore in this chapter develop contrasting interpretations of the role of Confucius and the nature of the *Analects* from this common starting point. Many see the text as essential to developing a true Japanese "national character," while some develop explicitly religious—not just civil religious—interpretations of Confucius and the *Analects*. In this sense, Japanese interest in the *Analects* does involve inculcating specific habits of the heart, and these beliefs, orientations, and feelings are thought to constitute something distinctively and authentically Japanese. This brings us to another distinguishing feature of the Japanese case. In Japan, the heightened interest in studying the *Analects*, whether as a more humanistic code of ethics or an expression of religious faith, is inextricably connected to a corresponding belief in the "loss" of Japan's true national character and the forsaking of traditional values.

It is worth investigating the philosophical and political background of this boom. Before proceeding with this investigation, let's consider some examples from leading Japanese business magazines in order to understand the nature and tone of the Confucian boom in Japan.

The *Nikkei Otona no OFF* published a special feature on the *Analects* in the October issue of 2011. On the opening page of this feature, we can find the typical tone:

> It is really a waste, if you have not read the *Analects* since you learned it in your school days. The *Analects* is a book which moves the heart of adults with considerable experience of life. Confucius is never a saint beyond our reach. He is a man who persisted in his way of life, while struggling through difficulties and conflicts, in the chaotic era of the *Spring and Autumn Period*. As concrete wisdom for living through the present day, his teachings still support us.[1]

As this citation shows, Confucius and the *Analects* provide us with a "concrete wisdom for living through the present day." And the Japanese are expected to have acquired this wisdom in our "school days" through education. We can characterize this feature or aspect of the Confucian revival as *kyōyō-shugi* 教養主義 or *kyōyō*-ism (educationalism).

Kyōyō (education) is a term that indicates the basic cultural setting for an educated person in modern Japan, especially in a number of high schools in the old system of education. The most important aim of *kyōyō* is to cultivate and achieve one's personality. Like *xiushen* 修身 or *xiuyang* 修養 (cultivation of the self) in the Chinese tradition, it often is accompanied by bodily practices like Zen meditation or reciting phrases from classic texts aloud. This practice of *kyōyō*, which is clearly religious in character, is now being revived as part of the Confucian boom in contemporary Japan.

This is welcomed not only by conservatives but also by liberals. *AERA*, a liberal magazine in Japan, introduces "Children's Education in the *Analects*" (*kodomo Rongo juku* こども論語塾), an educational program for children. It advocates bodily practices based upon recitation and memorization of some phrases in the *Analects*. The promoter of this educational program is Yasuoka Sadako 安岡定子. She is a granddaughter of Yasuoka Masahiro 安岡正篤 (1898–1983), who was a scholar of the Chinese classics in modern Japan and was very influential among politicians, high officers, and business leaders, especially in the prewar period. *AERA* reports on Yasuoka Sadako's ideas in the following way:

> Before knowing the contents [of the *Analects*], it is important to memorize the phrases bodily. Once the sounds of the passages in the *Analects* are ingrained in child's body, it is expected that they will develop into flesh and blood as the child grows up . . . The *Analects* that teaches the heart about benevolence and modesty, I think, fits the sensibility of what the Japanese originally had. In former times, there were many "adults with firm principle" based upon the teachings of the *Analects*, but they are gone now. In the background of reevaluating the *Analects*, there must be a social tendency to recover the sensibility that the Japanese originally had in this bewildered world.[2]

By repeating the prewar conception of *kyōyō-shugi*, Yasuoka's discourse presupposes both an ideal past and a cultural essentialism. There is neither an explanation of why there were many "adults with firm principle" in the past nor an elucidation of why the Chinese classics fit an "original" Japanese sensibility. If we push this discourse to its limit, there must appear the conclusion or aim of making the Japanese into Confucians. However, both in prewar *kyōyō-shugi* as well as in its current form, its advocates only use the *Analects* for the cultivation of moral character. Becoming a Confucian, that is, regulating one's whole existence in the manner of Confucian ritual, is never regarded as important. They never imagine making the Japanese into Confucians in terms of living a Confucian life but instead try to extract a Confucian "spirit" to support moral improvement.

Japanese Cultural Essentialism to Reappropriate the *Analects*

Such a conception of *kyōyō* as part of the Confucian boom seems widespread in Japan. High school teachers and university professors also support it.[3] Let's take up and explore one example from Saitō Takashi 齋藤孝, professor at Meiji University.

> Such an effort [of embodying the thought of the *Analects*] formed the lofty morality and ambition of the Japanese, and made the literacy rate the highest in the world in the later part of the Edo period. I think that such an accumulation [of literacy] caused the Meiji Restoration, which made Japan succeed in becoming the most rapidly modernized nation in Asia. The driving force of Japanese modernization consists in the high cultural standard

> of its people through education. One educational practice is a way of bodily memorizing excellent classics such as the *Analects* by reciting them.[4]
>
> The Japanese have been practicing the "trust" [*xin* 信] described in the *Analects*, that is, the correspondence of one's word with one's conduct or trust in other people, and have made these a part of their national temperament. In other words, the Japanese have appropriated the ideals of the *Analects* as their national character over a period of more than one thousand years.
>
> However, for present-day Japanese, the *Analects* seem to have become a classic without any practical use in everyday life. We have lost the habit of reading the *Analects* and referring to the phrases of Confucius in our daily lives. If we let things remain as they are, the crisis will spread, which means the virtue of the Japanese, which has been cultivated over many years, will fade and eventually we will lose trust, and our world will be filled with sorrow.
>
> Probably because people find themselves in such a situation, in recent years, they pay attention to the classics and philosophical books such as the *Analects*. This attention is motivated by a sense of despair and uneasiness toward the present age. The other side of the coin is that there is an elevated tendency among the Japanese to pursue spiritual maturity or mental satisfaction.[5]

This is a typical discourse concerning reappropriation of the *Analects* into the Japanese "national character." If we Japanese appropriate the essence of the *Analects* once again, we can survive this crisis of the world and recover a deep spirituality. In this discourse, too, the heteronomy of the *Analects* or Confucian teachings is completely excluded, while the cultural essentialism of Japan is stressed too heavily. We can easily find an echo from prewar Japan, when it was commonly said that we Japanese understand the essence of the *Analects* better than the Chinese. In fact, *AERA* magazine reports an interview with Hu Mei 胡玫, the film director of *Confucius* (2010), as follows: "I am astonished that the Japanese understand Confucius and the *Analects* much better. In particular, the Japanese spirit of ritual [*li* 禮] is beyond the reach of the Chinese."[6] What Hu Mei expressed here is nothing more than the discourse of *kyōyō-shugi*, which has existed since prewar Japan. What is absolutely astonishing is its repetition without any critical perspective from the prewar Japanese discourse on Confucianism.

The *Analects* as Pharmakon

There are few criticisms against this current discourse of *kyōyō-shugi*, and we can find a moderate counterargument in Katō Tōru 加藤徹, professor at Meiji University.

> In recent years, interest in the *Analects* has been booming in China as well as in Japan. In various places, private schools have been restored, which reevaluate the goodness of an education based upon recitation and encourage children to memorize the *Analects*. However, those who spar with the *Analects* are remarkably fewer in number.
>
> In fact, the *Analects* is a dangerous book. It can be a poison as well as a medicine. After understanding this character of the *Analects*, we have to spar with it. Our ancestors read it in this way.[7]

The most important point in Katō's criticism against the current discourse of *kyōyō-shugi* is that it consciously or unconsciously forgets the dangerous or critical aspects of the *Analects*, that is, that it is a book of revolution. If we trace back Japanese history, the *Analects* was used to strengthen the governing structure in the Tokugawa Shogunate, while it gave energy to those who overthrew the Tokugawa regime at the same time.

The ruling class of the Tokugawa Shogunate recognized the dangerous or critical aspect of the *Analects*. Confucian fundamentalists were severely persecuted by the Shogunate, while "Confucianism diluted with water,"[8] that is, *ruxue* 儒學, was promoted. Katō explains the rationale as follows:

> Until the sixteenth century, Confucian thought about loyalty and filial piety proved useful as a means to halt the vicious circle of the forcible displacement of a superior by his inferior in Japanese society, and to change the thinking of the samurai. However, in Confucianism, there is a dangerous side effect for its establishment too. If the thought of the *Analects* is interrogated to its limits and applied to Japanese society in the Edo period, what will happen? The question of whether the Japanese monarch is the Emperor in Kyoto or the Shogun in Edo could be raised.
>
> The relationship between Emperor and Shogunate is equivalent to that between monarch and the Sanyuan clans in

> Lu.[9] According to Confucian justification, the ways the Shogun can choose are twofold: to immediately return sovereignty to the Emperor or to become the Son of Heaven by receiving the heavenly mandate.[10]
>
> If we understand it seriously, Confucianism touches on the legitimacy of politics. That is why the Tokugawa Shogunate let the samurai merely recite and memorize the *Analects*. The establishment neither wanted to let them understand the real thought of the *Analects* nor let them become Confucians.[11]

If we follow Katō's argument, the discourse of *kyōyō-shugi* in the present day can be regarded as a prolongation of "Confucianism diluted with water." It seems very supportive of the present establishment. However, once we recognize the dangerous or critical aspect of the *Analects* and Confucianism, we can use it as a tool to change the status quo.

To Make Confucianism a Religion: Shirakawa Shizuka 白川靜

By pointing out the revolutionary thought in the *Analects*, Katō intentionally regards Confucianism as an ancient religion[12] and the group consisting of Confucius and his disciples as a kind of cult.[13] It is worth paying attention to what informs this viewpoint. Katō refers to the scholars who tried to religionize Confucianism in the supplement to his book. They are Shirakawa Shizuka and Kaji Nobuyuki 加地伸行.

Shirakawa published the *Life of Confucius* (*Kōshiden* 孔子伝) in 1972. This book cut a conspicuous figure, because it presented the religious aspect of Confucius and Confucianism against the modern Japanese interpretation of Confucius and the *Analects*, which had praised the rational personality of Confucius[14] and regarded his humanist attitude as important.[15] Shirakawa says:

> Confucius is the bastard of a shaman. He is a godsent child as it were.[16]
>
> Confucius is the child of a shaman. He is a bastard who does not know the name of his father. It seems unusual that he was born after his mother prayed to Mount Ni (*Nishan* 尼山). Like the Nazarene, God chooses such a child by preference. Confucius is a chosen man. That is why it is natural that nobody

> knows the first half of his life before he rises in the world. God imposes deep agony on the one who is chosen by God and lets him becomes aware of God's trust. One who becomes aware of God's trust becomes a saint.[17]

Shirakawa compares Confucius with Christ here and regards him as a "god-sent child." In other passages, he explains Confucius's dream of Duke Zhou as being equivalent to the voice of the *daemon* in Socrates.[18] The references to Christ and Socrates have been a cliché in the modern Japanese interpretation of Confucius, especially in that of Watsuji Tetsurō. However, Watsuji intentionally set Confucius apart from the religious aspect expressed in Christ and Socrates,[19] while Shirakawa is eager to find a similar religious aspect in Confucius.

Why does Shirakawa religionize Confucius and Confucianism? The answer is that he wants to find in them the possibility of rebellion against the establishment.

> The end of Spring and Autumn is a moment when the ancient regime collapsed and there appeared a fierce fluidity. Then a new social class was born out of the previous establishment. Confucians and Mohists emerged from this new social class. That is why their intellectual movements took the form of religious organizations or strongly association-oriented groups. Because of its starting point, the character of the religious organization of Confucius is naturally opposed to the establishment or status quo. In the beginning, the religious organization directed by Confucius fought political power in the real world. However, fighting political power in the real world means that they stood in the same order as their opponents. In this sense, the exile of Confucius offered the opportunity of renaissance to this religious organization.[20]

In this respect, Katō's viewpoint follows the idea of Shirakawa's interpretation. However, Shirakawa carefully sublimates the character of political rebellion in Confucius and Confucianism into an order beyond the understanding of common people.[21] Concretely speaking, he does not want to apply the power of rebellion in Confucianism to the contemporary political situation, thereby regarding the student movement as a revolution.[22] On the contrary, like the later Confucius, he devotes himself to constituting his academic world apart from the "real world."[23]

To Make Confucianism a Religion: Kaji Nobuyuki

Kaji Nobuyuki inherits Shirakawa's idea of making Confucianism a religion. He appeals to Shirakawa's distinction of the original Confucians into two types: the shaman who practices religious prayer and funeral on the one hand, and the recorder of rituals and oral tradition on the other.[24] Then, he describes Confucius as a philosopher who systematizes previous religious practices into a social theory of morals and rituals, because Confucius not only has an element of the shaman but also that of the recorder: "Confucianism does not leave shamanism at a stage of prayer, but makes it a philosophy in order to make a theory that fits real society. Probably it is only Confucianism that succeeds in doing this in the world. Original Confucianism turns out to be Confucianism. It is Confucius who promotes it as a central figure."[25] How can Confucius succeed in philosophizing the original Confucianism into a systematized theory of Confucianism? Kaji looks for the reason in Confucius's self-awareness:

> I argue that Confucius becomes aware of his theory of a life based upon filial piety through his appreciation of death. This is an important point. Confucius's self-awareness is important. It is natural that there were many prominent Confucians before Confucius. However, they just inherited the deeds coming from earlier times such as the worship of ancestors, filial piety, and producing offspring. Confucius becomes aware of it radically, and he theorizes and systematizes it from this self-awareness; this is when Confucianism becomes a mode of thought that will remain in history.[26]

According to Kaji, Confucius's self-awareness of "his theory of a life based upon filial piety" was derived from "his appreciation of death." Without this "appreciation of death," Confucianism never could have succeeded as a religious system. In other words, Kaji finds two origins of the religiosity of Confucianism: the original Confucianism based upon shamanism and Confucius's "appreciation of death." When he says that "Confucianism is a religion deeply connected to death," we have to recall these two origins of its religiosity.[27]

What is Kaji's purpose in making Confucianism a religion? It is very apparent that he has a strong political standpoint and the aim of restoring conservative values against modern Western values like democracy, individualism, and feminism. In this regard, his efforts and aims are quite similar to certain Mainland Confucians in China today.

> There is a possibility to form a new Confucian morality in contemporary society by reconstituting (reinterpreting) Confucianism as a whole from the religiosity of Confucianism.[28] The present day is an epoch of democracy. As in every epoch, an ideology controls an epoch. Now, the ideology of democracy controls the present day.
>
> The ideology of an age determines how justice in that epoch is defined, and what is contrary to this conception of justice is propagandized as error. However, it is not certain that "what is contrary to democracy" is truly wrong.[29] Individualism produces an increase of the homeless, ill treatment of the elderly, and the instability of the family (nuclear family). I think that countries and societies based upon the family are better that those based upon individualism.[30]

Kaji uses religious Confucianism as an antiestablishment tool. His political opponents are modern Western values and the Japanese status quo that is based upon them. If we return to Katō's definition of the *Analects* as a book of revolution, Kaji aims to develop a kind of conservative reform.

The Combination of Kyōyō-shugi and Conservative Reform: Yasuoka Masahiro

It is noteworthy that Kaji's aim of conservative reform comes closer to the background idea of *kyōyō-shugi*. As a final case of Japanese contemporary Confucianism, I would like to explore the example of Yasuoka Masahiro, grandfather of Yasuoka Sadako.

Yasuoka Masahiro published many books on the Chinese classics and was influential for business persons, politicians, and bureaucrats, especially in prewar Japan but also in postwar Japan. He established the Gold Rooster Academy (*Kinkei Gakuin* 金雞學院) in 1927 and the Safeguard the Nation Association (*Kokuikai* 國維會) in 1932 in order to reform state politics by appealing to an amalgam of Confucianism and Japanism. The New Bureaucrats (*Shin Kanryō* 新官僚) gathered in these institutions. Yasuoka was a central figure of conservative reform in prewar Japan. In the postwar period, the Supreme Commander for the Allied Powers (SCAP) purged him from public office until 1952, when he was rehabilitated. Nonetheless, he did not change his ideas regarding Confucianism and retained his influence on the Liberal Democratic Party up until his death.

Yasuoka himself does not go so far as to call for real revolution or radical reform of the establishment but supports conservative reform, serving as a spiritual master for those engaged in such work. In 1932, he gave a lecture on *The Consequence of the Movements to Reform Japan*. The conclusion states: "I believe that against the revolutions both of left and right wing, there must be a reform performed by the Japanese Spirit, which is pure and mellow."[31]

In order to realize this conservative reform by the Japanese Spirit, he advocated the idea of producing a person with a good conservative personality refined by culture or *kyōyō*.

> It is necessary to enhance the Japanese Spirit truly, to enlarge the way of the Japanese Emperor among the oriental nations, and to construct a greater Asia with Japanese leadership. We do not want the Japanese to show off Japanese Spirit and the way of the Emperor immoderately, but the Japanese should embody them modestly in personality and culture.[32]

This idea remains unchanged in the postwar period. Let's read his 1972 lecture on the *Doctrine of the Mean*:

> Generally speaking, we cannot deny the fact that the scantiness of *kyōyō* within the Japanese ruling class is a weak point of contemporary Japan, but this is not only true for the ruling class; students also lack *kyōyō* terribly. Confusion and decadence become more serious by the day. Nonsensical decadence that would have been extinguished immediately had it taken place just after the Great War as well as radical revolutionary movements gain force. What the Red Army or the Revolutionary Marxist Faction do is complete nonsense. We cannot call them revolutionary movements. If we do not escape from them, the true epoch will not come. It is best to conclude that this is a matter of *kyōyō*.[33]

Kyōyō is necessary to allow the "true epoch" to come. The ruling class, students, and so-called revolutionary movements all lack it terribly. In order to reconstitute it, we have to read the authentic Chinese classics again.[34]

For Yasuoka, what is the content of *kyōyō*, especially in Confucianism? He does not need to define Confucianism as a religion in order to find a radical revolutionary passion against the establishment. It is sufficient for him to find a good character in Confucius and use this as a foundation for *kyōyō*. That is why he describes Confucius as follows:

> Confucius does not take the attitude or intention to live in faith to the Absolute, transcending human beings (e.g., God or Heaven), but he tries thoroughly to find Heaven in human beings and to establish the authority of character and freedom.
>
> We have to say that he is not a so-called man of religion, but a great moralist or a practical philosopher. No, he should be a great complete man.[35]

Confucius is not a man of religion, but a philosopher or a moralist. Here we go back to the well-known figure of Confucius that Watsuji describes. Yasuoka is also a product of his time and place.

Conclusion

In the preceding study, we see different aspects of Confucianism in contemporary discourses in Japan. The discourse of *kyōyō-shugi* in education survives, while the discourse stressing the revolutionary aspect has been powerful enough to gain some degree of popularity. These discourses seemingly confront each other, but if we trace their genealogies, we can find their fusion in Yasuoka Masahiro. In other words, we are still in the circle of the modern Japanese problematic.

The most important task for the Japanese is to escape from this circle. As a way they might do so, I would like to propose the notion of "Critical Confucianism." Critical Confucianism asks us to deconstruct the modern problematic of Confucianism and find a new approach to Confucianism. By undertaking a critical investigation of Confucianism, we can reinterrogate its philosophical and political meaning, at least in Japan. My hope is that we now stand at the starting point of a coming age of Critical Confucianism.

Notes

1. *Nikkei Otona no OFF* 10 (Tōkyō: Nikkei BP Sha, 2011): 10.
2. *AERA* 46 (Tōkyō: Asahi Shinbun Shuppan, 2011): 51.

3. As an example of a high school teacher, see the publications of Saku Yasushi 佐久協, who taught Chinese classics at Keiō high school for more than thirty years. Saku Yasushi,『高校生が感動した「論語」』(The *Analects* by which High School Students Are Moved) (Tōkyō: Shōdensha, 2006).

4. Saitō Takashi,『声に出して読みたい論語』(The *Analects* Should Be Recited) (Tōkyō: Sōshisha, 2011), 225–226.

5. Ibid., 229.

6. *AERA* 46 (Tōkyō: Asahi Shinbun Shuppan, 2011): 50.

7. Katō Tōru,『本当は危ない『論語』』(The *Analects* as a Really Dangerous Book), (Tōkyō: NHK Shuppan, 2011), 241.

8. Ibid., 201.

9. Confucius criticized the Sanyuan clans such as Jisun, Shusun, and Mengsun who exercised their power over Lu, ignoring the monarch of Lu and usurping his power.

10. Katō, *The* Analects *as a Really Dangerous Book*, 202.

11. Ibid., 203–204.

12. Ibid., 42–43.

13. Ibid., 114.

14. The representative scholar to praise the rational personality of Confucius is Watsuji Tetsurō 和辻 哲郎 (1889–1960). See Watsuji Tetsurō, *Confucius* (Tōkyō: Iwanami Shoten, 1938).

15. Yoshikawa Kōjirō 吉川幸次郎 (1904–1980) advocates the humanist aspect of Confucius in postwar Japan. See Yoshikawa Kōjirō, *The Analects*, 2 vols. (Tōkyō: Asahi Shinbunsha, 1959, 1963) and『論語について』(On the *Analects*) (Tōkyō: Kōdansha, 1976).

16. Shirakawa Shizuka, 『孔子伝』(*Kōshiden*, Life of Confucius) (1972) in *The Works of Shirakawa Shizuka*, vol. 6 (Tōkyō: Heibonsha, 1999), 299.

17. Ibid., 324.

18. Ibid., 323–324.

19. Watsuji Tetsurō,『孔子』(*Confucius*) (1938) in *The Complete Works of Watsuji Tetsurō*, vol. 6. (Tōkyō: Iwanami Shoten, 1962), 337–340.

20. Shirakawa, *The Works of Shirakawa Shizuka*, 404.

21. Ibid., 404.

22. Shirakawa regards the student movement in 1968 as what brings "unmendable cracks in the educational world." Ibid., 494.

23. Satō Masayuki 佐藤將之 severely criticizes the method of Shirakawa by saying that "the feature of Confucius that Shirakawa describes are presented as hypotheses about hypotheses." Satō Masayuki,「『論語』なき孔子思想の探究：日本近代『論語』研究の問題」[The Search of the Thought of Confucius without the *Analects*: Problems of Modern Japanese Research on the *Analects*] (unpublished manuscript presented at the Kyōto Forum Between the *Analects* and the *Zhuangzi* on September 17, 2011, 3).

24. Kaji Nobuyuki,『儒教とは何か』(*What Is Confucianism?*) (Tōkyō: Chūōkōronsha, 1990), 56–57.

25. Ibid., 96.

26. Ibid., 69.

27. Ibid., 24.

28. Kaji Nobuyuki, 『沈黙の宗教 — 儒教』 (Silent Religion: Confucianism) (Tōkyō: Chikuma Shobō, 1994), 114.

29. Ibid., 107–108.

30. Ibid., 264.

31. Yasuoka Masahiro, 『日本改造運動の帰趨』 (The Consequence of the Movements to Reform Japan) (Tōkyō: Nihon Kōgyōkurabu Keizai Kenkyūkai, 1932), 65.

32. Yasuoka Masahiro, 『日本精神の真義と帰趨』 (The True Meaning and Consequence of Japanese Spirit) (Tōkyō: Keimeikai, 1935), 41.

33. Yasuoka Masahiro, 『論語に学ぶ』 (Learning from the *Analects*) (Tōkyō: PHP Institute, 2002), 122.

34. Ibid., 123.

35. Yasuoka Masahiro, 『論語の活学』 (Lively Study of the *Analects*) (Tōkyō: President Sha, 1987), 250–251.

9

The Bildungsroman of the Heart

Thick Naturalism in Robert Bellah's *Religion in Human Evolution**

Yang Xiao

Introduction

The publication of Robert Bellah's book *Religion in Human Evolution: From the Paleolithic to Axial Age* in 2011 is one of the most important intellectual events of our time. It is the most important systematic and historical treatment of religion since Hegel, Durkheim, and Weber. I believe it will become one of the basic texts in our public and global discourses on human nature, culture, history, as well as modernity and secularism. In order to truly understand its significance, we need to consider another important book by Bellah and his coauthors, *Habits of the Heart: Individualism and Commitment in American Life*, published in 1985.[1] I may also justify this move by mentioning that the title of our conference is A Habit of the Heart: Confucianism and Contemporary East Asia, which is, very appropriately, an allusion to the title of this book.

Habits of the Heart is one of the most important and influential books on contemporary American society. I still remember vividly the powerful sense of moral urgency I felt when I first read the book in the 1990s. One of the most important things we can learn from *Habits of the Heart* is how to do what may be called "history of the present."[2] Bellah and his coauthors argue that to understand the present American society and to shape its future, one must understand its past; furthermore, to heal contemporary American sickness, one must draw upon its diverse and rich civic and religious traditions. They argue that one can find four traditions in American history: utilitarian individualism, expressive individualism, biblical religion, and civic republicanism. They blame most of our problems on the tyranny and dominance of the first two traditions: utilitarian and expressive individualism. They argue that Americans should draw upon the other two traditions, our "second languages" of biblical religion and civic republicanism.

Inspired by Bellah and his coauthors, especially their emphasis on the importance of the tradition of civic republicanism, I have argued that to heal certain contemporary Chinese sicknesses, such as domination and corruption, we need to retrieve what may be called the "Chinese tradition of civic republicanism."[3] The fact that Bellah and his coauthors' approach can have global implications is not a coincidence. Richard Madsen, one of the coauthors, is a China expert, and Bellah's original field was actually East Asian studies.[4] In fact, Bellah's study of America is informed and shaped by his study of East Asia. For example, his 1967 essay "Civil Religion in America," which made him famous and turned him eventually into an Americanist, was particularly influenced by his study of religions in East Asia.[5]

One of the main points I want to make in this chapter can be put as follows: Bellah is trying to do with global civil society in *Religion in Human Evolution* what he and his coauthors have done with American society in *Habits of the Heart*.[6] We should read Bellah's new book as a general theory of human nature as "habits of the heart" or culture, of which religion is an essential dimension. It offers a general theory of religion as a cultural system by providing a general theory of culture. One should not be misled by the word "religion" in the title of Bellah's book to think that it is just a book about religion. The emphasis should be on the word "human" in the title. It is a book about humanity or human nature. Since, as I shall argue, Bellah believes that human nature is largely second nature, namely, culture, not surprisingly, this is a book about culture as much as it is about religion.

In her 2003 lecture tellingly entitled "Who Owns 'Human Nature'?" Marjorie Garber observed that the natural sciences now dominate the public discourse on human nature:

> Humanists have, by and large, abandoned their claims to an interest in this most interesting of problems [regarding human nature], tending in recent years to regard the phrase *human nature* as a reductive mode of fuzzy thinking. . . . But this shift in the disciplinary custody of "human nature" has serious consequences for the value of that amorphous enterprise called "the humanities." For if the place to investigate "human nature" is not "the humanities," what is the use of the humanistic disciplines? What else gives them cultural authority?[7]

We can find in Bellah a compelling answer to Garber's question, which is that human nature should not be understood as a purely biological concept. Natural scientists do not own human "nature"; human beings are historical and cultural animals and an *animal symbolicum*. In other words, human nature should include our "acquired second nature," to put it in John McDowell's terms.[8] In fact, human nature is "largely second nature," as McDowell would put it. By "second nature," McDowell means *Bildung* (culture, upbringing, education). Bellah's theory of human nature is a nonreductive naturalist one, similar to McDowell's "naturalism of second nature."[9] The differences between McDowell and Bellah might be that Bellah takes history more seriously than McDowell, and this is why his theory of human nature should also be read as a "history of the present" on a global scale.

Bellah as a Nonreductive Humanistic Naturalist versus the New Naturalists

We have been witnessing some dramatic developments in our culture. It was predicted at the beginning of the twenty-first century that the next big thing would be religion. But few foresaw that the public discourse on religion in the first decade of the new century would be dominated by reductive naturalist atheists such as Richard Dawkins, Sam Harris, Christopher Hitchens, and Daniel Dennett, debunking religion as an irrational illusion.[10] Their atheism is "reductive naturalist" because they believe that naturalistic theory of human nature offered by the natural sciences can tell us everything about religion. Religion should—and eventually will, as they predict—be replaced by our scientific and secular worldview. This is a typical attitude of "scientism."

Interestingly enough, religion also has its naturalist defenders, such as Stewart Guthrie, Pascal Boyer, and Scott Atran.[11] Unlike the naturalist atheists, they do not try to explain religion away as an irrational illusion. Following Barbara Herrnstein Smith, I call them "New Naturalists."[12] Although these two groups of people, the debunkers and defenders of religion, hold opposite views on religion, they share the same narrow reductive naturalist framework and the typical attitude of scientism: They all assume that natural sciences tell us everything about reality.

Future histories may report that the public discourse on religion was dominated by reductive naturalism until Robert Bellah's *Religion in Human Evolution* appeared in 2011. One of the most distinctive features of Bellah's book is his extensive use of the latest developments in the natural sciences, such as biology, cognitive science, evolutionary psychology, and developmental and child psychology. His use of empirical studies of animal play in his constructing a theory of culture is just one example. One of his purposes is to show, as he puts it, "how deeply we are shaped by a very long biological history."[13] This might give the wrong impression that Bellah's approach is similar to that of the New Naturalists. I believe Bellah's approach is better characterized as a nonreductive humanistic naturalism, which is a synthesis of the humanistic (interpretative, social, and historical) understanding of religion and the naturalist approach. Bellah belongs to a long and rich humanistic tradition of sociological, anthological, and philosophical study of religion that can be traced back to Hegel, Durkheim, Mauss, Weber, Cassirer, Schutz, Voegelin, Ricoeur, and Geertz. Bellah also draws upon the "experiential-expressive" tradition founded by Schleiermacher, William James, and Paul Tillich, taking seriously the mental, emotional, and experiential dimensions of religion. Bellah's book should remind us of a maxim by Marquis de Vauvenargues: An original book is the one that makes one love old truth.

It is interesting to note that most of the aforementioned thinkers, such as Hegel, Cassirer, Schutz, Voegelin, Ricoeur, Schleiermacher, and James, are usually labeled "philosophers." In fact, it is better to characterize what Bellah does in the book as "philosophy of religion," in which "philosophy" is understood as a "humanistic discipline" as Bernard Williams defines it.[14] Bellah and Williams have very different views and temperaments when it comes to religion.[15] However, they share one thing in common: they respect the natural sciences and recognize their limits at the same time. In other words, they respect the sciences but reject scientism. As Williams puts it, "Philosophy should certainly be interested in the sciences and some philosophers may well be involved in them and nothing I say is meant to deny it." However, as he insists, "Scientism is, rather, a misunderstanding of the relations between philosophy and the natural sciences which tends to assimilate philosophy to the aims, or at least the manners, of the sciences."[16] I believe Bellah would have agreed completely with what Williams has to say about the relation between the sciences and philosophy (and the humanities), especially in the following passage:

> Philosophy should get rid of scientistic illusions, that it should not try to behave like an extension of the natural sciences (except in the special cases where that is what it is), that it should think of itself as part of a wider humanistic enterprise of making sense of ourselves and of our activities, and that in order to answer

> many of its questions it needs to attend to other parts of that enterprise, in particular to history.[17]

Both Bellah and Williams emphasize the importance of history in a humanistic approach to the study of human nature. We should not be misled by the word "evolution" in the title of Bellah's book. Bellah uses the term in a very broad sense so it includes history (and culture). This is another important respect in which he is different from the New Naturalists.

Bellah has overcome almost all the problems and limits of the New Naturalism that Barbara Herrnstein Smith has identified. Smith has argued that "there are better and worse ways of pursuing the naturalistic study of religion,"[18] and Bellah's humanistic naturalism is exactly this "better" naturalist approach Smith has envisioned. However, before I show why Bellah's approach is superior to the New Naturalist's, I have to give a brief summary of Bellah's seven-hundred-page-long book. Given the extraordinary complexity and richness of Bellah's book, this is almost an impossible task.

To take a big risk and to put it crudely, we may say that Bellah's book argues for two related themes or theses, and the book can be divided into two parts, each of which is devoted to one of the themes. The first is that religion is a cultural system, which is the topic of the first part of the book (chapters 1–2). It offers a general theory of religion as a cultural system by providing a general theory of culture. One of Bellah's most innovative and interesting ideas in this part of his work is that play gives rise to culture, especially ritual and myth, which are the key components of religion. Here he draws upon Johan Huizinga's classic *Homo Ludens: A Study of Play-Element in Culture*, Schiller's *On the Aesthetic Education of Man*, as well as contemporary empirical studies of animal play, summarized in Gordon Burghard's fascinating book *The Genesis of Animal Play*.

Bellah's second theme is that religion has evolved from the Paleolithic Age to the axial age around the world. This is the focus of the second part of the book (chapters 3–9), an epic narrative of the evolution of religions and cultures. Adopting Merlin Donald's account of the evolution of human cognition and culture,[19] Bellah's story of religious evolution is given as part of a general theory of cultural evolution in three stages: mimetic, mythic, and theoretic. Bellah's second thesis offers an important qualification of his first thesis. Religion is indeed a cultural system, but at the same time, religion is also always *embodied, social, personal, emotional, experiential, developmental,* and *historical.* These two interconnected theses also serve as a fundamental heuristic device that governs and organizes the interpretations of the extremely rich and diverse data of the empirical, historical, and ethnographical materials.

The second part of the book can be further divided into two sub-parts: chapters 3–5 deal with tribal and archaic religions, and chapters 6–9 cover the four axial religions in ancient Israel, Greece, China, and India. When he discusses tribal and archaic religions, Bellah focuses on the first two stages of cultural evolution, namely, mimetic and mythic. He gives an account of how our capacities for mimetic and mythic culture come about as a result of a long evolutionary process. In the part dealing with the four axial religions, Bellah focuses on the last stage of cultural evolution, that is, theoretic culture, which is developed in the axial age.

Now let me turn to three major differences between Bellah's and the New Naturalist's approach and show how and why Bellah is superior to the New Naturalists in all these aspects. First, Bellah has a much larger and better set of data. The New Naturalists tend to focus on religious *beliefs*; more specifically, they tend to focus rather narrowly on beliefs in monotheistic religions, such as beliefs in immortality, life after death, and the existence of supernatural agents such as God and spirits. Bellah's book, on the other hand, is one of the most comprehensive and global-minded studies of all types of religious beliefs and practices that have existed. It is a massive synthesis of various archeological, anthropological, and ethnographical studies of religious *beliefs* as well as *practices*. Bellah's "general theory of religion" is solidly based on empirical and historical case studies. The book can be said to consist of close examinations of a wide range of historical cases from around the world: the Australian Aborigines, the Brazilian Kalapalo, the North American Navajo; the religious practices in Tikopia, Polynesia, Hawaii, ancient Mesopotamia and Egypt, Shang and Western Zhou China; and finally religions in the four axial civilizations in ancient Israel, Greece, China, and India. Bellah's general theory is built on these concrete cases and is further tested, modified, and developed through the articulations and interpretations of these cases. One could argue that Bellah is doing better "science" of humanity partly because he has a much larger and more reliable set of data than the New Naturalists.

The second difference between Bellah and the New Naturalists is that Bellah has an adequate solution to, whereas the New Naturalists are not aware of and have no adequate solution to, what Bernard Williams calls the "problem of representation," which arises in any accounts that involve the relations between biology and human practices, such as evolutionary psychology or biological accounts of human practices. Williams formulates the problem as follows: "How is a phenotypic character which would present itself in other species as a behavioral tendency represented in a species which has a culture, language, and conceptual thought?"[20] Williams's view is similar to Bellah's. Let me cite a full passage from Williams here:

> Virtually no behavioral tendency which constitutes genuine action can just show up in a cultural context "as itself." Where there is culture, it affects everything, and we should reject the crude view that culture is applied to an animal in a way which leaves its other characteristics unmodified. . . . None of this is to deny that there is a biological basis for elements in human behavior which are culturally affected, moulded, and elaborated. It is not to deny that some culturally elaborated behavior can usefully be explained from a biological perspective. It is simply to recall the fact that almost all human behavior, at least that which deserves the name of "action," is in fact culturally moulded and elaborated.[21]

The New Naturalists are not aware of this problem. They tend to focus on mental modules, and religion is often explained in terms of a "module for supernatural being." They assume that there are immediate and direct causal connections between a mental mechanism and a religious belief, which indicates that they do not see the possibility that human believing as action and practice is culturally molded and elaborated. Furthermore, they do not see religion as a cultural system of *meaning*, mediated by—and expressed in—various modes of representations. Instead, as Smith points out, they see religious beliefs as "the automatic outcome of the activity of a universal cognitive mechanism responding to the inherent properties of some domain of stimuli,"[22] and they are not aware of what Smith calls "more than a century of relevant work in social theory and sociology of religion."[23] Pascal Boyer's 2002 book *Religion Explained* is a good example here. As Smith puts it, Boyer

> identifies interpretation with intellectual approaches cast as intrinsically nonscientific. Thus it is not surprising that terms like "symbol" or "represent" do not appear anywhere in his discussion of rituals or that he treats references to their "meaning" so dismissively there. Indeed, according to Boyer, rituals, contrary to the accounts of them given by many anthropologists and participants, are virtually meaningless.[24]

Smith's book *Natural Reflections* was published before Bellah's book. I think she certainly would have made use of Bellah's book as a positive model to show how to make sense of rituals and symbols. Bellah gives a comprehensive—and hence much richer—picture of various modes of religious representation: unitive representation, enactive representation, symbolic representation (such as iconic, musical, and poetic symbolization), and conceptual representation. For Bellah, religion is primarily about meaning; mimetic culture (ritual) and mythic culture (symbol and narrative) are essential parts of religious practice. For example, this is his definition of symbol: "It is always possible that an object, person or event in the world of daily life may have a meaning in another reality that transcends the world of working. If so we call it a *symbol*" (8). Bellah calls this approach "cultural-linguistic." Hence, Bellah's solution to what Williams called the "representation problem" can be put as follows: we must take the biological approach and the cultural-linguistic approach as "coordinate approaches," to borrow a phrase he uses in a similar context (12). I come back to Bellah's idea of coordinate approach later.

The third difference between Bellah and the New Naturalists is really an important implication of the second difference, which is that Bellah can give an adequate account of the particularities and varieties of religions throughout human history, whereas the New Naturalists take particular religions as mere manifestations of the same universal and ahistorical mental module for supernatural beings. The New Naturalists are unable to do justice to the cultural and historical differences among religions.[25]

Bellah is aware of a set of problems on various levels, which have the same structure as that of what Williams called the "representation problem." I have mentioned that Bellah draws upon the "experiential-expressive" tradition, which assumes that there is "a general human capacity for religious experience that is then actualized differently in different religious traditions" (11). Bellah is aware that this approach may have the tendency to take particular religions as simply "surface manifestations of this deep panhuman experiential potentiality" (11).

Bellah's solution to this problem is similar to his solution to the representation problem we have mentioned earlier, which is that we should take the "experiential-expressive" and the "cultural-linguistic" as "coordinate approaches." As he puts it, "We need to move back and forth between them to understand the phenomenon of religion" (12). Bellah emphasizes that the "cultural-linguistic representation" can have a looping effect on human experience. In other words, for Bellah, religion is not just about the mind (the beliefs and the mental modules). It involves the heart-mind, as well as the habits of the heart-mind that are shaped and formed by social practices and by linguistic-symbolic representations.

Since the New Naturalists focus on the mental modules, overlooking linguistic-symbolic representations, they are not even aware of this possibility that the latter can influence and shape the former. In sharp contrast, Bellah emphasizes the interaction between "cultural-linguistic representation" and "experiential/mental experience." He says the cultural-linguistic approach, "which derives from cultural anthropology, particularly from Clifford Geertz, takes symbolic forms as primary, seeing them not so much as expressions of underlying religious emotions, but as themselves *shaping religious experiences and emotions*" (11). This enables Bellah to accommodate the multiple aspects of particular religions, especially the cultural and historical particularities of various religious practices. Let me cite an important and representative passage here:

> Thus when I characterize widely different expressions as examples of Being cognition, I am not arguing that there is a subsistent reality of Being experience that simply comes out in different forms on different occasions. Rather, I am recognizing that there are some common human experiential potentialities that have recognizable similarities, but are inchoate until given shape by symbolic form. Once so shaped, their similarities are always qualified: the differences may be crucial. I am also fully in agreement with Lindbeck that cultural traditions not only shape, they even call forth emotional experiences. In short, we cannot disentangle raw experience from cultural form. Nevertheless we can see them as equally essential, like the Aristotelian notions of matter and form, and not have to choose one approach as primary. (12)

This passage provides the reason why Bellah's general theory of religion in the early chapters is able to accommodate the great diversity of so many particular religions from around the world from the Paleolithic to the axial age discussed in the later chapters.

Human Nature is Largely Second Nature (*Bildung*)

Bellah's book is so far the most comprehensive investigation into the "reality of life in the religious mode" (xxii). If we want to find another work that equals the scope, ambition, depth, and rigor of Bellah's book, the closest might be Hegel's *Lectures on the Philosophy of Religion*[26] or Weber's sociology of world religions. Here I focus on Bellah and Hegel.

There are several striking characteristics shared by both Hegel's and Bellah's projects. First, both projects were produced at the pinnacle of two magnificent careers, at the most mature stage of their intellectual lives. The second common feature is that Bellah's book matches Hegel's *Lectures* in terms of scope, ambition, and weight. Hegel's *Lectures* might be the only other major work, in addition to Max Weber's sociology of world religions, which covers the same wide range of themes as Bellah's: a general theory of religion and culture, as well as religions of ancient Israel, Greece, China, and India. Hegel's *Lectures* represents the final and in some ways the decisive element of his entire philosophical system, and the same can be said about Bellah's book regarding its place in his system of thought. In his concluding chapter, Bellah characterizes his book as belonging to the genre of "universal history." Even though Bellah emphasizes that his history is quite different from the traditional Hegelian "universal history" in many aspects (more of this later), it is still a *universal* history.

The third common feature of Hegel's and Bellah's work is the most important one, which is that Bellah's guiding heuristic that "nothing is ever lost" is a Hegelian idea (I say more about this later). The Hegel passage Bellah has chosen as one of the three epigraphs for his preface is very telling: "Those moments which the spirit appears to have outgrown still belong to it in the depths of its present. Just as it has passed through all its moments in history, so also must it pass through them again in the present" (ix). Both Hegel and Bellah try to tell the universal history of religion as *Bildungsroman* of humankind. And they see it as an essential part of human *Bildung* through which a *particular* individual becomes a *universal* individual, which is the goal of *Bildung* (culture or education). This is how and why human nature is largely second nature. In other words, human nature is largely human culture (*Bildung*). I believe Bellah would have agreed with what McDowell says in the following: "Our nature is largely second nature, and our second nature is the way it is not just because of the potentialities we were born with, but also because of our upbringing, our *Bildung*."[27] It is interesting to note that both Bellah and McDowell rely on the Hegelian idea of *Bildung*. If McDowell is indeed right that our nature is largely second nature, our next task should then be exactly what Bellah has accomplished, which is to articulate a nuanced theory and narrative of human second nature.

What would be the implications for education, according to this naturalism of second nature? To become truly *human*, we must, as Bellah puts it, "live again those moments that belong to us in the depths of our present, to draw living water from the well of the past" (xxiv). I speculate that this might have been one of the reasons Bellah changed the original title of his book manuscript from *Religious Evolution* (which is also the title of his celebrated 1963 essay) into *Religion in Human Evolution.*[28] This is why Bellah's book is a must read for anyone who considers herself/himself an educated human being.

The "Spontaneous Becoming in Different Spaces" in Bellah's Universal History

Although there are many similarities between Hegel's and Bellah's universal history, there are important differences. For instance, Bellah's universal history is more "critical" than Hegel's in the sense that he has corrected a major dogma in Hegel's system, which is Hegel's Eurocentrism. Bellah breathes new life into universal history by making ancient China and India indispensable parts of a grand narrative of human religious evolution. People today tend to be suspicious about any evolutionary story, for they often assume that an evolutionary project must commit itself to the teleology of progress and Eurocentrism. I believe one of Bellah's major achievements is to have rescued universal history from its traditional provincial and Eurocentric dogmas. For example, Bellah shows that what is common to all of the four axial religions in ancient Egypt, Greece, Israel, China, and India is that they all have grown through the three stages of human evolution: mimetic, mythic, and theoretic. One implication of this is that there is what Feuerbach calls "*spontaneous becoming in different spaces*" in Bellah's narrative, which is exactly what is missing in Hegel's universal history. Let me explain.

According to Hegel, the World Spirit marches on progressively in time, and it would eventually reach its end—its actualization—in modern Europe. For Hegel, this is a world history in the sense that each nation or culture gives its specific contribution in a linear temporal manner in this process. In Hegel's script for this grand play called "World History," China and India appear in the first act only; they contribute something primitive at the beginning of world history, for China and India only represent "Nature Religion." They are then "frozen" in these moments in the infancy of humankind; there is never development or evolution *in* China or India because the World Spirit only goes *through* them, moving on to Jewish and Greek religions, which are "Religion(s) of Spiritual Individuality."

Interestingly, Feuerbach has anticipated Bellah's critique. In fact, he might have been the first critic of Hegel to point out that Hegel does not really have a concept of spontaneous becoming in different places. Let me quote Feuerbach here:

> Hegel determines and presents only the most striking differences of various religions, philosophies, times, and peoples, and in a progressive series of stages, but he ignores all that is common and identical in all of them. The form of both Hegel's conception and method is that of exclusive time alone, not that of tolerant space; his system knows only subordination and succession; coordination and coexistence are unknown to it.[29]

What we find in Bellah's book is exactly this "tolerant space" and "coordination and coexistence" that Feuerbach found wanting in Hegel. In Bellah, what is common to all axial religions is that they all grow through the same three stages of human evolution. To put Bellah's point in Hegel's terms, world spirit does not march *through* places, but rather it dances *in* each and every place in the world. Bellah has produced a *Bildungsroman* of the human spirit on a truly global scale.[30]

The Hegelian Heuristic Device: "Nothing Is Ever Lost"

The idea that nothing is ever lost is the guiding heuristic device of Bellah's book.[31] For instance, this is very much the idea that guides Bellah's discussion of individual developmental psychology: nothing in the early stages of an individual's psychological life is "ever lost" in the later stages. And this is also the case on the level of human history. As he puts it, "The view that 'nothing is ever lost' can, as we shall see, also be brought to bear on religious history" (13). Indeed, this heuristic guides Bellah's discussion of Merlin Donald's thesis that human culture has evolved through three stages: mimetic, mythic, and theoretic. Bellah argues that the early stages are never lost in the later stages.

For example, when he discusses Mesopotamian culture, which is supposed to be a "dead civilization" (a phrase that appears in the title of Leo Oppenheim's book on Mesopotamian civilization), Bellah insists that "in an important sense, all culture is one: human beings today owe something to every culture that has gone before us. Mesopotamian culture certainly had an influence on its neighbors, notably Persia, Israel, and Greece" (225). While discussing the gods in Egyptian religion, Bellah says,

> Since "we" are the product of all previous human culture, we have, at some level "already" experienced those gods, as we have "already" experienced the powerful beings of tribal peoples. If

> we are truly to understand ancient Egyptian religion (or any religion) it will be part of our task to "remember" what we have forgotten, but which in some sense we already know. (228).

The idea that nothing is ever lost is also the guiding heuristic in the chapters on the axial religions. What makes the axial religions *axial*? How should we understand the Axial Age? According to Bellah, there are two defining features of the axial age: the emergence of a reflective and critical standpoint (what Jaspers calls "reflexivity," what Momigliano calls "criticism"), and the emergence of theoretic culture (especially "theory-construction"). Bellah makes a compelling case for a general similarity among the four axial religions, which is that all forms of culture—mimetic, mythic, and theoretic—coexist in each of the axial religions, and they form what Merlin Donald calls a "hybrid system" even after the emergence of theoretic culture.[32] In other words, the first two forms of culture are not replaced by the theoretic culture, which is the last stage. Instead, the theoretic culture "grows out of and significantly criticizes, but never abandons, the early stages [of mimetic and mythic culture]" (118). I call this Bellah's "hybrid system" thesis.

In the case of early China, Bellah's "hybrid system" thesis makes even better sense. Here are two pieces of evidence: First, narrative is a major part of many Chinese texts in the Axial age.[33] Second, most early Chinese thinkers in the axial age argued that ritual was indispensable.[34] In other words, after the emergence of the theoretic culture in axial China, mythic culture (narrative) and mimetic culture (ritual) are not being replaced. Unlike in the case of ancient Greece, it is relatively much easier to show that ancient China is a cultural "hybrid system" that includes all three cultures at once. However, when we move to Plato, we tend to assume that philosophy as theory-construction has completely replaced myth and narrative. This is perhaps why Bellah devotes a substantial part of the ancient Greece chapter arguing that the "hybrid system" thesis applies to Plato as well. As he puts it:

> My point is that the power of Plato is his reform of the whole of what Donald called the cultural "hybrid system," the system that includes mimetic, mythic and theoretic in a new synthesis, but not the replacement of mimetic and mythic by the theoretic alone. Such a replacement is an experiment that no one central to the axial transition in any of the four cases undertook; that awaited the emergence of western modernity in the seventeenth century. (394–395)

"Looking for Friends in History": Bellah's Mencian Friendship-Based Hermeneutics

Bellah's reading of Plato is just one example of what may be called Bellah's "friendship-based hermeneutics," which is practiced throughout the book. Here we are using Aristotle's definition of friendship: a friend is another self. In this sense, Plato is still our friend, and this might be the reason why he is still speaking to us today. Bellah believes that there is "friendship between the ancients and the moderns":

> This book asks what our deep past can tell us about the kind of life human beings have imagined was worth living. It is an effort to live again those moments that belong to us in the depths of our present, to draw living water from the well of the past, *to find friends in history who can help us understand where we are.* (xxiv; emphasis added)

The last phrase is an allusion to a passage from the *Mencius* (5B8), which Bellah uses as one of three epigraphs for his preface. In this passage, Mencius is essentially saying that the right way to read the writings of the ancients is very much like "finding friends in history." This Mencian friendship-based hermeneutics is further illustrated by a moving passage in Bellah's acknowledgments:

> It perhaps goes without saying, but I will say it anyway, that I owe much to the friends in history that Mencius talked about, not least to Mencius himself, but to all the creators of the great traditions that I deal with in the later chapters of this book, as well as to the reciters of myth and the dancers of ritual in the tribal and archaic traditions, who must remain anonymous, but who have been, not merely my examples, but my teachers in this enterprise. (xxvii)

If we contrast Bellah's "the ancients-as-friends" hermeneutics with the antagonistic hermeneutic approach to the past that is articulated in Harold Bloom's *The Anxiety of Influence*, it is illuminating that we don't see any "anxiety of influence" here. Much could be said about Bellah's uniquely calm and generous voice in this book. There is no anxiety in his engagement with the ancients; there is instead magnanimity.[35]

I have said earlier that the idea that nothing is ever lost is the guiding *heuristic* for Bellah. I intentionally used the term "heuristic" because Bellah does not take it to be literally true with regard to everything in history. As Bellah puts it, "I also believe that there are types of religion and that these types can be put in an evolutionary order, not in terms of better or worse, but in terms of the capacities upon which they draw" (xviii). In the following passage, Bellah makes it very clear that the slogan "nothing is ever lost" means that the *capacities* are never lost. This crucial insight allows Bellah to hold the view that there is "progress" in the sense that new capacities are acquired as humankind moves from tribal and archaic religions to axial age religions. Yet he can at the same time reject the view that there is progress in all aspects in general:

> Religious evolution does not mean a progression from worse to better. We have not gone from "primitive religion" that tribal peoples have had to "higher religions" that people like us have. . . . Religious evolution does add new capacities, but it tells us nothing about how those capacities will be used. It is worth remembering, as Stephen J. Gould pointed out, that complexity is not the only good. (xxii–xxiii)

In other words, Bellah is able to take seriously the grand universal narrative of the development of *human capacities* without falling into the traps of a modernist and triumphalist history of religion, which were popularized in the nineteenth century, often assuming a hierarchy of religions, from "primitive" to "advanced." Bellah does not assume the teleological primacy of "progress" in religious evolution; instead he pays great attention to the evolution of new "capacities" in each religious tradition on its own terms.

Bellah's book seems to be a sign that postmodernism is on its way out, and grand narrative has returned. Postmodernism can mean too many things these days, but its initial and defining meaning, as Jean-François Lyotard has claimed, is really its complete rejection and distrust of any grand narrative or universal history. However, as Bellah would certainly remind us, since nothing is ever lost, postmodernism cannot be completely forgotten. What we find in Bellah's book is *critical* universal history because it has absorbed the postmodernist critique of the traditional, dogmatic, and provincial "universal history."

Again the chapter on ancient China is a great example here. It is clear that one of Bellah's goals is to use the case of ancient China to test his general theory of religion and cultural evolution. However, the China chapter is much more than that. Any reader will be impressed by Bellah's genuine curiosity and fascination about the historical, social, and cultural details of ancient China, many of which are not necessarily relevant for the purpose of confirming Bellah's general theories and theses. It seems that Bellah wants to tell the story of early China and its religions and philosophies for its own sake, trying to do justice to its particularities and diversities.[36] The same can be said about the chapters on the other axial civilizations. The generosity and breadth of Bellah's empathy with and curiosity about humanity is on full display on every page. One will never see human history and our contemporary world the same after reading Bellah's magnificent book.

Conclusion

The subtitle of Bellah's book, *From the Paleolithic to the Axial Age*, indicates that it is about religions between the Paleolithic and the axial ages. Bellah explicitly states that this is "not a book about modernity" and that he plans to write another, smaller book on modernity (xxiv). The tentative title for the smaller book is *The Modern Project in the Light of Human Evolution*. It is a great loss that Bellah had not finished the book when he passed away in 2013. However, in a very important sense *Religion in Human Evolution* is about modernity as well. Keep in mind that his original intention was to write a book that covered from the Paleolithic Age to modernity. It was after thirteen years of working on it with the result of a one-thousand-page-long manuscript that he realized that he needed to stop and send it to the publisher and write another smaller book on modernity. We can assume that the key idea in the book on modernity would be the idea that there are necessary links "between past and present," and that "nothing is ever lost."

In his 2007 book *A Secular Age*, Charles Taylor has identified "secularism's subtraction stories" as the central dogma of secularism and modernism. They are, as Taylor puts it, "stories of modernity in general, and secularity in particular, which explains them by human beings having lost, or sloughed off, or liberated themselves from certain earlier, confining horizons, or illusions, or limitations of knowledge."[37] Obviously, Bellah's "nothing is ever lost" theme-based *Bildungsroman* of human religion implies a rejection of secularism's dogmatic assumption, which is that theoretic culture can be the *only* sources of knowledge, representation, criticism, and meaning, and that it can completely replace mimetic and mythic cultures.

Since Taylor focuses on telling the stories about what has happened between the sixteenth and twentieth centuries in Europe, he does not have much to say about the early history of religion in a global setting. From this perspective, Bellah's and Taylor's books complement each other perfectly. They will certainly become two landmark texts in our ongoing discourse on modernity and secularism in the twenty-first century.

Notes

*I am grateful to P. J. Ivanhoe and Sungmoon Kim for inviting me to be part of the conference in honor of Robert Bellah at the City University of Hong Kong in December 2011. Special thanks go to Lindsay Waters for his generous encouragement. My deepest gratitude goes to my first reader Anna Sun, as always.

1. Robert N. Bellah, Richard Madsen, William M. Sullivan, Ann Swidler, and Steven M. Tipton, *Habits of the Heart: Individualism and Commitment in American Life* (Berkeley: University of California Press, 1985). The Chinese translation was published in 1991: 心灵的习性 (Beijing: San Lian Press, 1991). It was reprinted by a different press in 2011 (Beijing: Zhongguo shehuikexue Press, 2011).

2. This is what Hannah Arendt calls the "critical interpretation of the past," which, as she puts it, is "an interpretation whose chief aim is to discover the real origins of traditional concepts in order to distill from them anew their original spirit which has so sadly evaporated from the very key words of political language." *Between Past and Future: Eight Exercises in Political Thought* (New York: Viking Press, 1968), 15. This is not entirely dissimilar with the "hermeneutics of restoration through criticism" in Paul Ricoeur and Josiah Royce; please see Bellah's discussion of them in *The Robert Bellah Reader*, ed. Robert N. Bellah and Steven M. Tipton (Durham: Duke University Press, 2006), 216–217 and 313–314. As I argue in this essay, this idea of "history of the present" is implied by Bellah's Hegelian idea that "nothing is ever lost" in *Religion in Human Evolution.*

3. Yang Xiao, "Rediscovering Republicanism in China: Beyond the Debate between New Leftists and Liberals," *Contemporary Chinese Thought* 34.3 (Spring 2003): 18 34; please see especially my discussion of *Habits of the Heart* on p. 26. Please also see Yang Xiao, "Republican Beginnings: Liberty as Non-Domination in the Chinese Republican Tradition," *Republicanism in Northeast Asian Context*, ed. Jun-Hyeok Kwak and Leigh Jenco (London: Routledge, 2014), 137–157.

4. Bellah's PhD is a joint degree in sociology and what was then called "Far Eastern languages" at Harvard University, and his dissertation was later published as *Tokugawa Religion: The Cultural Roots of Modern Japan* in 1957. Bellah continued to write about Japan while writing about America. *Imagining Japan: The Japanese Tradition and Its Modern Interpretation*, a collection of his essays on Japan, was published in 2003.

5. Bellah was the first to have acknowledged this; in the first footnote of the essay on civil religion in America, he asked the question of "why something so obvious [civil religion in America] should have escaped serious analytical attention." He then says, "Part of the reason this issue has been left in obscurity is certainly due to the peculiar Western concept of 'religion' as denoting a single type of collectivity of which an individual can be a member of one and only one at a time. The Durkheimian notion that every group has a religious dimension, which would be seen as obvious in southern or eastern Asia, is foreign to us. This obscures the recognition of such dimensions in our society." "Civil Religion," *Beyond Belief: Essays on Religion in a Post-Traditionalist World* (Berkeley: University of California Press, 1991), 187n1.

6. It is important to note that how to imagine a global civil society is the theme of Bellah's keynote speech presented as the University Distinguished Lecture at the City University of Hong Kong in 2011 and is included as the final chapter in this volume.

7. This passage is from her second lecture, Marjorie Garber, "Who Owns 'Human Nature'?" *A Manifesto for Literary Studies* (Seattle: Walter Chapin Simpson Center for the Humanities, 2003), 19–20.

8. John McDowell, "Two Sorts of Naturalism," *Mind, Value and Reality* (Cambridge: Harvard University Press, 1998), 167–197. McDowell's critique of what he calls "bald naturalism" is applicable to the New Naturalism.

9. John McDowell, *Mind and World* (Cambridge: Harvard University Press, 1991), 86.

10. Please see Richard Dawkins, *The God Delusion* (Boston: Houghton Mifflin, 2006); Sam Harris, *The End of Faith: Religion, Terror, and the Future of Reason* (New York: W.W. Norton, 2004); Christopher Hitchens, *God Is Not Great: How Religion Poisons Everything* (New York: Twelve, 2007); and Daniel Dennett, *Breaking the Spell: Religion as a Natural Phenomenon* (New York: Viking, 2006).

11. Please see Stewart Guthrie, *Faces in the Clouds: A New Theory of Religion* (New York: Oxford University Press, 1993); Pascal Boyer, *Religion Explained: The Evolutionary Origins of Religion* (New York: Basic Books, 2001); Scott Atran, *In Gods We Trust: The Evolutionary Landscape of Religion* (New York: Oxford University Press, 2002); and Justin Barrett, *Why Should Anyone Believe in God* (Lanham: AltaMira Press, 2004).

12. Barbara Herrnstein Smith, *Natural Reflections: Human Cognition at the Nexus of Science and Religion* (New Haven: Yale University Press, 2009). Smith takes Boyer and Atran as representatives of this approach. Her book is one of the best books on science and religion, and she offers a penetrating critique of the New Naturalists.

13. Robert N. Bellah, *Religion in Human Evolution: From the Paleolithic to the Axial Age* (Cambridge: Harvard University Press, 2011), 83. Hereafter, reference to this book will be cited in the text by page number.

14. Bellah's "philosophy of religion," if we do use this term to characterize what he is doing, is very different from the philosophy of religion practiced by analytic philosophers in the English-speaking countries, in which the focus in on

the logical analysis of concepts and reconstructions of arguments, especially the arguments for the existence of God and the logical solutions of theological problems such as the problem of evil. Obviously, no one would deny that this is an important part of a study of religion. But to believe that this is all there is in the philosophy of religion is a serious mistake.

15. Bellah has been greatly influenced by Alasdair MacIntyre and Charles Taylor, and there are deep affinities among their views on religion and ethics. Williams is generally considered to be quite different from MacIntyre and Taylor, and perhaps Bellah as well. But the agreements among them are often overlooked. For example, all four of them reject scientism and take history to be necessary and essential in any attempt to make sense of humanity. In an edited volume in honor of Williams, Taylor contributed a chapter on Williams's critique of modern moral philosophy. In his reply to Taylor, Williams characterized the similarities and differences among him, MacIntyre, and Taylor as follows: "If Taylor and MacIntyre will forgive me putting them into mere cartoon sketch, one set of relations between our positions might perhaps be put like this: Taylor and MacIntyre are Catholic, and I am not; Taylor and I are liberals, and MacIntyre is not; MacIntyre and I are pessimists, and Taylor is not (not really)." Bernard Williams, "Replies," *World, Mind, and Ethics: Essays on the Ethical Philosophy of Bernard Williams*, ed. J. E. J. Altham and Ross Harrison (Cambridge: Cambridge University Press, 1995), 222n20. If we take Bellah into account, we may say the following: Bellah, Taylor, and MacIntyre are Christians, and Williams is not; Bellah, Taylor, and Williams are liberals, and MacIntyre is not; MacIntyre and Williams are pessimists, and Bellah and Taylor are not. Bellah and Taylor's Hegelian belief that nothing is ever lost makes them non-pessimists. I say more about this later in the chapter.

16. Bernard Williams, "Philosophy as a Humanistic Discipline," *Philosophy as a Humanistic Discipline* (Princeton: Princeton University Press, 2008), 182.

17. Ibid., 197. By the phrase "except in the special cases where that is what it is," Williams refers to sub-disciplines in philosophy such as the philosophy of quantum mechanics which may be rightly considered as an extension of the sciences.

18. Smith, *Natural Reflections*, 121. She calls this "one of my central points in this book" (121).

19. Merlin Donald, *Origins of the Modern Mind: Three Stages in the Evolution of Culture and Cognition* (Cambridge: Harvard University Press, 1991) and *A Mind So Rare: The Evolution of Human Consciousness* (New York: W.W. Norton, 2001).

20. Bernard Williams, "Evolution, Ethics, and the Representation Problem," *Making Sense of Humanity* (Cambridge: Cambridge University Press, 1995), 102.

21. Ibid.

22. Smith, *Natural Reflections*, 93.

23. Ibid., 86–87.

24. Ibid., 54.

25. Since I have been very critical of the New Naturalists, here let me say that this kind of research has its value in that they give a good account of the *psychology* of certain religious *beliefs*. This is a rather limited contribution to the *comprehensive*

study of religion as both beliefs and *practices*. It is a contribution nevertheless. The limits of these scholars' contribution do not necessarily come from their personal failings as scholars. Rather, they come from the limits of their disciplines (psychology and evolutionary psychology) when applied to study religion, which is more than a psychological phenomenon. Furthermore, we should differentiate the New Naturalists from another group of people who try to give vulgar "scientific" proofs of God; please see Dean Hamer, *The God Gene: How Faith Is Hardwired into Our Genes* (New York: Anchor, 2005); Matthew Alper, *The "God" Part of the Brain: A Scientific Explanation of Human Spirituality and God* (New York: Rogue Press, 2001); Andrew Newberg, Eugene D'Aquili, and Vince Rause, *Why God Won't Go Away: Brain Science and the Biology of Belief* (New York: Ballantine Books, 2002); Andrew Newberg and Mark Waldman, *Born to Believe: God, Science, and the Origin of Ordinary and Extraordinary Belief* (New York: Atria Books, 2007). In these books, religion is explicitly reduced to certain type of peak experience in the brain.

26. G. W. F. Hegel, *Lectures on the Philosophy of Religion, Volume I Introduction and the Concept of Religion*, ed. Peter Hodgson (Berkeley: University of California Press, 1984): G. W. F. Hegel, *Lectures on the Philosophy of Religion, Volume II Determinate Religion*, ed. Peter Hodgson (Berkeley: University of California Press, 1987); G. W. F. Hegel, *Lectures on the Philosophy of Religion, Volume III The Consummate Religion*, ed. Peter Hodgson (Berkeley: University of California Press, 1985).

27. McDowell, *Mind and World*, 87–88.

28. I have had the privilege and honor to read the draft of the chapters whenever Bellah finished one. I read the draft of the first chapter fifteen years ago; the original title of the book at the time was *Religious Evolution*.

29. Ludwig Feuerbach, "Towards a Critique of Hegel's Philosophy," *The Fiery Brook: Selected Writings of Ludwig Feuerbach*, trans. Zawar Hanfi (New York: Anchor Books, 1972), 54.

30. Bellah makes similar corrections to Weber's comparative sociology of world religions. At the center of Weber's project is a rather narrow question that motivates and frames his work: What had enabled the West—and only the West—to produce a rational form of capitalism, namely, modern capitalism? After completing *The Protestant Ethic and the Spirit of Capitalism*, Weber embarked on analyzing other world religions in order to answer this question. As Bellah points out, "For Weber it was not just Protestant Christianity, but what he called 'ascetic Protestantism,' . . . against which all other religions were to be measured and found more or less wanting, beginning with Catholicism, but then going on to the religions of China and India" (603). However, although Bellah shares Weber's belief that to know only one religion is to know none, and that world religions must be studied comparatively, he does not use modern capitalism as the only goal or standard to measure the axial age religions.

31. Bellah gives other formulations of this idea as well, one of which is the following: "religion is one because every expression of religion is historically related, somehow, to every other" (xxvi).

32. Donald, *Origins of the Modern Mind*, 368.

33. For a discussion of the importance of narrative in the *Analects*, as well as in the long tradition of its commentaries, see Yang Xiao, "How Confucius Does Things with Words: Two Paradigms of Hermeneutic Practice in the *Analects* and Its Exegeses," *Journal of Asian Studies* 66.2 (May 2007): 497–532. For an excellent study of narrative in the *Zuozuan*, see Wai-yee Li, *The Readability of the Past in Early Chinese Historiography* (Cambridge: Harvard University Asia Center, 2007).

34. This has been emphasized by many Western scholars, most notably Herbert Fingarette, *Confucius: The Secular as Sacred* (New York: Harper Torchbooks, 1972). For an excellent articulation and defense, see P. J. Ivanhoe, *Confucian Reflections: Ancient Wisdom for Modern Times* (London: Routledge, 2013). As MacIntyre puts it, "In no Aristotelian catalogue of the virtues, for example, indeed in no Western catalogue of the virtues, do we find any mention of *li*, the Chinese name of the virtue of ritual propriety. . . . What is missing, when ritual is absent, is the unity of inner thought and feeling with outward bodily expression that constitutes integrity. . . . It is in and through ritual, thus understood, that our dispositions to respond adequately and relevantly to particular social situations and to communicate to others the character of our responses are exhibited. Hence, it is not just that without the exercise of *li* we cannot possess *ren*. It is that without the exercise of *li*, we cannot genuinely possess *any* virtue." Alasdair MacIntyre, "Once More on Confucian and Aristotelian Conceptions of the Virtues," in *Chinese Philosophy in an Era of Globalization*, ed. Robin Wang (Albany: State University of New York Press, 2004), 152, 156, 157. MacIntyre's claim about the uniqueness of the Confucian virtue of ritual may need to be qualified if we take into account the virtue of decorum in Cicero and Seneca; please see Nancy Sherman's discussion of the Stoic view that "decorum is inextricably woven into the fabric of virtuous character. . . . [And the emphasis on] the crucial role of emotional demeanor in acts of kindness and gratitude." Nancy Sherman, "Of Manners and Morals," *British Journal of Educational Studies* 53.3 (September 2005): 273.

35. I wish I had the space to say more about the style of writing in Bellah's book, but this is already a long essay. Much could have been said about Bellah's uniquely calm, patient, and generous often magnanimous voice in this book.

36. As Bellah puts it, "The religion of each person, group, or tradition is unique and can never be captured adequately with general terms such as 'Christianity' or 'Confucianism,' right up to the term 'religion' itself" (xxvi).

37. Charles Taylor, *A Secular Age* (Cambridge: Harvard University Press, 2007), 22.

10

Can We Imagine a Global Civil Religion?

Robert N. Bellah

In my essay "Civil Religion in America," first published in *Daedalus* in 1967, over forty years ago, which, unfortunately, quite a few people think is the only thing I ever wrote, I did discuss toward the end the possibility of what I called a "world civil religion."[1] Naïve though it may sound today, the idea of a world civil religion as expressing "the attainment of some kind of viable and coherent world order" was the imagined resolution of what I then called America's third time of trial, an idea later developed in my book *The Broken Covenant*.[2] The first time of trial was concerned with the question of independence and the second with the issue of slavery, but the third, as I then put it, was concerned with America's place in the world, and what kind of world it would have a place in. That "viable and coherent world order" for which I hoped, would, I believed, require "a major new set of symbolic forms." So far, I argued, "the flickering flame of the United Nations burns too low to be the focus of a cult, but the emergence of a genuine transnational sovereignty would certainly change this." A genuinely transnational sovereignty? Quite remarkably, just last month the Vatican released a document calling for just such a transnational institution to oversee the global economy and even tax banks to pay for its activities. Not surprisingly this idea was apoplectically rejected by the American right wing. This apparently utopian idea is something we will have to think about later. But I did hold that, though the idea of a world civil religion would be in one sense the fulfillment of "the eschatological hope of American civil religion," nonetheless "it obviously would draw on religious traditions beyond the sphere of biblical religion alone."

When P. J. Ivanhoe first consulted me about my attendance at this week's conference, he referred to Confucianism as "a habit of the heart" in

East Asia, and a possible civil religion there. I expressed my problems with the term "civil religion," but in thinking further about the possible religious dimensions of a global civil society, I was intrigued by Ivanhoe's use of Alexis de Tocqueville's term "habits of the heart" to refer to Confucianism, and I thought it might be worthwhile to consider the implications of trying to translate that term into Chinese. Translators of the classical word for heart, *xin* 心, are often worried that the reader may take the term in its colloquial English sense of feelings as opposed to intellect and so translate it as "heart and mind" or "heart/mind." Yet I think that when Tocqueville used the term "heart" he did not mean feelings alone. He used it in the deep biblical sense of *leb* in Hebrew, which has been said to mean "the core of the person" and to include "personality, emotions, intellect, will, and relationship with God." Yet we could use this rich and complex meaning of "heart" in biblical religion to translate *xin*, possibly changing relationship with God to relationship with Heaven, but catching the deep and rich meaning of heart in Mencius, say, and in both cases realizing that the term is beyond simple translation in any English word.

When Tocqueville used the term "habit" he probably didn't have a biblical term to draw from, but without necessarily being conscious of it, the word *ethos*, in ancient Greek philosophy, meant variously a person's character; for the Stoics, source of behavior, as well as what we more commonly think of as habit. Here the fit is not as close as with "heart," but if we think of *li* 禮 as a possible Chinese translation of habit in Tocqueville's profound sense, then we will actually enrich the Western term, for *li*, which originally meant ritual, came to mean the appropriate way to relate to others and the world, carrying a depth of ethical meaning that our word "habits" barely touches. Nonetheless if the term "habits of the heart" could sum up some absolutely central ideas in East Asian and Western religion and philosophy, we might indeed see them as a possibly universal entry into something like the spiritual dimension of a global civil society, if not a global civil religion.

Returning to my original essay and its extraordinary vision of a possible global civil religion might make it seem that that essay of forty years ago was hopelessly out of touch with reality—the resolution of the third time of trial being no closer today than it was then, perhaps even farther away—unless one realizes that much of the actual text of that essay was a severe criticism of an America that had gone badly astray and was not helping the world toward a viable and coherent world order at all. I included a long quotation from Senator J. William Fulbright about "the arrogance of power."

Still we can hope; perhaps hope is all we have. Times of trial in human history have often been protracted, have lasted a hundred years or more, and if ours seems to have no end in sight, we can still imagine the possibility, even the necessity, of a viable and coherent world order if our catastrophe—ecological, political, economic—is not to become total.

One thing I learned from the complex discussion of the 1967 essay is that for many, particularly religious believers but also secularists, the idea of "a civil religion" is viewed as a threat, one religion competing with and threatening to displace other religions, even being established. All my Durkheimian arguments that any really existing social group necessarily has a religious dimension never quelled the opposition, to the point where, by about 1980, I stopped using the term "civil religion" and talked about the same issues using other language, language that did not involve me in endless, futile, discussions of definition. So if American civil religion is a bad idea, a global civil religion can only be worse, and I can answer the question of my title, which itself was meant to provoke as much as to describe, in the negative: no, a global civil religion is not possible.

But for the creation of a viable and coherent world order a world civil society is surely an essential precondition, and, dare I say it, any actual civil society will have a religious dimension, will need not only a legal and an ethical framework but some notion that it conforms to the nature of ultimate reality. The biggest immediate problem is the strengthening of global civil society, and it is on that that I want to focus, but I will have some hints and suggestions that perhaps the religious communities of the world may have something to contribute to that global civil society, and that their participation may be essential for its success.

But first I think I have to raise the serious question, one not on the table in 1967, as to whether we don't already have a global civil religion. Harvey Cox raised this issue starkly in his essay "Mammon and the Culture of the Market," a contribution to my *Festschrift* published in 2002. In his first paragraph he says, "My thesis is that the emerging global market culture—despite those who do not, or choose not, to see it—is generating an identifiable value-laden, 'religious' world-view." The market, Cox argues, is not seen as a human creation but as a power beyond human control. In this view the market is omnipotent, omniscient, and omnipresent. All we have to do, as individuals or nations, is to bow down to it. Its demands are beyond question.[3]

Although many are suffering under the rule of this deity, those who celebrate it can be found all over the world, in China and India as well as the West, and, for the moment they seem without serious opposition. But if the worship of Mammon is the new global religion, it is not one that can create a viable and coherent world order or a global civil society that might make that possible. On the contrary, it seems to make our grave problems, environmental catastrophe and the greatest inequality in human history, worse, not better. Can we understand what is happening and can we see any alternative?

I want to use some statements of Michael Walzer as a foil for my argument. I have learned much from him, have taught some of his books, so it was with some surprise that I found myself raising serious questions about his book *Thick and Thin: Moral Argument at Home and Abroad.* I was amazed to learn from him that humanity in effect does not exist. He writes:

> Societies are necessarily particular because they have members with memories not only of their own but of their common life. Humanity, by contrast, has members but no memory, and so it has no history and no culture, no customary practices, no familiar life-ways, no festivals, no shared understanding of social goods. It is human to have such things, but there is no singular human way of having them.[4]

And later in the book he writes, "Our common humanity will never make us members of a single universal tribe. The crucial commonality of the human race is particularism: we participate, all of us, in thick cultures that are our own."[5] This is especially news to me since I have spent much of my life, particularly the last ten years, writing the history of humanity in a book entitled *Religion in Human Evolution.* And I have argued that the fact that religion has characterized all human societies means that religion is a kind of common culture, religion in the singular as I learned from my teacher Wilfred Cantwell Smith, even though it is also, as is all human culture, at the same time indelibly particular.

What I would question in Walzer's position is the idea that the global and the particular are mutually exclusive, that one lives in one and only one community, which, were it true, would surely make the idea of membership in "a single universal tribe" impossible. I would argue, on the contrary, that humans have almost never lived in one and only one community, that we almost always, and in modern times necessarily always, live in many overlapping communities, and, under the rule of Mammon, none of them may be particularly thick. To affirm that humanity has no memory, no history, and no culture, seems to me remarkable at a time when there is widespread popular interest in human origins, in human evolution, and, since the pioneering work of William McNeill, in world history. And if the Olympic Games and, for much of the world, the World Cup, aren't global festivals, what are they? According to the *Wikipedia*, 715 million people watched the 2006 World Cup.

Harold Berman has eloquently argued for the existence of world law, which necessarily implies at least the beginnings of world politics and world civil society.[6] While we have no world state, and wouldn't want one, the beginnings of world governance, which is not the same thing as a world state, we certainly have. A remarkable example is the fact that air traffic control and the rules for landing and taking off at airports, even the language used between pilots and controllers, are the same all over the world. Even more obviously, our global economy would be impossible were there not a plethora of rules, some legal, some customary, governing global trade and capital transfers. We will need to sort out what is ominous and what is promising in this growing array of world law and world regulation, but that world society doesn't exist and each of us is stuck in his or her particularistic tribe, as Walzer affirms, seems to me remarkably far from the truth.

That there is no world culture seems to me an idea that can come only from the reification of the nation-state. World culture can be traced all the way back. The bow and arrow, for example, had been adopted everywhere except in Australia, long before history. Stith Thompson has traced motifs in folklore that can be found in every continent. There has never been a time when human culture has not been shared; we do not come in hermetically sealed boxes. Even the nation-state is a cultural form that has been transmitted with remarkable fidelity over the entire world since the nineteenth century, as the works of John Meyer and his associates have abundantly shown.[7] Wilfred Smith has traced shared stories and practices throughout the world religions, most of which themselves have been disseminated over very wide areas and have influenced and been influenced by those they have not converted.[8] Hinduism spread throughout Southeast Asia, leaving, for example, a remarkable degree of Sanskrit vocabulary in modern Indonesian. Buddhism spread throughout East Asia, as well as Southeast Asia, and had a considerable impact on Chinese Confucianism, acting as a stimulant to the formation of Neo-Confucianism. Christianity and Islam have spread all over the world and mutually influenced all the cultures they contacted. Nonetheless, global culture, which I would insist is a deep feature of human history, is not the same thing as global civil society or global governance. World empires, beginning with the Achaemenid Persian Empire in the middle of the first millennium BC, have played a significant role in human history but have never succeeded in becoming the universal empires that they aspired to be. Civil society is a relatively late idea, only emerging for the first time in the West in the eighteenth century.

It is worth noting that world trade, often the carrier of world culture, can be traced back into the deepest recesses of human history but was growing in importance since classical times, when China and India were linked in a variety of ways with the Middle East and Europe. After the European discovery of the New World, trade truly became global. The degree to which market economies were embedded in states and societies has been a subject of wide-ranging historical argument that I do not need to get into, but a principled independence of the market from state and guild monopolies was a feature of the early modern period, pioneered by Britain but rapidly diffusing to other societies and making possible the emergence of modern capitalism.

The idea of an economy independent of the polity is already present in germ in Locke, for whom economic life precedes the social contract, whose purpose is to a considerable degree to guarantee the pursuit of economic ends with some security. But with Adam Smith the idea of a self-regulating economy in which the invisible hand guarantees positive social outcomes even when economic actors pursue only their own interests becomes a moral ideal and a practical project. We should not, however, forget that Smith thought such an autonomous economy could operate only within an ethical and political framework organized around noneconomic motives, thus implying the need for an enlightened civil society and an enlightened polity. An economic liberal he certainly was; a neoliberal he certainly was not.

Developing only slightly later, but overlapping the disembedding of the economy, was the emergence of civil society or the public sphere, a realm of thought, argument, and association independent of the state but leading to the formation of what came to be called public opinion, which politicians could ignore at their peril. Jürgen Habermas's early work *The Structural Transformation of the Public Sphere* helped us understand this newly independent realm.[9]

I will use civil society as virtually synonymous with public sphere in a way that has become common in recent writings to refer to forms of communication and association that have been disembedded from the state and from established religions that could be used for state purposes and are not directly controlled by the market. In the eighteenth century the main problem was to achieve independence from the state and state religion, and the institutionalization of human rights was the essential precondition for an independent civil society. The First Amendment to the American Constitution guaranteeing freedom of religion, speech, and assembly is the legal basis that makes civil society possible, and similar developments have followed, not without much struggle and backsliding, elsewhere ever since, even where such rights, though included in constitutions, are consistently violated in practice. This again suggests that culture and even law have spread where institutions and practices have not as yet fully developed.

Civil society, though oriented to the discussion and advocacy of political issues, lacks the capacity to make binding decisions. Nonetheless it is closely related to another eighteenth-century idea, the sovereignty of the people. It was Robespierre who first gave the idea of democracy a positive meaning after centuries during which it was usually a pejorative term. Democracy as a way of exercising the sovereignty of the people gave civil society the right not to make political decisions but to elect those who would. This idea has now achieved global legitimacy even when it is often honored in the breach.

Most writing about civil society has taken the nation-state as the basic frame of reference, though of late a discussion of global civil society has emerged. In principle human rights were often expressed in universalistic terms, but in practice they were usually viewed as only applicable within nation-states. Alejandro Colas has made the useful point that civil society was in principle international virtually from the beginning. Though it may have originated in Britain in the eighteenth century, it was already disseminated to the American colonies, whose actions in turn were widely influential on the continent, as were British practices. The emergence of civil society in France, therefore, was not some pristine innovation but was deeply indebted to Anglo-American exemplars.[10] In fact, all the great modern ideologies—liberalism, nationalism, socialism—were international and involved not only cross-national communication of a variety of sorts but many international associations. We may think of nationalism as antithetical to globalism, but nationalism has always been an international phenomenon. Colas cites the interesting example of Giuseppe Mazzini, the most important theorist of Italian nationalism, establishing in 1847 the People's International League, whose objectives he defined as: "to disseminate the principles of national freedom and progress; to embody and manifest an efficient public opinion in favour of the right of every people to self-government and the maintenance of their own nationality; to promote a good understanding between the peoples of every country."[11]

While many have argued that the rapid growth of NGOs since World War II is an indication of the growth of global civil society, Colas suggests the limitations of NGOs in that they represent only limited memberships and are usually oriented to single issues rather than to structural problems, whereas social movements that cross national boundaries more closely approximate a genuine global civil society. His examples include socialism, feminism, and environmentalism.

Mass communication, but particularly the internet, has made possible the organization of global public opinion to a degree unimaginable only a few years ago. Adam Lupel has described a remarkable event:

> On 15 February 2003 across North America, Europe, the Middle East, Asia and Australia as many as 30 million people took to city streets to express opposition to the planned invasion of Iraq. It seemed an extraordinary moment for global civil society, perhaps for the first time living up to its name. The anti-war movement appeared to accomplish in a day what four years of transnational activism against neo-liberal globalization could not. It brought together constituencies from East and West, North and South into a broad-based movement with a common clear objective: stop the US-led drive for war. The next weeks saw what was perhaps a Pyrrhic victory for global civil society. The protests no doubt contributed to the Bush Administration's defeat in the UN Security Council. But in the end they also contributed to the heightened sense that the United Nations and global civil society were impotent next to the hegemonic power of the United States. . . .
>
> Global public opinion, as best it could be determined, was overwhelmingly opposed to the war, and yet by most accounts war seemed inevitable from the very start. For all the advances in international communications and the spread of international law in the twentieth century, there remains no institutional mechanism to effectively channel the transnational communicative power of an emerging global civil society.[12]

Using this example in both its positive and negative aspects as a starting point, we can ask where we are. Granted that there is a global economy, global culture, global law, global civil society, even global festivals, why are global institutions both so promising and so weak? I will turn to Jürgen Habermas, Europe's leading social philosopher, for help, particularly in his remarkable essay of 1998, "The Postnational Constellation and the Future of Democracy."[13] Habermas organizes his discussion around the tension between two central facts in our present situation: 1) The nation-state is the largest form of society that has been able to create a sense of common membership powerful enough to convince a majority of its citizens that they have a responsibility for all, including the least advantaged, thus giving rise to significant redistribution in what we have come to call the welfare state; and 2) the rise of the global neoliberal market ideology and practice has everywhere threatened the capacity of nation-states to carry out the responsibilities inherent in the notion of common membership. Habermas begins his essay with an epigraph from Robert Cox that sums up the present dilemma: "All politicians move to the centre in order to compete on the basis of personality and of who is best able to manage the adjustment in economy and society necessary to sustain competitiveness in the global market. . . . The possibility of an alternative economy and society is excluded."[14]

What Habermas is describing is a double disparity between economics and politics: economics is seen as the realm of the natural, not the social, whereas politics is the sphere of intentional social choice. But when nations are the sole locations of effective politics and the economy has become global, then the disparity in power between global economy and even the strongest state means that it is the economy that will in the end determine outcomes. In this situation Habermas asks whether "we can have a politics that can catch up with global markets" in order to avert the "natural" disaster that an uninhibited market economy seems to entail.[15] That idea is opposed by those who view the economy not as a human creation but as a force of nature, as something that can only be accommodated, never controlled, ideas that make global market culture into a god that can only be worshiped. Habermas sees this as an enormous challenge to citizens of all countries to form a global civil society: "Only the transformed consciousness of citizens, as it imposes itself in areas of domestic policy, can pressure global actors to change their own self-understanding sufficiently to begin to see themselves as members of an international community who are compelled to cooperate with one another, and hence to take one another's interests into account." What we need, he argues, is "an obligatory cosmopolitan solidarity."[16] He stresses the need for a "world domestic policy," because we are now living in a world, not in nation-states alone, and the world market requires such a policy.[17]

The most fundamental question that Habermas is raising is whether a global civil society and some forms of global governance are possible, a civil society and governance that would not replace nation-states but would place some limits on their autonomy, as the global economy already does. And here there is a question of what kind of people we are. Could we as

Americans or Chinese accept the notion of common global membership such that we would be willing to give up something of ours for the sake of Mexicans or Vietnamese? It is at this point that I think we have to ask, What are the cultural resources for thinking of global citizenship that would go along with global economics and moderate its excesses? Is abstract constitutional patriotism enough? It is here that we have to consider philosophical and religious resources for thinking about membership in global civil society, membership that would entail at least short-term sacrifice, though as we look at global warming and the growing numbers of failed states, the Tocquevillian idea of self-interest rightly understood is not to be ignored.

Since we actually have since the United Nations Universal Declaration of Human Rights and its subsequent elaborations something that can be called a global ethic, sometimes referred to as a human rights regime, we can ask how much help we can derive from this consensus, one that is not simply an ideal but that has significant legal weight, though by far not enforceable everywhere, not even in the original home of legal human rights, the USA.[18] And we can ask whether the questions raised by non-Western and non-Christian thinkers about the adequacy of an exclusive emphasis on human rights can be answered, as well as the question whether an exclusive focus on human rights may not be part of our problem, however much in the end it must surely be part of a solution.[19]

Christian arguments for civil rights have always focused on the sacredness of the individual, created in the image and likeness of God; this emphasis has never stood alone. When Desmond Tutu was writing about human rights in a Christian perspective, after affirming the freedom to choose that must be guaranteed for individuals, he also affirmed the necessity of "a caring and compassionate, a sharing and gentle society," because many people are in fact, and for reasons beyond their control, not able to exercise the autonomous agency that is their right.[20] Even the Universal Declaration of Human Rights, though its focus is on the classic demands of liberalism, that is, freedom from interference with the autonomy of the individual, also contains concerns for the conditions that make that autonomy possible, such as a reasonable standard of living, education, rest and leisure, that can be seen as social freedoms, not merely freedom from external interference. Still in the discourse on human rights the autonomous individual is usually in the foreground.[21]

Let me make it clear that although I think the extraordinary primacy placed on the individual and the backgrounding of society is a problem, I don't think it is an irremediable problem, but one that we have significant resources at hand to rectify. I don't accept either the assertion that the emphasis on human rights is indelibly "Western" and so inapplicable in the rest of the world, or the assertion that such claims are characteristic of "modernism" and so inappropriate in a postmodern world.

Since human rights, emancipation, and enlightenment are a part of the modern project, ethically construed, they are shared by significant actors all over the world. They are not the concerns of Westerners as opposed to non-Westerners (indeed they have Western as well as non-Western opponents), nor are they limited to the modern seen as a finite and completed period in human history.

But we must remember that the market, the individual as autonomous agent who is free to choose, the consumer, are also global, and that there is a relation between the global market culture that Harvey Cox warned us was taking on religious functions and the very tradition that named Mammon as the great alternative to God. We cannot get out of the conundrum by denouncing "European Universalism" as simply an ideological cover for the exercise of power over non-European peoples, as Immanuel Wallerstein comes close to doing.[22] European universalism has so often provided the ideological tools for resistance to European oppression that, again, we can no longer think of it in simple geographical terms. Even so, those who suggest that non-Western traditions have resources that would help ameliorate the radical individualism of the current human rights regime are not to be dismissed out of hand.

Let us consider Confucianism, because it is one of the most frequently mentioned alternatives to "Western" ways of thinking, and particularly to our radical individualism. Henry Rosemont has stated the contrast starkly when he wrote:

> For the early Confucians there is no *me* in isolation, to be considered abstractly. I am the totality of the roles I live in relation to specific others. I do not *play* or *perform* these roles; I *am* these roles. When they have all been specified I have been defined uniquely, fully, altogether, with no remainder with which to piece together a free, autonomous self.[23]

I am ready to go almost all of the way with Rosemont, except that I would point out that some of those roles that fully constitute the person in early Chinese thought *require* that the individual act alone, if need be at the cost of his life, to stand for justice and human dignity, and that these values are as universal in Confucianism as they are in Christian or modern thought. Indeed the very next essay in the same book where Rosemont's appears,

Human Rights and the World's Religions, is by W. Theodore de Bary, entitled "Neo-Confucianism and Human Rights," and gives numerous examples of individuals who acted on those principles in imperial China.[24]

P. J. Ivanhoe and Tu Weiming have raised doubts about the term "role" in connection with views like those of Rosemont, that is, if we take the role as applying to empirical roles that the individual has experienced and internalized, we might be led to the notion that the individual is "programmed" by society. But I think Confucians offer a different understanding of role. This is clear in many places in Confucian thinking but quite obviously in the teaching that is most often referred to as "the rectification of names." Such rectification requires that the (empirical) ruler really be a ruler, that is, one who conforms to the Confucian virtues of *ren* 仁 and *li* 禮, and the same thing holds for the role of father and the other central roles. I think that is why Rosemont says, "I do not *play* or *perform* these roles; I *am* these roles." To play a role would be to mimic an external conception of what one should be. But to be a role means that the role expresses the spiritually developed self who understands what the role should be, however badly it is played in the environing society. In this sense an ethical understanding of roles makes up the self; the self is not programmed by external models but is responsible for carrying out those roles in an ethically exemplary way. In this way the first Confucian commandment, to cultivate the self, is fulfilled, not denied, by this understanding of role. Actually, the West, where it has become common to reject the notion of role altogether in the quest for a radically autonomous self who is answerable to no one, might be usefully instructed that a self without ethically understood roles is no self at all.

Let me return to the way Habermas poses the problem: how we can create a global civil society that will have the same capacity of citizens to identify with the plight of fellow citizens as already exists in nation-states, and to his example of the immediate task of creating such a civil society that would include the whole European Union. While accepting Habermas's framework, let me offer a couple of caveats. 1) Under the regime of the neoliberal market it is not always easy to get even the citizens of the same nation to identify with all other citizens (in the United States it has never been easy). 2) The situation in which such identification has been most effective has usually been war: we are all in this together because we have a mortal enemy that we must defeat. If we can't assume the ability to identify with all fellow members of civil society even in advanced democracies and the conditions that have made that possible have usually involved war, we can see that the task of generalizing such identification beyond the nation-state will never be easy.

It is for these reasons that I wonder if Habermas's abstract constitutional patriotism will ever be enough. It is one thing to believe in abstract principles. It is another to mobilize the motivation to put those principles into institutional practice. Hans Joas has recently pointed out, following the pioneering work of Georg Jellinek, that, though ideas about human rights go way back in Western history, and include Classical, Catholic, Lutheran, and Calvinist thinking, it was only when the American sectarian Protestants in the eighteenth century, mainly the Baptists and Quakers, were willing to insist on them that they were included in the American Constitution.[25] Religious fervor is always problematic because it has so often been used for evil as well as good purposes, but it may be that only such powerful motivation could make human rights genuinely practical. And though Christianity has a big contribution to make, it surely is not alone. Confucians hold on to the basis of the *Analects* of Confucius that "all within the four seas are brothers." Buddhists identify not only with all human beings but with all beings in the universe, natural as well as human—all have the Buddha nature. For millennia these deep commitments have been held but never effectively institutionalized. Can the world's religions now mobilize their commitments so that they can at last have genuine institutional force?

Moving to the next question as to whether human rights as vested exclusively in individuals are enough, we may ask whether Kantian moral universalism alone can provide sufficient guidance. Perhaps it will require substantive religious motivation to see that human rights without a humane and caring society will be empty, incapable of fulfillment. And there remains the question of some functional equivalent to the powerful mobilization of human aggression by nation-states as a basis for solidarity. Early in the twentieth century William James raised the question of the moral equivalent of war.[26] We have seen the use of war as a metaphor in such things as the war on poverty, the war on drugs, and so forth, but the metaphor never seems to be as effective as real wars. I suppose it would be too much to ask if we could mobilize a religious war against selfishness, ignorance, and sinfulness in each of us according to our own faith, in part because, I suppose, we have been fighting that war all along. In any case there are enormous threats on the horizon and a popular culture that seems more apprehensive than at any time in my life, with fear of the future replacing the certainty of progress. But anxiety and fear have often fueled extremely regressive movements and there is no certainty that they will move people in the right direction. There is also the great danger that anxiety and fear can immobilize rather than stimulate to action. It is a delicate balance.

Surely secular philosophies have ways of dealing with the fragility of solidarity, even at the national level, and the ease with which humans can be frightened into a negative solidarity against alleged enemies. But if, as I have argued, the religions may have capacities to strengthen and generalize a sense of solidarity so that it reaches truly global proportions, they can do so only in and through self-criticism. Let me say plainly what I have already implied: Christianity, and especially Protestant Christianity, has contributed significantly to the institutionalization of human rights and human solidarity—I have given the American example of the religious roots of the Bill of Rights, but I must add the significant role of Evangelicals in leading the social gospel movement that helped (with the assistance of Catholics motivated by Catholic social teachings) to create in the middle years of the twentieth century what became the beginnings of a welfare state in the United States. Yet Christianity and especially Protestant Christianity have contributed to an emphasis on individual piety that makes the secular notion of radical autonomy attractive. Max Weber saw the relation between the Protestant Ethic and the Spirit of Capitalism. Webb Keane has shown the relation between global Protestantism and neoliberal economics. It is in these regards that I have said that religion is part of the problem as well as part of the solution. And if Christianity can make a contribution to the creation of global solidarity only through self-criticism, such is the case with all the other religions, and secular philosophies as well. There is no way of sorting out the good guys from the bad guys in our present world crisis. We all need each other, but we need critical reason and profound faith reinforcing each other.

What the world requires now must go on at many levels, religious, ideological, political at the global, national, and local levels. But one thing Habermas's scenario requires is very evident, however difficult to achieve. We must now turn the idea of being citizens of the world into a practical citizenship, willing to be responsible for the world of which we are citizens. I truly believe that there are millions of citizens of the world in every country, willing to make the necessary commitments. Whether they are anywhere in the majority so that the politicians will listen to them instead of pandering to the short-term interests of their constituents is doubtful. What we need is to turn a growing minority into an effective majority.

Because I see neoliberalism as the source of our deepest global problems, it might be thought that I am opposed to it altogether. That would be as foolish at this point in history as to be opposed to capitalism altogether. What I worry about is the destructive consequences of the naturalization of neoliberalism so that it has no effective challenge. I agree with Habermas (and now, apparently, the Vatican) that world politics needs to catch up with the world economy so that an effective structure of regulation can be created that will protect the environment and the vulnerable of the earth who are paying the price while only a few are reaping the benefits. If this is a political challenge, it is also a religious challenge. I am convinced that religious motivation is a necessary factor if we are to transform the growing global moral consensus and the significant beginnings of world law into an effective form of global solidarity and global governance, an actually existing global civil society with a spiritual dimension drawing from all the great religions of the world.

Notes

Presented as the University Distinguished Lecture at City University of Hong Kong, December 12, 2011.

1. "Civil Religion in America" has been most recently reprinted in Robert N. Bellah and Steven M. Tipton, eds., *The Robert Bellah Reader* (Durham: Duke University Press, 2006), 225–245.

2. Robert N. Bellah, *The Broken Covenant: American Civil Religion in Time of Trial*, second ed. (Chicago: University of Chicago Press, 1992 [1975]).

3. Harvey Cox, "Mammon and the Culture of the Market: A Socio-Theological Critique," in *Meaning and Modernity: Religion, Polity, and Self*, ed. Richard Madsen, William M. Sullivan, and Ann Swidler (Berkeley: University of California Press, 2002), 124–135. The best treatment I have seen of what Cox calls the emerging global market culture is David Harvey's *A Brief History of Neoliberalism* (New York: Oxford University Press, 2005).

4. Michael Walzer, *Thick and Thin: Moral Argument at Home and Abroad* (Notre Dame: University of Notre Dame Press, 1994), 8.

5. Ibid., 83. For a recent and much more balanced treatment of the relation between universalism and particularism, see Michael Walzer, "Morality and Universality in Jewish Thought," in *The Globalization of Ethics*, ed. William M. Sullivan and Will Kymlicka (Cambridge and New York: Cambridge University Press, 2007), 38–52. Matteo Bortolini pointed out to me that in the same year that *Thick and Thin* was published, Walzer edited a book called *Toward a Global Civil Society* (Providence: Berghahn, 1994). It would be hard to imagine a book whose contents were more at odds with its title. Not a single one of the book's twenty-six chapters deals with global civil society; all remain concerned with civil society within nation-states. Walzer mentions "international civil society" only in one paragraph in his introduction (5–6) and then qualifies it by suggesting that the real decisions are made by states. In his own chapter in the book, "The Concept of Civil Society" (7–27), he describes civil society only within nation-states and even then emphasizes the particularism of its constituent associations.

6. See, for example, Harold J. Berman, "World Law," *Fordham International Law Journal* 18.5 (1995): 1617–1622, and "Faith and Law in a Multicultural World," *The Journal of Law and Religion* 18.2 (2002–2003): 297–305. See also Daniel Philpott, "Global Ethics and the International Law Tradition," in *The Globalization of Ethics*, 17–37.

7. See, for example, George M. Thomas, John W. Meyer, Francisco O. Ramirez, and John Boli, *Institutional Structure: Constituting State, Society and the Individual*, (Newbury Park: Sage, 1987).

8. Wilfred Cantwell Smith, *Towards a World Theology* (Philadelphia: Westminster, 1981).

9. Jürgen Habermas, *The Structural Transformation of the Public Sphere: An Inquiry into the Category of Bourgeois Society* (Cambridge: MIT Press, 1989 [1962]).

10. Alejandro Colas, *International Civil Society: Social Movements in World Politics* (Cambridge: Polity, 2002), 49–58 and passim.

11. Ibid., 55.

12. Adam Lupel, "Tasks of a Global Civil Society: Held, Habermas and Democratic Legitimacy beyond the Nation-State," *Globalizations* 2.1 (2005): 117–118.

13. Jürgen Habermas, "The Postnational Constellation and the Future of Democracy," *The Postnational Constellation: Political Essays* (Cambridge: MIT Press, 2002 [1998]), 58–112.

14. Quoted in ibid., 58.

15. Ibid., 109.

16. Ibid., 55.

17. Ibid., 54.

18. Jeremy Waldron discusses the tradeoff of liberty for security since 9/11: "But after a while we start to wonder what security can possibly mean, when so much of what people struggled to secure in this country—the Constitution, basic human rights, and the rule of law—seems to be going out the window." Jeremy Waldron, "Is This Torture Necessary?" *New York Review of Books* 54.16 (October 25, 2007): 40–41; 44.

19. Hans Küng has been actively concerned with building a consensus for a global ethic, one that emphasizes human rights but includes social issues not easily defined as rights. He drafted the Chicago Declaration toward a Global Ethic, endorsed by the Parliament of the World's Religions in 1993 (for the text see Sullivan and Kymlicka, *The Globalization of Ethics*, 236–246). Küng has developed his thought further in his *A Global Ethic for Global Politics and Economics* (New York: Oxford University Press, 1998).

20. See the preface by Desmond Tutu in Jared Genser and Irwin Cotler, eds., *The Responsibility to Protect: The Promise of Stopping Mass Atrocities in Our Time* (New York: Oxford University Press, 2011), xiii.

21. An excellent discussion of the problems with an overly individualistic conception of human rights from an Asian perspective is Onuma Yasuaki, "Towards an Intercivilizational Approach to Human Rights: For Universalization of Human

Rights through Overcoming of a Westcentric Notion of Human Rights," *Asian Yearbook of International Law* 7 (1997): 21–81. Onuma avoids using an Asian perspective to defend authoritarian governments and acknowledges the validity of individualistic values when combined with social concerns.

22. Immanuel Wallerstein, *European Universalism: The Rhetoric of Power* (New York: The New Press, 2006). I say "comes close to doing" because Wallerstein builds his book around the debate between Las Casas and Sepulveda in sixteenth-century Spain over whether the American Indians should be treated as human equals or subordinated to Spanish coercion, thus indicating that the issues with which he is concerned had been European from the beginning. His solution rests in "a multiplicity of universalisms that would resemble a network of universal universalisms" (84), which, though well intentioned, is a little hard to conceive.

23. Henry Rosemont, Jr., "Why Take Rights Seriously? A Confucian Critique," in *Human Rights and the World's Religions*, ed. Leroy S. Rouner (Notre Dame: University of Notre Dame Press, 1988), 177.

24. W. Theodore de Bary, "Neo-Confucianism and Human Rights," in *Human Rights and the World's Religions*, 183–198.

25. Hans Joas, "Max Weber and the Origin of Human Rights," in *Max Weber's* Economy and Society: *A Critical Companion*, ed. Charles Camic, Philip S. Gorski, and David M. Trubek (Stanford: Stanford University Press, 2005), 366–382. Jellinek's book, *The Declaration of the Rights of Man and of Citizens: A Contribution to Modern Constitutional History*, was published in German in 1895 and in English translation by Henry Holt in 1901.

26. William James, "The Moral Equivalent of War," first published, February 1910, in William James, *Writings 1902–1910* (New York: Library of America), 1281–1293.

Contributors

Robert N. Bellah was Elliott Professor of Sociology Emeritus at the University of California at Berkeley. He began teaching at Harvard in 1957 and left there as Professor of Sociology in 1967 when he moved to Berkeley to become Ford Professor of Sociology. His publications include *Tokugawa Religion, Beyond Belief, The Broken Covenant, The New Religious Consciousness, Varieties of Civil Religion, Imagining Japan: The Japanese Tradition and Its Modern Interpretation, The Robert Bellah Reader*, and most recently (2011) *Religion in Human Evolution: From the Paleolithic to the Axial Age.* In 1985 he published *Habits of the Heart: Individualism and Commitment in American Life*, in collaboration with Richard Madsen, William M. Sullivan, Ann Swidler, and Steven M. Tipton, and in 1991, with the same collaborators, *The Good Society*. In 2000, Professor Bellah was awarded the National Humanities Medal by President Clinton.

Sébastien Billioud is Professor of Chinese studies at University Paris Diderot, Sorbonne Paris Cité. His work focuses on the multiple fates of Confucianism in modern and contemporary China with an interdisciplinary approach in intellectual history/philosophy and anthropology. His most recent publications include *Thinking through Confucian Modernity, A Study of Mou Zongsan's Moral Metaphysics* (Brill, 2012) and *Le Sage et le peuple, le renouveau confucéen en Chine / The Sage and the People. The Confucian Revival in China*, co-authored with Joël Thoraval (CNRS Editions, Paris, 2014 and Oxford UP, 2015, forthcoming). He is currently working on a book project exploring the appropriation of Confucianism by syncretistic religious organizations.

Do-Hyun Han currently serves as Professor of Sociology and Director of the Institute for Modern Korea at the Academy of Korean Studies. He served as Director for the Strategic Initiative for Korean Studies, which supports long-term Korean studies in Korea and abroad (2007–2010), was a member of the Korean Studies Development Committee, and also a member of the Committee for Humanities and Social Sciences in the Ministry of Education, Science, and Technology. He received his PhD in sociology from Seoul National University in 1992. Professor Han was a Stanley Junior Fellow of the Center for Asia-Pacific Studies at the University of Iowa and a visiting scholar at the Harvard-Yenching Institute. His research spans such fields as historical sociology, civil society, and comparative sociology. His major publications include: *Corporate Citizenship and the Civic Community*, *Religion and the Civic Community*, *Local Voluntary Associations and the Civic Community*; *Grassroots Leaders and Civic Community*, *Advancing the Rule of Law in Contemporary Korea*, *An Alternative Model against the Fordist Food System: A Social Relations Approach*, "A Comparative Study of Rural Social Organization in Traditional Korea and Vietnam," "Colonial Corporatism," and "Globalization and the Quality of Life of Korean Farmers." He translated Joong-Seok Seo's book from Korean into English with Pankaj Mohan (*Korean Nationalism Betrayed* [London: Global Orient, 2007]).

Philip J. Ivanhoe is Chair Professor of East Asian and Comparative Philosophy and Religion at City University of Hong Kong, where he is a member of the Department of Public Policy and Director of the Center for East Asian and Comparative Philosophy (CEACOP) and the Korean Philosophy in Comparative Perspectives Laboratory. He specializes in the history of East Asian philosophy and religion and its potential for contemporary ethics. Among his publications are: *Confucian Reflections: Ancient Wisdom for Modern Times*, *The Daodejing of Laozi*, *Confucian Moral Self Cultivation*, *Working Virtue: Virtue Ethics and Contemporary Moral Problems* (with Rebecca Walker), *Readings in the Lu-Wang School of Neo-Confucianism*, *The Essays and Letters of Zhang Xuecheng*, and *The Reception and Rendition of Freud in China: China's Freudian Slip* (with Tao Jiang).

Sungmoon Kim is Professor of Political Theory at City University of Hong Kong. He attained his PhD from the University of Maryland at College Park (political science) and taught previously at the University of Richmond. He specializes in comparative political theory, democratic political theory, and East Asian political thought. His research has appeared in the journals such as *American Political Science Review*, *British Journal of Political Science*, *Constellations*, *Contemporary Political Theory*, *Critical Review of International Social and Political Philosophy*, *History of Political Thought*, *Journal of the*

History of Ideas, *Philosophy East and West*, *Philosophy & Social Criticism*, and *Review of Politics*, among others. Kim is the author of *Confucian Democracy in East Asia: Theory and Practice* (Cambridge UP, 2014) and the editor of *Confucianism, Law, and Democracy in Contemporary Korea* (Rowman & Littlefield International, 2015).

Richard Madsen is Distinguished Professor of Sociology at the University of California, San Diego, and was a codirector of a Ford Foundation project to help revive the academic discipline of sociology in China. Professor Madsen is the author, or coauthor, of more than a dozen books on Chinese culture, American culture, and international relations and has written scholarly articles on how to compare cultures and facilitate dialogue among them. He has written extensively on the sociology of morality, religion, and politics in both the United States and Asia. His latest book is *Democracy's Dharma: Religious Renaissance and Political Development in Taiwan*.

Takahiro Nakajima is Associate Professor of Chinese Philosophy at the Institute for Advanced Studies on Asia. His publications include *The Philosophy of Evil: Imaginations in Chinese Philosophy*, *Practicing Philosophy between China and Japan*, *Praxis of Co-existence: State and Religion*, *Deconstruction and Reconstruction: The Possibilities of Chinese Philosophy*, *The Zhuangzi*, *Philosophy in the Humanities*, *The Reverberation of Chinese Philosophy: Language and Politics*, and *The Chinese Turn in Philosophy*. Professor Nakajima's current research focus is the phenomena associated with the contemporary revival of Confucianism in China and Japan.

Guoxiang Peng is the Qiu Shi Distinguished Professor of Chinese Philosophy, Intellectual History, and Religions at Zhejiang University. He was Arthur Lynn Andrews Chair Visiting Professor at the University of Hawai'i (2003–2004), Visiting Professor at Chinese University of Hong Kong (2010), a visiting scholar at Harvard University (2004; 2007–2008) and Wesleyan University (2006), a visiting research fellow at National Taiwan University (2009) and the Max Planck Institute for the Study of Religious and Ethnic Diversity (2012), a Humboldt Fellow at Ruhr-University Bochum (2009, 2010), and a distinguished visiting scholar at National University of Singapore (2012). He has received numerous fellowships and awards, including the Friedrich Wilhelm Bessel Research Award bestowed by the Humboldt Foundation and the Ministry for Education and Research of Germany. He is Vice President of the International Society for Comparative

Studies of Chinese and Western Philosophy, board member of the International Confucian Association, and on the editorial boards of several leading journals. His publications include *The Unfolding of the Learning of the Innate Goodness: Wang Longxi and Wang Yangming's Teaching in the mid-late Ming* (Taipei 2003; Beijing 2005), *Confucian Tradition: Between Religion and Humanism* (Beijing 2007), *Confucian Tradition and Chinese Philosophy: Prospect and Retrospect in a New Century* (Shijiazhuang 2009), *Interpretation and Speculation of Confucian Tradition: From Classical Confucianism to Neo-Confucianism and Contemporary New Confucianism* (Wuhan 2012), *Reconstruction of This Culture of Ours: Confucianism and Contemporary World* (Beijing, 2013) and numerous articles.

Anna Sun is Assistant Professor of Sociology at Kenyon College. Her teaching and research interests include sociology of knowledge, sociology of religion, social theory, and sociology of East Asia. As a coprincipal investigator of the John Templeton Foundation funded research project The Empirical Study of Religions in China (ESRIC), 2006–2009, she has been studying the revival of Confucianism as a religion in contemporary China, as well as the larger conceptual and methodological issues in studying Asian religions. In addition to her scholarly publications, Sun's work has appeared in *Harvard Review* (2000) and *The London Review of Books* (2004). A MacDowell Colony Fellow in 2001, she is currently a consulting editor of *The Kenyon Review*. Her award-winning book *Confucianism as a World Religion: Contested Histories and Contemporary Realities* was published by Princeton University Press in 2013.

Yang Xiao is Professor of Philosophy at Kenyon College. His primary research interests are in ethics and moral psychology, Chinese philosophy, philosophy of language, and political philosophy. Professor Xiao received his BA in theoretical physics, MA in philosophy from the Chinese Academy of Social Sciences, and his PhD in philosophy from the Graduate Faculty of The New School for Social Research. Professor Xiao has been a Postdoctoral Fellow at the Center for Chinese Studies, UC Berkeley, 1999–2000, and at the Fairbank Center, Harvard University, 2002–2003. In 2010–2011 he was a visiting scholar at the Institute for Advanced Study in Princeton. Professor Xiao has been the book review editor of *Dao: A Journal of Comparative Philosophy* since 2005.

Fenggang Yang is Professor of Sociology and Director of the Center on Religion and Chinese Society at the Department of Religious Studies at Purdue University. His research focuses on religious change in China and immigrant religions in the United States. He is the author of *Religion in China: Survival and Revival under Communist Rule* and *Chinese Christians in America: Conversion, Assimilation, and Adhesive Identities*, and coeditor of *Social Scientific Studies of Religion in China: Methodology, Theories, and Findings* (with Graeme Lang), *Confucianism and Spiritual Traditions in Modern China and Beyond* (with Joseph Tamney), *State, Market, and Religions in Chinese Societies* (with Joseph Tamney), and *Asian American Religions: The Making and Remaking of Borders and Boundaries* (with Tony Carnes). He has received two distinguished article awards for his essays "The Red, Black, and Gray Markets of Religion in China" (*The Sociological Quarterly* 47.1) and "Transformations in New Immigrant Religions and Their Global Implications" (with Helen Rose Ebaugh) (*American Sociological Review* 66.2).

Index

Acton, Lord, 38
afterlife, 32, 100, 105, 188
Ames, Roger, 114
Analects (*Lunyu*), 17–18, 25, 128–29, 217; Japanese interest in, 17–18, 169–74, 177; study groups for, 50–52, 73, 75–76, 78, 82n5
ancestor worship, 36, 64, 105, 176
Anderson, Lisa, 145
Angle, Stephen, 90
Anglican Church, 34
Arendt, Hannah, 199n2
Aristotle, 196
Asian Financial Crisis (1997), 164
atheism, 26, 27, 36, 44n5, 89; in Nationalist China, 101, 102; "reductive naturalist," 185
Atran, Scott, 185
Axial Age religions, 20, 187, 188, 192, 193, 195

Ba Jin, 40
Barber, Benjamin, 118
Bell, Daniel, 113
Bellah, Robert N., 18–22, 37–39, 162, 223; *Broken Covenant*, 205; "Can We Imagine a Global Civil Religion?," 20–22, 99–100, 205–19; "Civil Religion in America," 93, 94, 184, 205; *Religion in Human Evolution*, 19–20, 22, 96, 183–99, 208; *Tokugawa Religion*, 23n7, 199n4. See also *Habits of the Heart*
Berman, Harold, 209
Billeter, Térence, 62
Billioud, Sébastien, 7–8, 47–66, 92, 95, 223
Blair, Tony, 89–90
Bloom, Harold, 196
Book of Changes (*Yijing*), 4, 76
Bortolini, Matteo, 219n5
Boyer, Pascal, 185, 189
Buddhism, 8, 95, 217; afterlife in, 32; Chinese, 40, 65, 100; Confucianism and, 8, 100–101, 103; globalization of, 12, 81, 99–100, 104–5, 108–9; individualism and, 104–5; Neo-Confucianism and, 209; reform movements in, 102; Tibetan, 90; in United States, 99–100, 104–5
Buddhist Compassion Relief Society, 99
Burghard, Gordon, 187
Burns, James M., 146
Bush, George W., 212

Cai Lixu, 54
capitalism, Confucian, 115, 129–31
Cassirer, Ernst, 186
Chang, Mi-Kyung, 141
Chechnya, 107
Chen Ming, 8, 31, 58–59, 92

China, 26–27; Buddhism in, 40, 65, 100; Christianity in, 39–40; civil religion for, 37–41; Confucian-inspired groups in, 50–53, 95; Confucian revivals in, 47–66, 71–82; Nationalist, 53, 61–62, 101–3, 106
China Confucius Foundation (CCF), 73–74, 82n2
Chinese Communist Party (CCP): atheism of, 11, 26, 27, 44n5, 89, 101; Confucian studies sanctioned by, 73–74, 78–79; Cultural Revolution of, 26–27, 61, 102, 106, 113; Kuomintang and, 62; religious antipathies of, 8–13, 63, 72; schools of, 32, 76. *See also* Marxism-Leninism-Maoism
Chinese People's Political Consultative Conference (CPPCC), 63
Chinese Spiritual Life Survey (2007), 33
Choi, Bong-Dae, 141
Choi, Yang-Bu, 141
Christianity, 37, 39–40, 209; characteristics of, 34, 36, 41; Confucianism and, 7, 10–11, 25–26, 42–43, 81; historical Jesus movement in, 101, 102; human rights and, 214, 218; Qufu Church Controversy and, 10–11, 63, 86–87, 90, 96
civil religion, 3–7, 37–41, 57–66, 71; definitions of, 1–2, 8; in France, 95; global, 20–22, 99–100, 205–19; politics of, 91–96; scholarly debates on, 58–60; *tianxia* as, 26, 41–44, 60, 92–93; in United States, 37–39, 95, 207
Colas, Alejandro, 211–12
"common religion," 64–66, 69n58
Community Compact (*hyang'yak*), of *Saemaul* Movement, 15, 139, 146, 149, 150, 158, 163
Concordia Association, 61
Confucian classics education, 7–10, 29, 50–56, 71–72, 77–82; in Chinese universities, 75–77; commercialization of, 77–78, 81; in Japan, 17–18, 169–74, 177–79; retrospective on, 72–75
Confucian Prize, 107
Confucian revivals, 7–10, 45n11; Billioud on, 47–66; Madsen on, 107; Nakajima on, 61; Peng on, 71–82
"Confucian Way," 61, 109–10
Confucianism, 31–36, 87–88, 174–79; antipathy toward, 26–27, 57–58, 62, 63; Buddhism and, 8, 100–101, 103; Christianity and, 7, 10–11, 25–26, 42–43; "Critical," 18, 82n5, 179; Daoism and, 100–101, 103; democracy and, 13–15, 107, 113–16, 122–32; globalization of, 12, 42–43, 81–82, 86, 99–110, 205–19; individualism and, 103–5, 109–10, 215–16; metaphysics of, 14, 31, 33; nationalism and, 11, 90–91, 101, 103; politics of, 14–15, 18, 72–73, 78–79, 88–96, 106–8; "postmodern," 14, 115–30, 134n12; as Western term, 110n2
Confucius Institutes, 62, 80–81
Confucius statue, in Tiananmen Square, 10–11, 62, 74, 86, 88, 96
Cox, Harvey, 21, 207–8, 215, 219n3
Cox, Robert, 213
cultural-linguistic approach, 119, 190, 191
Cultural Quality Education Courses, 76
Cultural Revolution, 26–27, 61, 102, 106, 113

Dalai Lama, 99
dalu xinrujia. *See* Mainland New Confucians

Daoism, 90; afterlife in, 32; Confucianism and, 100–101, 103; globalization of, 12, 81, 99, 104–5, 109; individualism and, 104–5
Dawkins, Richard, 185
de Bary, William Theodore, 33, 80, 83n8, 216
democracy, 37, 40, 80, 211; Confucian, 13–15, 107, 113–16, 122–32; individualism and, 30; pluralism and, 96
Deng Xiaoping, 26, 102–3
Dennett, Daniel, 185
Descartes, René, 116–18
Dewey, John, 118, 132
Doctrine of the Mean (*Zhongyong*), 55
Donald, Merlin, 187, 194, 195
Durkheim, Émile, 35, 37, 57, 200; Bellah on, 207; Ji Zhe on, 93; Yang Xiao on, 183, 186
Dutournier, Guillaume, 54

Eck, Diana, 98n22
education, 54, 76–77; as *Bildung*, 185, 191–93; as *kyôyô*, 17–18, 169–74, 177–79; in *Saemaul* Movement, 146–50. *See also* Confucian classics education
Enlightenment, European, 13, 26, 40. *See also specific philosophers*
environmentalism, 21, 22, 148, 208, 212, 219
epistemology, 14; Cartesian, 116–17; onto-, 14, 117, 121, 123, 128–29; politics of, 11, 12, 87–88
ethnocentrism, 34

Fan Zhongyan, 82n5
Fang Keli, 28
Feuerbach, Ludwig, 193–94
filial piety (*xiao*), 40, 176
Fingarette, Herbert, 103, 203n34
folk religion, 32, 100, 101; characteristics of, 36; shamanism and, 174, 176
folklore, 209
Foucault, Michel, 119, 120, 123–29
Fröhlich, Thomas, 56, 64
Fulbright, J. William, 206

Garber, Marjorie, 184
Geertz, Clifford, 186, 191
gender roles, 108, 135n36, 212
Gesellschaft/Gemeinschaft, 118
Ginsberg, Allen, 99
globalization, 210; of Buddhism, 12, 81, 99–100, 104–5, 108–9; of civil religion, 20–22, 99–100, 205–19; of Confucianism, 12, 42–43, 81–82, 86, 99–110, 205–19; of Daoism, 12, 81, 99, 104–5, 109
Gongyang studies, 53
Gould, Stephen J., 197
Great Learning (*Daxue*), 55
Gu Mu, 73
guajiao (national religion), 23n9, 25, 44n1, 60
Guthrie, Stewart, 185

Ha, Sa-Yong, 142, 151, 157
Habermas, Jürgen, 22, 210, 212–13, 216–19
Habits of the Heart (Bellah et al.), 19, 23n4; Billioud on, 47–57, 65–66; Xiao on, 183–84
"habits of the heart" (Tocqueville), 2, 5, 130–31, 205–6; in Korean villages, 140, 145
Hacking, Ian, 88
Hahm Chaibong, 14, 115–22
Hai Rui, 106
Hall, David, 114
Han Do-Hyun, 13, 15–16, 139–64, 223–24
Han, Seung-Mi, 141, 145

"harmonious society" concept, 9, 16, 62–63, 79, 107
Harris, Sam, 185
Hartog, François, 48
Harvey, David, 219n3
Hattori Unikochi, 61
Hegel, G. W. F., 19–20, 183, 186, 191–93
Heidegger, Martin, 119–20
Hinduism, 106, 123, 188, 193, 209
Hitchens, Chistopher, 185
Hobbes, Thomas, 117–18
Hou Hsiau-hsien, 110
Hu Jintao, 86
Hu Mei, 172
Hu Shi, 80
Huizinga, Johan, 187
human nature, 19, 41, 183–87, 192, 208–9
human rights, 80, 107, 214, 218
hyang'yak (Community Compact), of *Saemaul* Movement, 15, 139, 146, 149–50, 158, 163

imagination, social, 49–57, 66
imperial examination system (*keju*), 29
individualism, 6–7, 13, 127–28, 183–84; Confucianism and, 103–5, 109–10, 215–16; democracy and, 30; Descartes on, 116–17; moral, 137n55
Indonesia, 209; Confucianism in, 33–34, 36
ingan (value), 120–22
"inner peace and life direction" (*anshen liming*), 50, 59
Inoue Tetsujiro, 61
Institute of World Religions (IWR), 26, 27, 44n5
International Confucian Association (ICA), 73–75, 82n2
Iraq War, 212
Islam, 90, 123, 209; characteristics of, 36; Confucianism and, 81; in Singapore, 106
Ivanhoe, Philip J., 1–23, 205–6, 216, 224

James, William, 22, 186, 217
Jang Hyeon-geun, 134n9
Japan, 61, 91; Confucianism in, 16–18, 61, 91, 169–79
Jaspers, Karl, 195
Jellinek, Georg, 217
Jeong, Kab-Jin, 142
Ji Zhe, 8, 53–54, 59, 92, 93
Jiang Qing, 7–8, 51–53, 60, 91, 92
Jin Yong, 110
Jingkon, Venerable Master (Xu Yehong), 8, 53, 54
Joas, Hans, 217
Jobs, Steve, 99

Kaji Nobuyuki, 18, 174, 176–77
Kang Xiaoguang, 8, 60, 91, 92
Kang Youwei, 24n9, 34, 36, 82
Kant, Immanuel, 217
Kateb, George, 127
Katô Tôru, 17–18, 173–75
Keane, Webb, 218
Kim, Dae-Yong, 141
Kim, Jong-Seop, 141
Kim, Ki-Myeong, 142, 149, 157–58
Kim Seok-geun, 134n9
Kim, Sun-Gyu, 141
Kim Sungmoon, 1–23, 113–32, 224–25
Kim, Yeong-Mi, 141, 142
KMT. *See* Kuomintang
Koh, Won, 141
Kong Xiangling, 86
Korea, South, 13–16, 100, 109; Christians of, 43; Confucian democracy in, 13–15, 107, 113–16, 122–32; flag of, 4. See also *Saemaul* Movement
Kuhn, Thomas S., 3
Küng, Hans, 220n19
Kuomintang (KMT), 61–62, 101–3, 106

kyôyô, 17–18, 169–74, 177–79. *See also* education

Las Casas, Bartolomé de, 221n22
Lee Ang, 110
Lee, Chun-Man, 149
Lee, Jae-Yong, 142
Lee Kwan-yu, 106
Lee, Sang-Gil, 149–50
Lee, Se-Yeong, 141, 142, 147
Lew Seokchoon, 134n9, 134n13
Li Shen, 27, 28
liangzhi (innate cognitive capacity), 56, 65
liberal arts education, 76–77
Lim, Weon Sang, 149
Lin Yusheng, 40
linguistic turn in philosophy, 119, 190, 191
Liu Xiaobo, 103, 107
Locke, John, 117–18, 128, 210
Lupel, Adam, 212
Lyotard, Jean-François, 197

MacIntyre, Alasdair, 201n15, 203n34
Madsen, Richard, 12–13, 99–110, 184, 225
Maine, Henry, 118
Mainland New Confucians (MNC), 6–8, 14–15; for civil religion, 25–44; Japanese revivalists and, 18
Mao Zedong, 4–6, 102, 106; Institute of World Religions and, 26; nostalgia for, 48; personality cult of, 4, 27
market economy, 30
martial arts, 110
Marxism-Leninism-Maoism (MLM), 6, 9; canonical works of, 72; relgious character of, 36; religious beliefs and, 26, 28, 30–31, 44n5. *See also* Chinese Communist Party
Mauss, Marcel, 186
May Fourth Movement, 29, 40; antitraditionalism of, 72, 80, 103, 108
Mazzini, Giuseppe, 211
McDowell, John, 185, 192
McNeill, William, 209
Mencius, 94, 100, 108, 169, 196, 206
Meyer, John, 209
Mill, John Stuart, 135n36
Mingde Guoxue Guan (organization), 75, 82n3
MLM. *See* Marxism-Leninism-Maoism
Monstesquieu, 117–18
Mou Zongsan, 8, 52, 83n12

Nakajima, Takhiro, 16–18, 61, 169–79, 225
Nan Huaijin, 54
National Foundation for Humanities and Social Sciences, 79
"national learning" (*quoxue*), 48, 73, 75, 78, 81
nationalism, Confucian, 11, 90–91, 101, 103
Nedostup, Rebecca, 89
Neo-Confucianism (of Song dynasty), 102, 120, 123, 129; Buddhism and, 209; cosmology of, 14, 123; ethics of, 137n55; ontology of, 121; politics of, 131
New Confucianism (of 20th century), 102; in Japan, 18; in Korea, 115, 134n9; Mainland, 6–8, 14–15, 25–44
New Culture Movement, 26, 29, 40, 80
New Life Movement, 62, 106
"New Naturalists," 185–91, 201n25
new religious movements (NRMs), 55, 82n3
New Village Movement. See *Saemaul* Movement
Nozick, Robert, 128

Oestreich, Gerhard, 126
Oh, Yoo-Seok, 141
Okin, Susan M., 135n36
Onuma Yasuaki, 220n21

Oppenheim, Leo, 194

Park Chung-Hee, 15, 16, 139, 145, 147, 159–63
Park Jin-Hwan, 140, 160
Parliament of World Religions (1893), 12, 101
Peng Guoxiang, 8–10, 71–82, 225–26
People's International League, 211
Persian Empire, 209–10
Plato, 175, 195, 196
pluralism, 34, 41, 95–96; Eck on, 98n22; Hahm on, 123–24, 132, 136n41
"postmodern" Confucianism, 14, 115–30, 134n12
postmodernism, 20, 35, 119–20, 124, 128, 197
Pu Yi, 61
Pure Land Buddhism, 53
Putin, Vladimir, 107

Qian Mu, 73, 102
Qufu Church Controversy, 10–11, 63, 86–87, 90, 96

Rawls, John, 132
"redemptive societies," 101–2
religion(s), 26–28; characteristics of, 35, 36; communist banning of, 26; ethnocentrism of, 34
Ren Jiyu, 26–28, 44n5
Ricci, Matteo, 42, 43
Ricoeur, Paul, 186, 199n2
River Elegy (TV series), 103
Robespierre, Maximilien, 211
Rosemont, Henry, 215–16
Rousseau, Jean-Jacques, 37, 57, 59; Ji Zhe on, 93–94; social contract theory and, 94, 117–18, 125, 128, 210
Royce, Josiah, 199n2
Rules for Disciples (*Dizigui*), 54
rushi (scholar-officials), 32, 83n5, 100–101, 110n2
Russia, 107

Saemaul (New Village) Movement, 15–16, 139–64; Community Compact of, 15, 139, 146, 149, 150, 158, 163; developmental methods of, 150–56; leadership training for, 146–50, 158–59; scholarship on, 140–42; successes of, 139–40, 156–58; women of, 139, 155–56, 162. *See also* Korea
Saitô Takashi, 17, 171–72
Satô Masayuki, 180n23
Schiller, Friedrich, 187
Schleiermacher, Friedrich, 186
Schneewind, Sarah, 100–101
scholar-officials (*rushi*), 32, 83n5, 100–101, 110n2
scientism, 185–87
self-cultivation, 16, 122, 128–29, 170; in Confucian classics, 48–50, 52, 54–56; Daoism and, 105; Foucault and, 137n55; in *Saemaul* Movement, 146–47, 159
Sen, Amartya, 80
Sepúlveda, Juan Ginés de, 221n22
shamanism, 174, 176. *See also* folk religion
Sherman, Nancy, 203n34
Shin Saimdang, 23n8
Shinto, 61, 91
Shirakawa Shizuka, 18, 174–76, 180n23
Singapore, 32, 33, 43, 106
Smith, Adam, 210
Smith, Barbara Herrnstein, 185, 187, 189–90, 200n12
Smith, Wilfred Cantwell, 87–88, 208
Snyder, Gary, 99
social contract theory, 94, 117–18, 125, 128, 210. *See also* Rousseau, Jean-Jacques
Song Bok, 134n9
South Africa, 99, 214
Stoicism, 203n34, 206

Sun, Anna, 10–12, 67n67, 85–96, 226
Sun Yatsen (Sun Zhongshan), 43, 61

taeguk (Supreme Ultimate) symbol, 4
Taiwan, 106–10; Buddhists of, 99; Christians of, 43; Confucians of, 32, 33, 102; Yiguandao in, 55
Tang Junyi, 56, 64, 83n12, 102
Taylor, Charles, 35, 118, 198–99, 201n15
Thompson, Stith, 209
Tiananmen Square: Confucius statue near, 10–11, 62, 74, 86, 88, 96; protests of 1989 in, 101, 103, 106
Tiandijiao sect, 33
tianxia, as civil religion, 41–44, 60, 92–93
Tibet, 90
Tillich, Paul, 186
Tocqueville, Alexis de, 2, 5, 131, 140, 145, 206; on self-interest, 214; on U.S. churches, 37
Tu Weiming, 33, 44, 102, 216
Tutu, Desmond, 214
Tzu Chi (organization), 99

Unborn Mother tradition, 55, 56
United Nations, 205, 209, 212, 214
United States, 37, 39, 40, 95, 205; Buddhism in, 99–100, 104–5; church-state separation in, 34, 37; civil religion in, 37–39, 95, 207; Confucianism in, 28, 42–43, 100; Confucius Institutes in, 80–81; Constitution of, 211, 218; Daoism in, 28, 104–5; Iraq War of, 212

Vauvenargues, Marquis de, 186
vocation cults, 36

Waldron, Jeremy, 220n18
Wallerstein, Immanuel, 215, 221n22
Walzer, Michael, 21, 208, 209, 219n5
Wang Caigui, 8, 50, 52–53
Watsuji Tetsurô, 175, 179
Weber, Max, 126, 186, 192, 202n30, 218
Willaime, Jean-Paul, 8, 60, 63, 64
Williams, Bernard, 186–90, 201n15
Wittgenstein, Ludwig, 119
Wu Han, 106

Xiao, Yang, 19–20, 183–99, 226
Xu Guangqi, 43
Xu Yehong (Venerable Master Jingkon), 8, 53, 54
Xuandi, Chinese emperor, 80
Xuanyuanjiao sect, 33
Xunzi, 169

Yang, C. K., 36
Yang, Fenggang, 6–8, 14–15, 25–44, 59–60, 92–93, 226–27
Yasuo Fukuda, 78
Yasuoka Masahiro, 170, 177–79
Yasuoka Sadako, 17, 18, 170–71
Yi Hwang, 4
Yi I, 4, 23n8
Yidan Xuetang (organization), 75, 82n3
Yiguandao sect, 33, 55, 56
Yijing (*Book of Changes*), 4, 76
Yoo, Jeong-Mi, 141
Yoshikawa Kôjirô, 180n15
Yu, Byeong-Yong, 141
Yu Dan, 17–18, 73, 78–79
Yu, Yeong-Mo, 142
Yu Yingshi, 80
Yu Yingshih, 44
Yuan Shikai, Chinese emperor, 29, 36, 80
Yuandi, Chinese emperor, 80

Zen Buddhism, 99, 104
Zhongyong (*Doctrine of the Mean*), 55
Zhou Enlai, 102
Zhu Xi, 129, 169

www.ingramcontent.com/pod-product-compliance
Lightning Source LLC
LaVergne TN
LVHW050151080826
844660LV00002B/163

* 9 7 8 1 4 3 8 4 6 0 1 3 0 *